ADVENTURES IN SINGING

A Process for Exploring, Discovering, and Developing Vocal Potential

Fourth Edition

Clifton Ware

University of Minnesota-Minneapolis

Boston   Burr Ridge, IL   Dubuque, IA   Madison, WI   New York   San Francisco   St. Louis
Bangkok   Bogotá   Caracas   Kuala Lumpur   Lisbon   London   Madrid   Mexico City
Milan   Montreal   New Delhi   Santiago   Seoul   Singapore   Sydney   Taipei   Toronto

This book is dedicated to the many students who have used and currently use *Adventures in Singing*. May each student's ongoing adventures in singing provide the requisite inspiration and means for assisting with development into well-balanced, expressive individuals.

Higher Education

ADVENTURES IN SINGING: A PROCESS FOR EXPLORING, DISCOVERING AND DEVELOPING VOCAL POTENTIAL, 4/E
Published by McGraw-Hill, a business unit of The McGraw-Hill Companies, Inc., 1221 Avenue of the Americas, New York, NY, 10020. Copyright © 2008, 2004, 1998, 1995 by The McGraw-Hill Companies, Inc. All rights reserved. No part of this publication may be reproduced or distributed in any form or by any means, or stored in a database or retrieval system, without the prior written consent of The McGraw-Hill Companies, Inc., including, but not limited to, in any network or other electronic storage or transmission, or broadcast for distance learning.
Some ancillaries, including electronic and print components, may not be available to customers outside the United States.

This book is printed on acid-free paper.

3 4 5 6 7 8 9 0 QPD/QPD 0 9 8

ISBN: 978-0-07-297759-2
MHID: 0-07-297759-0

Vice President and Editor-in-Chief: *Emily Barrosse*
Publisher: *Lisa Moore*
Sponsoring Editor: *Christopher Freitag*
Developmental Editor: *Beth S. Ebenstein*
Editorial Assistant: *Marley Magaziner*
Executive Marketing Manager: *Pamela Cooper*
Managing Editor: *Jean Dal Porto*
Senior Project Manager: *Emily Hatteberg*
Art Director: *Jeanne Schreiber*
Senior Designer: *Gino Cieslik*
Lead Media Project Manager: *Marc Mattson*
Senior Production Supervisor: *Jason I. Huls*
Composition: *11/13 Janson, Thompson Type*
Printing: *45# Scholarly Matte Plus, Quebecor Dubuque*
Cover Illustration: *Beppe Giacobbe*

Library of Congress Control Number: 2006937623

The Internet addresses listed in the text were accurate at the time of publication. The inclusion of a Web site does not indicate an endorsement by the authors or McGraw-Hill, and McGraw-Hill does not guarantee the accuracy of the information presented at these sites.

www.mhhe.com

Contents

SONG ANTHOLOGY

*Songs with music and/or accompaniment on
Web site. See listing on p. v.

For more adventures in singing go to
Web site songs (www.mhhe.com/ais4):

Group, Patriotic, and Warm-up Songs

The Star-Spangled Banner (American) Music and
   orch. acc.
Vocalizing Fun (American/Ware) Piano acc.
We Are Singing (American/C. Ware) Orch. acc.

We Sing of America (American/Ware) Music and
   orch. acc.
Zum Gali, Gali (Palestinian)

Folk Songs

Down in the Valley (American) *Low Key-E♭;
High Key-G*
Long Time Ago (American) *High Key-A*
O Shenandoah (American) *Low Key-D*
Simple Gifts (American Shaker) *Low Key-E♭;
High Key-G*

Art Songs and Arias

A Memory (R. Ganz) *Low Key-D*
Infant Joy (D. E. Thomas) *Medium Key-G*
Bois epais (J. B. Lully) *Medium/Low Key-E♭*
Blow, Blow, Thou Winter Wind (T. A. Arne)
   Medium Key-F
Cara, Cara e Dolce (A. Scarlatti) *Medium/High Key-C*
Caro mio ben *Medium/High Key-E♭*
Nel cor piu non mi sento (G. Paisiello) *Medium/
Low Key-C*
Preach Not Me Your Musty Rules (T. A. Arne)
   Medium/High Key-F
Sehnsucht (F. Mendelssohn Hensel), *Medium Key-C*
Da Unten in Tale (J. Brahms) *Low Key-D; High Key-F*
Heidenroslein (F. Schubert, 2 keys) *Low Key-C;
High Key-C*

Musical Theater Songs

Tipsy Song (Offenbach) *Low Key-C*

Novelty Songs (*Sweet Love Suite*)

Genteel Love (C. & B. Ware) *Medium Key-F*
Solemn Love (C. & B. Ware) *Medium Key-fm*
Fickle Love (C. & B. Ware) *Medium Key-E♭*
Wholesome Love (C. & B. Ware) *Medium Key-E*

Preface

Adventures in Singing is a comprehensive instructional package that includes a textbook with song anthology, a two-CD set of song accompaniments, and a support Web site (www.mhhe.com/ais4). The Web site, which has been expanded, provides additional anatomical illustrations, supportive information for teachers, a video of a warm-up routine for developing effective vocalism, extra songs and song information, orchestrated and keyboard accompaniments for selected songs, and links to relevant Web sites. Although intended primarily for beginning voice students, these materials will be useful to anyone interested in learning about the singing process or exploring new vocal repertoire.

Some of the major features and advantages of the text are (1) methodical voice-building techniques, beginning with the speaking voice and progressing to more challenging singing tasks; (2) foundational preparations, including mind-body health and an overview of how the voice works; and (3) self-assessment questions at the end of most chapters to help students think critically about the material discussed. Most importantly, appropriate exercises are provided in conjunction with discussions related to the vocal process (how the voice works) and basic performance skills. The subject matter is systematically presented, beginning with mind-body preparations (relaxing and energizing) and continuing with a study of the entire vocal process (respiration, phonation, resonation, and articulation). The primary goal of *Adventures in Singing* is to help guide students in discovering and developing their *authentic* voices, the desired result of learning efficient voice production and expressive singing skills.

As pointed out in the Group Voice Instruction guidelines (available on the Web site), chapters can and should be rearranged to accommodate the students' needs, as determined by the instructor. For instance, chapters 11 and 12 can be introduced earlier, according to the instructor's wishes. Teachers also have options as to how much emphasis to place on textual content, from using the text primarily as adjunct reading material, with minimal discussion, to requiring more detailed learning, including quizzes and written assignments. At the University of Minnesota, for instance, class voice students are typically required to read a chapter weekly and take a brief quiz in class (see sample on Web site), following the instructor's brief discussion of the chapter's most significant information, all of which relates to the quiz. The total time spent presenting the material and managing the quiz is 20–25 minutes per week, with most of class time (three-fourths) devoted to singing activities.

Every attempt has been made to offer a comprehensive and well-balanced anthology of songs suitable for most beginning- and intermediate-level singers taking voice class and/or private lessons. Although most songs are set in medium keys suitable for the majority of male and female students, a few songs include keys for high and low voices. In addition, some songs in higher and/or lower keys are located on the Web site (see table of song contents). Standard song repertoire representative of musical historical periods, nationalities, languages, and styles are included. Information provided in Appendix B includes guidelines used in selecting songs, background and interpretive comments on all songs. International Phonetic Alphabet transcriptions and literal translations of foreign language song texts are provided in Appendix C.

Two compact discs of keyboard accompaniments serve as a learning aid for students lacking strong musical skills, as well as providing a built-in professional accompanist. A low-volume instrumental (flute) rendition of the vocal line is included as a learning aid. When using a stereo playback system, it is possible for the singer to adjust dynamic levels of either the voice line or the accompaniment simply by manipulating right or left stereo channels or the balance control knob. The right channel features the flute solo instrument playing the voice line, and the left channel features the keyboard accompaniment. In addition, songs with foreign language texts are recited on a separate track following the playing of keyboard accompaniments.

Adventures in Singing is perhaps most notable for its general emphasis on holistic learning, with the intention of providing greater potential for self-improvement in the process of learning how to sing. Topics directly stressing this holistic approach include positive mental attitudes, constructive learning habits, and the role of singers as vocal athletes. The overall goal of *Adventures in Singing* is to assist the student in achieving effective and lasting results, both as a vocal performer and as a human being.

Acknowledgments

Major influences in my life and career have been teachers and students—teachers with whom I have studied and students from whom I have learned. Since 1980, this text has been developed and class tested by more than 2,000 students at the University of Minnesota, for two decades instructed by four to five graduate students annually under my supervision. Their comments and continuing feedback—plus my hands-on experience in teaching group voice for the past 25 years—have shaped the form, content, and methods of these instructional materials.

Beginning with voice lessons at age 15 and continuing throughout my vocal career, I am indebted to several teachers/mentors whose encouragement and instruction kindled within me an intense desire to continue developing as an artist-teacher. My principal mentor was Roy A. Schuessler, who helped me gain, during the second decade of my teaching career, a broader and more profound understanding of the human voice, both its function and its intimate connection to personality. This book is written as a testament to his continuing legacy.

Following the untimely death of Professor Schuessler, I began a collegial collaboration with Harris Balko (University of Wisconsin–Superior) that involved informal explorations in developing efficient vocal technique. I greatly appreciate the many stimulating pedagogical discussions and learning opportunities we have shared, especially as related to his expert "vocal ear" and profound influence in my vocal life.

Several other people have played significant roles in bringing this project to fruition. Above all, my wife, Bettye, provided valuable assistance with reading and proofing, arranging folk songs, editing piano accompaniments on several songs, and providing accompaniments for the compact discs. Her personal contributions, encouragement, and moral support helped me to complete this ongoing, long-term project.

I was fortunate in securing the services of Deirdre ("D.D.") Michael, Ph.D, speech pathologist at the University of Minnesota Hospital's Otolaryngology Clinic, who served as medical and scientific consultant. And my voice colleague, Lawrence Weller, who teaches voice and diction at the university, graciously read the manuscript and offered criticism related to diction.

The first, second, and third editions of the Song Anthology involved the valuable expertise and collaboration of several individuals not mentioned in this edition. Primary contributors include Bettye Ware, who provided arrangements of three new songs, Tim Almen, the electrotechnician responsible for the CD accompaniments, and A-R Editions, Inc., the company that provided the final music that appears in the book. Moreover, *Adventures in Singing* would never have been published by McGraw-Hill without the professional expertise, advice, and encouragement of Paul Nockleby, my agent and general editor. I also wish to thank key persons of McGraw-Hill's Higher Education Division, especially Chris Freitag, who served as chief facilitator of the project throughout the publishing process. Other key persons include Emily Hatteberg, who served as project manager, development editor Beth Ebenstein, copyeditor Barbara Hacha, editorial assistant Marley Magaziner, and all the people who worked behind the scenes to make this publication a reality.

I wish to express my genuine thanks for the collective effort of everyone associated with producing all four editions of *Adventures in Singing*. I hope this improved fourth edition will continue to assist singers in the technical and artistic development of singing.

Finally, the publisher and I would like to express special appreciation to the people listed below who served as insightful reviewers of *Adventures in Singing* 3/e in preparation for this edition. In recognition of their valued input, I tried faithfully to incorporate as many suggestions as feasible. Unfortunately, it was not possible to accommodate every request, for the only way to completely satisfy all users would be to provide custom-made individualized publications. I sincerely hope most reviewers are satisfied with the final results.

Susan Goldman-Moore,
University of Tulsa

Jeffrey Hess,
Normandale Community College

Nathan J. Kreitzer,
Santa Barbara City College

Kelly MacGregor,
Florida School of the Arts

William McCrary,
The University of Texas
at San Antonio

Thomas E. Miller,
Victor Valley College

Noelle Noonan,
University of Minnesota

Margaret Sears,
California State University-Bakersfield

Karla J. Stroman,
North Hennepin Community College

Nina Tober,
Susquehanna University

Clifton Ware

ABOUT THE AUTHOR

Clifton Ware is Professor Emeritus (1970–2007) of Vocal Pedagogy and pedagogy chair of the Roy A. Schuessler Vocal Arts Center in the School of Music at the University of Minnesota in Minneapolis. In his pedagogy position, he directed a Vocal Pedagogy Certificate program cosponsored by the School of Music and the Vocal Arts Center.

The author's accomplishments and honors include a D.M. degree in vocal performance from Northwestern University (Evanston, Illinois), former leadership positions as president of the National Opera Association and the Minnesota Chapter of the National Association of Teachers of Singing, member of the NATS Foundation board, and listings in several *Who's Who* publications. In 2000 he received the Schubert Club's "Teacher of the Year Award."

As tenor soloist, Dr. Ware has performed with more than 60 major music organizations in North America and Europe. His repertoire includes 53 opera, operetta, and musical theater roles, 76 major works with orchestra and chorus, more than 25 solo recitals, and several chamber music recitals. He can be heard in recordings of Benjamin Britten's *St. Nicolas* (MHS), *Paul Bunyan* (Virgin Records), and Franz Schubert's *Intende voci orationis* (Millsaps). His most recent performance venture has been associated with his unique creation, *Vocal Explorations*, which includes the *Best Loving Tenor Contest*, a humorous parody of stereotypical tenor voice productions in both pop and classical vocal styles, all based on variations of "Twinkle, Twinkle, Little Star." A demonstration CD of this work was produced in 2003.

As an author, Dr. Ware has produced *Voice Adventures* (Harmony Publications, 1988), which has been revised and expanded into *Adventures in Singing* (McGraw-Hill, 1995, 1998, 2004), a beginning-level voice text and song anthology with CD accompaniments and a support Web site (2004). He also has produced a popular vocal pedagogy text, *Basics of Vocal Pedagogy: The Foundations and Process of Singing* (McGraw-Hill, 1998). He has written many articles, including a series that focuses on the various roles of singers, titled "High Notes," for the National Opera Association's *Opera Journal.* The articles were later compiled and organized into a book: *The Singer's Life: Goals and Roles,* published by Birch Grove Publications in 2005 (see Web site: http://www.birchgrovepublishing.com).

Although Dr. Ware enjoys the challenges of working with students at all levels of vocal development, his teaching has mostly involved undergraduate and graduate voice majors. The author has more than 25 years of experience teaching voice class through the continuing education program of the university. In addition to teaching a group voice pedagogy class annually, he has supervised graduate voice teachers in elective-level instruction, including several voice classes per semester.

Dr. Ware collaborates with his wife, Bettye, a private piano instructor, organist, and keyboard accompanist, in numerous music-related projects. The couple has three adult sons and three grandchildren. Clif and Bettye share a long-term interest in developing and maintaining a balanced, healthy lifestyle.

For more information about Dr. Ware, please consult his personal Web site (http://www.tc.umn.edu/~warex001/).

CHAPTER 1

Preparing for the Journey

> Of all the ways to express oneself in the classical arts, singing is the most personal, and the one from which you cannot separate yourself, because it's coming from inside of you. As hard as a lot of singers try, they can't separate that.
>
> —Patrick Summers, conductor

> I made a careful study of the qualities [of singers] I admired and did my best to emulate them.
>
> —Renée Fleming, soprano

At the outset of our vocal journey, we need to bear in mind three important points:

- Humans are genetically predisposed to communicate expressively through speech and singing, meaning that—with rare exceptions—*anyone can learn to sing*.

- Each of us has a unique vocal instrument, an *authentic voice*, that in good time and with dedicated effort can be realized through effective instruction and constructive learning skills.

- The process of singing, when undertaken under appropriate conditions, motivated by high aspirations, and moderated with reasonable expectations, can serve as a comprehensive self-improvement program for developing poised, healthy, and expressive individuals.

Four Questions for the Journey

Before starting out on any long trip, we first need to clarify and understand our reasons for wanting to do it: perhaps because we desire a personal challenge, a sense of adventure, or to learn new skills and gain more knowledge about things that interest us. Then we need to set a destination, arrange an itinerary, and make all necessary preparations, including gathering and packing everything that's needed. Likening the study of singing to a journey is an appropriate metaphor, and we can use it to distinguish the type of journey each of us desires, anywhere from a short-term excursion to a long-term expedition, depending on our personal goals and motivations. In all instances we need to answer four important questions: (1) "Why do I want to take this journey?" (2) "How much time and effort can I commit?" (3) "What resources do I have or need to assist me?" and (4) "Who will be my companions?"

Why Do I Want to Study Singing?

Like other worthwhile endeavors, singing requires lots of preparation. In addition to native talent and abilities, it helps greatly if there is a firm personal commitment that's motivated by a strong and lasting desire for learning. Thus, the most beneficial first step is to give an honest answer to the question, "Why have I decided to undertake the study of singing?"

When students are asked this question on the first day of class, they offer a variety of responses, such as: "I've been told I have a pleasant voice, so I thought I'd like to develop it"; "It fulfills a graduation requirement"; "It was the only course open when I was free to attend"; "I'm extremely shy and want to gain confidence as a performer"; and "I have vocal problems that need correcting."

Though each answer represents a valid motivation for enrolling in voice class, voice teachers are most heartened by the response: "I really enjoy singing, and I want to get better at it." Teachers appreciate this upbeat response because dedicated, self-directed student "travelers" tend to make steady progress toward their desired destination while enjoying every step along the way.

How Much Time and Effort Can I Commit?

The second most important decision involves the amount of time and effort you can commit to the learning process. Studies show that a distinctive characteristic of high achievers is an ability to clearly articulate realistic, worthwhile, prioritized goals that serve to order and channel efforts in a step-by-step game plan. Obviously, voice study must be balanced with other worthwhile commitments—personal, academic, and professional. Because singing demands considerable organized effort in the development of various skills, making steady progress will largely depend on time spent in disciplined study and practice, including the following activities:

- **Reading and reviewing** assigned text chapters until the contents are fully digested, which will take approximately one or two hours per week per chapter; this preparation saves valuable class time for singing, rather than spending too much class time discussing readings.

- **Practicing appropriate vocal warm-ups and exercises** assigned by your instructor, requiring a minimum of 20 to 30 minutes daily (five to six days weekly).

- **Studying assigned songs,** using such strategies as reading texts aloud dramatically, analyzing the music, and listening to recordings of song accompaniments, your own practicing, and performance of songs.

- **Learning from model singers** by listening to recordings and attending live performances to hear a variety of singers and voice types at various levels of development, as well as attending classical vocal solo events (recitals, opera, oratorio, and so on).

- **Writing and reflecting,** using a log/journal to record daily and/or weekly entries of your vocal activities and experiences (see the Web site for a log/journal form).

Each person's weekly time commitment will depend on at least three factors: the circumstances and conditions associated with the class, the instructor's expectations, and each student's abilities and needs. In general, the average time spent weekly will range from approximately four to eight hours, including one to two hours of class, an hour or two of reading and reviewing a chapter, one to two hours of technical work, another hour or two studying and performing song repertoire, and if required, approximately an hour with miscellaneous assignments, such as log/journal entries, attending solo vocal performances and writing performance critiques, and other assignments the instructor may require.

A weekly involvement of several hours may seem excessive, especially for beginning-level singers. However, because repetitious, routine practice is necessary for building appropriate automatic muscular responses in any intricately complex performance art or sport, you need to realize in advance that *there are no shortcuts in learning to sing well.*

What Resources Do I Bring to the Class?

Resources for the class consist of two kinds: internal know-how (knowledge and skills) and external resources (tools and equipment). Among one's internal resources are the levels of proficiencies already attained—the so-called state of learning readiness. Voice classes often include students with widely ranging expertise and experience, from individuals who have practically no formal musical training to those who have varying degrees of musical and/or vocal training. Relatively inexperienced singers should not feel apologetic for lack of training, but rather think of singing as a series of adventures into ever steeper, more challenging terrain—with the prospect of enjoying some exciting scenes and experiences ahead.

In addition to vocal experience, you have personal resources acquired through experience or education that contribute in some way to the composite personality you present to others when performing, including

- **General perceptions, attitudes, and beliefs** about singing, especially as related to your vocal image and identity.

- **Positive and negative memories,** from childhood to the present, of teachers, friends, and relatives who have influenced you, either by enhancing or lowering your self-esteem.

- **Cultural experiences,** such as notable concerts, theatrical events, and television programs featuring singers that have favorably impressed you with their musicianship, vocalism, and overall performing ability.

- **Knowledge and skills** gained from previous musical study or activities, from extracurricular activities (speech, drama, athletics), and from a variety of relevant areas (literature, history, arts).

We also bring to voice class some native resources—talents, endowments, and abilities—that may either enable or burden us, depending on the attitude we take toward them. The all-important question is, "What will you do with the unique vocal instrument you have inherited?" One goal of voice study is to help identify your uniqueness, strengths, and weaknesses, and to start you down the road toward self-fulfilling potential.

To save time and optimize efforts, the aspiring vocalist also needs certain tools. In addition to the personal resources you bring to voice class and the acquired instructional materials (text, song anthology, audiotape, notebook), the following basic tools are suggested for voice study:

- **A rehearsal space**—a private room that is pleasant, quiet, and has favorable acoustics.

- **A pitch-producing instrument**—preferably a well-tuned piano, although a guitar or pitch pipe can also be used.

- **A mirror**—preferably a full-length type for observing posture, breathing, muscle tension, mannerisms, and facial expressions (a penlight might also prove useful for viewing the inside of your mouth and throat).

- **A portable recorder/player**—to be used in lessons and practice sessions to record vocal progress, as well as song accompaniments.

- **A music stand and a metronome**—the stand for holding your music high enough to be viewed without strain, and the metronome for indicating and maintaining the designated tempi of songs.

Who Will Be My Companions?

The remaining issue in preparation for the course is: "What roles do my fellow students play in the learning process?" As you and your classmates will discover, a community of learners can serve as an effective support system for exploring and developing each student's vocal potential. Admittedly, performing in a group may seem somewhat intimidating to some students, especially at the beginning, but a healthy spirit of competition can help motivate learning.

Because performing regularly in front of one's peers can be nerve-wracking to some singers, we need to have a better understanding of performance anxiety or "stage fright." First, please realize that it's perfectly natural to suffer some slight discomfort when singing in the presence of others. Even the most experienced singers suffer from the "fight or flight" syndrome associated with public performance, although the intensity of symptoms individuals experience range widely, from noticeable perspiration (sweaty palms) and elevated heart beats to nausea and difficulty with breathing. Indeed, the mechanisms that trigger the "fight or flight" syndrome are the result of long-term developmental trends to help us cope effectively under stress. However, because no one wants to become paralyzed with fear, there are a few things that can be done to alleviate negative reactions to performance stress.

- **Do your vocal music homework,** which means spending whatever time it takes to prepare all song repertoire as thoroughly and as soon as possible, thereby avoiding the pitfalls caused by procrastination.

- **Observe precautionary stress-reduction measures,** particularly guidelines for good mind-body health, including eating well, exercising regularly, getting sufficient rest, and avoiding harmful substances and activities (see chapter 3 for details).

- **Develop mind-body stress-reduction strategies,** including breathing and meditation techniques (see chapters 2 and 3 for more information).

Bear in mind that the competition that occurs in class setting can be a healthy stimulus toward individual improvement. One of the most valuable aspects of the voice class experience is observing and hearing others perform, effectively providing a yardstick for measuring individual progress. Observing others in the act of discovering and developing their voices inevitably helps everyone develop higher performance standards. Almost every facet of the singing process—vocal technique, musicianship, musical and vocal style, and performance skills—is enhanced in a group-learning environment.

Finally, the power of social interaction and interdependence in the typical classroom cannot be underestimated. When each student comes to the class with a positive attitude and an open mind, learning is greatly enhanced for all students. As social creatures, we thrive on the synergy of working with our peers. With the motto "one for all, and all for one" as a guiding principle, voice class can function as a support group for promoting the welfare and edification of all participants.

Developing a Philosophy of Singing

It's obvious that in the same way *what* and *how* we think determines our behavior, the ideas and concepts we hold about singing affect our vocal study. This author's book, *The Singer's Life: Goals and Roles* (Birch Grove Publishing, 2005), begins with a chapter titled "The Singer as Philosopher" (pp. 3–18), in which 10 guidelines summarize one teacher's approach to singing and teaching singing. For the sake of brevity, only the titles of the 10 guidelines are included here:

1. Understand your potential for expressive communication.

2. Sing, and enjoy a challenging self-improvement program.

3. Develop a positive attitude to achieve optimal results.

4. Embrace learning and change.

5. Develop an *authentic voice* using efficient vocal technique.

6. Choose your vocal icons and voice production wisely.

7. Coordinate your voice to achieve the "Golden Mean" (balancing or integrating opposites).

8. Perform with artistry to achieve expressive communication.

9. Create a game plan, from short-range to long-range goals.

10. Work consistently and trust the process.

Singers adopting these or similar guidelines will build upon a philosophical foundation that enables steady, positive development. Moreover, they will tend to enjoy all aspects of the singing process throughout their vocal journey, gaining immeasurable satisfaction every step of the way. So let's get started!

Preparation Assessment Exercises

Exercises 1-1 and 1-2 will help you assess your learning readiness and establish some useful criteria for vocal study. Writing is suggested as the most effective way to reflect, organize, and express your thoughts.

Exercise 1-1   SOME FUNDAMENTAL QUESTIONS

Give some careful thought to answering these questions, preferably in writing: (1) "Why am I taking this course?" (2) "What do I expect to learn?" (3) "Who has especially encouraged or discouraged me in my voice use?" (4) "Who are the singers I most admire and why?" (5) "How do I feel about my voice?" (6) "What is my impression of what others think about my voice?" (7) "Do I truly enjoy singing and performing, or does it frighten me?"

Exercise 1-2 PERSONAL VOCAL HISTORY

Using the questions raised in Exercise 1-1 as a guideline, write a personal vocal history, tracing your development as vocal musician from earliest recollections to the present. Note primary influences, including musical experiences, teachers, and other persons.

Because it is impossible to sing well without having a good idea of excellent singing, students should listen frequently to audio and video recordings of reputable classical vocal artists, especially singers of similar voice type. Among the many outstanding examples of well-known contemporary singers, some of whom also perform classical pop repertoire, include sopranos Dawn Upshaw and Renée Fleming, mezzo-sopranos Susan Graham and Jennifer Larmore, tenors Rolando Varzon and Ramon Vargas, baritones Nathan Gunn and Thomas Hampson, and bass-baritone Bryn Terfel. In addition, crossover tenor Andrea Bocelli is an appropriate model for demonstrating ease of singing without artiface. Even better than listening to recordings or viewing video performances, you are strongly urged to attend some local live performances of operas, oratorios, and recitals that feature model singers. The more you listen and observe, the more equipped you will be to evaluate any singer's artistry and vocalism.

Exercise 1-3 LISTENING AND OBSERVING

I was never the person who got singled out or told that I had what it takes to be a singer. I was as surprised as anybody else to achieve this success . . . It just never occurred to me that I wouldn't get to do what I wanted if I was willing to work hard enough.

—Jerry Hadley, tenor

Attend a live performance or listen to a recording of a model singer. Ask yourself such questions as: "What makes this voice and performance unique?" "How does he or she differ from the other singers I have heard?" "What are my reasons for liking or disliking this voice?" "Can I understand every word, and do I get the meaning of the text?" Write an evaluation, commenting on such factors as: (1) *presentation*—general effectiveness, posture, and mannerisms; (2) *vocal tone*—intonation, quality, consistency, and range; (3) *musicianship*—rhythm, pitches, phrasing, and style; and (4) *diction*—pronunciation, clarity, and textual expression.

Go to www.mhhe.com/ais4 to learn about additional Web-based resources that supplement the content of this chapter.

CHAPTER

2 Getting Started

Why Learn About Our Voices?

In the same way that having a fundamental understanding of an automobile's mechanical functioning benefits automobile drivers in urgent situations, gaining a basic understanding of the vocal process, or how the vocal instrument functions, can aid singers throughout their vocal journey. Any driver who has experienced a car breakdown, including something as simple as changing a flat tire, knows how frustrating and helpless it feels to lack control over the situation. Conversely, drivers who *do* possess basic mechanical knowledge and skills are more confident in their ability to be more venturesome, by taking long auto trips—or even exploratory back-road trips into unknown territory—all the while secure in the belief they can manage effectively. Similarly, singers who know their voices very well are more capable of managing their instruments under a variety of situations, as when experimenting with new vocal techniques, learning challenging vocal repertoire, or dealing with voice problems due to illness or injury.

> When you're young, you must really pay attention to having a good basic technique. That is the most important thing you can do. But I also think about knowing vocal pedagogy . . . The more knowledge you have, the better it is for you.
>
> —Jennifer Larmore, mezzo-soprano

Though most young singers show little or no interest in teaching singing, the reality is that having teaching skills is extremely important, if for no other reason than *we must learn how to teach ourselves.* Because contact with a professional voice teacher is normally limited to a relatively short period weekly, students must assume responsibility for teaching themselves during all other study periods, which might amount to 75–90 percent of the total weekly learning time. Thus, the more knowledge and skills students have about their vocal instruments, in addition to mastering effective techniques and strategies, the more capable they will be in teaching themselves.

> Ultimately, it's the student who has to stand alone in the practice room and explore, using her creativity and imagination to flesh out the teacher's suggestions. In the end, singing isn't a science, but a highly cultivated, almost perverse use of our natural voices, and it requires patience.
>
> —Renée Fleming, soprano

Now that we understand the importance of learning as much as possible about our voices, let's begin our exploration of the vocal process.

7

The Vocal Process: How Our Voices Work

The human **larynx,** or "voice box," has developed from a mechanism designed by nature for protection (keeping foreign matter out of the lungs) and for thoracic pressure (lifting, defecation, and childbirth) to an instrument capable of wide-ranging oral and verbal expression. Because singing is an exaggerated extension of speech and, like speech, requires the development and coordination of many complex skills, our appreciation will be enhanced if we think of speech and singing as the products of a single instrument.

All musical instruments, including the voice, have in common three elements for the production of sound: an actuator, a vibrator, and a resonator. In addition to these three elements, the human voice includes a fourth: an articulator. The balanced coordination of these four elements produces a functionally efficient vocal tone. Because the impulse behind all intentional vocalization is mentally and emotionally based, we must also consider the decisive role of the brain and nervous system as the motivator of the vocal process.

What follows is a brief outline describing the five steps in the vocal process (Fig. 2-1), listed formally or conceptually (in bold) and functionally (in italic, as *physical cause > musical effect*).

1. **Volition** (*Motivator > Mind-body connections*). The brain and neurological system send commands to and receive messages from the body, resulting in muscular responses that control various aspects of the vocal process.

2. **Respiration** (*Actuator > Breath energy*). The body parts associated with breathing (trachea, lungs, bronchi, diaphragm, ribs, and abdominal and back muscles) act in coordination to control the inhalation and emission of air, the fuel for vocal tone.

3. **Phonation** (*Vibrator > Creation of fundamental tone*). The larynx, or voice box, consists of membranes, muscles, **ligaments,** and **cartilages** that coordinate in managing airflow and adducting (closing) the **vocal folds** to create a fundamental "buzz-tone."

4. **Resonation** (*Resonator > Enhancement of tone*). The combined resonance cavities, principally the throat, mouth, and nose, act as acoustical secondary vibrators for enhancing the fundamental buzz-tone of the vocal

Figure 2-1
The Vocal Instrument and Process

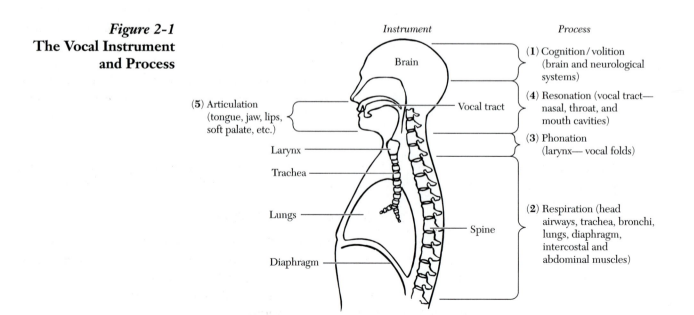

Instrument

Process

Brain

Vocal tract

(5) Articulation (tongue, jaw, lips, soft palate, etc.)

Larynx

Trachea

Lungs

Spine

Diaphragm

(1) Cognition / volition (brain and neurological systems)

(4) Resonation (vocal tract— nasal, throat, and mouth cavities)

(3) Phonation (larynx— vocal folds)

(2) Respiration (head airways, trachea, bronchi, lungs, diaphragm, intercostal and abdominal muscles)

folds. On a larger scale, the experience of singing in a shower (secondary vibrator) illustrates the effectiveness of a resonant chamber for voice enhancement.

5. **Articulation** (*Articulator > Shaping of tone into recognizable speech sounds*). The organs of speech (tongue, jaw, cheeks, teeth, lips, **hard** and **soft palates,** and dental ridges) coordinate in producing all the sounds normally associated with human verbal communication. As the only natural instrument equipped with an articulator, the human voice has the capacity to produce a seemingly infinite variety of sounds.

Individuals will vary in their degree of technical control over elements of the vocal process. A malfunction in any one of the parts will affect overall coordination and, hence, the final vocal product. For example, a singer might exhibit efficient breath functioning but inefficient phonation, resulting in an inadequately resonated tone. Another vocalist might be phonating well, but because of inadequate airflow, the voice will be deficient in resonance. The ultimate objective in both speaking and singing is a balanced coordination of the four physiological elements of the vocal process: respiration, phonation, resonation, and articulation.

From Speech to Singing

Although speech and singing are functionally analogous, dynamic singing requires more energy and a more outgoing manner. Singing simple folk and popular songs can be compared to ordinary conversation, but full-voiced singing used in **opera** and **oratorio** is analogous to dramatic acting and speaking; that is, the more energized voice levels used in sermons and public speeches. **Recitative** and **Sprechstimme** are hybrid forms of speech and singing. Because speech and singing are so closely related, we begin with a consideration of speech before launching into singing.

Our initial step is to find the voice's natural, comfortable, and efficient speaking pitch range, a task that can be hampered by a person's acquired speech habits. For instance, many people talk at lower pitch levels, possibly because of social and cultural conditioning. In some cultures, for instance, young men may believe that lower-pitch-level speaking is "manly," and women may think of a lowered voice as more "sensuous."

For those who have sung in choirs or studied voice, it is possible that well-meaning choral directors or voice teachers have unknowingly assigned voice classifications incompatible with your natural vocal abilities. Having your voice type incorrectly or prematurely classified can create an incongruity between your acquired and natural voice images that could become increasingly difficult to reconcile in future years. For this reason, an exploration of your natural **tessitura** (comfortable vocal range) is an important first step in the process of learning to sing.

Exercises for Exploring the Speaking Voice

The following techniques can help you explore and discover your natural speaking range, particularly if you can arrange to record them for critical listening.

Exercise 2-1 EXPLORE YOUR SPEAKING VOICE

1. Check your natural, uninhibited sound pitch levels by crying, laughing, coughing, yawning, and speaking "um-hum," or whatever expression you use instead of "yes" when responding to a close friend's question. These involuntary, uninhibited, unsophisticated sounds are clues for determining your natural vocal range.

2. With a friend or teacher at the piano, explore the comfortable extremes of your vocal range, beginning with the lowest pitches where the voice begins to "fry" or "crackle" and moving to the highest pitches (in the lighter-head mechanism). (**Vocal fry** is caused by insufficient breath flow and extremely relaxed folds on the lowest audible pitches). A range of approximately two octaves is typical for most people.

3. Using your normal speaking voice, locate your present speaking level by talking in normal quality while checking pitch levels on a pitch-producing instrument (piano, guitar, pitch pipe). Use such phrases as "My name is (*fill in*)," "I like to sing," or "How are you?"

4. Experiment with a higher speaking level by reading one stanza of a song using your current speaking level. Then gradually move to higher pitches with several successive readings, noting where your most comfortable, least-stressful range lies.

Speech levels will vary according to individual differences in **vocal range** (low to high pitches), **timbre** (color), and **volume** (loudness). Given the octave difference between male and female voices, as a rule most people should speak about a fourth to a fifth (pitch intervals) above their lowest singable tone, which allows spoken cadences to occur without hitting "gravel" or "frying."

Techniques for Improving Speech

A systematic exploratory routine for improving the speaking voice can also enhance one's singing voice. Throughout the following routine, note that the suggestions regarding the use of higher pitches is *not* intended to induce artificial-sounding archetypical voice types, such as the affected or ineffectual speech patterns associated with comical or stuffy-sounding persons. As we will learn later on, when our speaking and singing voices are fully resonated and supported by ample breath flow, all pitches sound lower perceptually, an acoustical phenomenon we will explore later in chapter 8. Accomplished vocalists can readily demonstrate this phenomenon: first, by speaking or singing in a mid-to-high-range using an artificial-sounding, ineffectual voice, and next, by speaking or singing the same lines using a fully resonated and supported voice. When using the full voice, the vocal tone should be warmer and fuller sounding, and the overall pitch level perceptually lower, perhaps by a considerable margin. A technique is recommended at the end of the exercise routine to help in exploring this phenomenon.

Exercise 2-2 VOICE EXPLORATION ROUTINE

1. Begin by repeating some short phrases, such as "My name is (*fill in*)," "I like to sing," or "How are you?" in a higher than normal voice. Note that it takes more breath energy (airflow or breath support) to speak in a higher range.

2. Use extreme speech variation (inflection, emphasis, stress) by shifting pitches from high to low in an animated, exaggerated manner. An easy way to exaggerate speech is to mimic persons who appear "out of their minds," that is, insane, crazed, drugged, or drunk.

3. Create an enthusiastic, "heady" sound with an awareness of sensations in the area above the roof of the mouth and surrounding the eyes and

bridge of the nose. The tonal sensation must be very light and in the head. Men get this feeling when singing head voice (less so in falsetto, which is weaker and breathier), and women can easily experience the same sensation when using their lighter, high-voice mechanism.

4. Allow this light feeling to grow dynamically by increasing airflow, especially in higher ranges of speaking. The feeling of exaggerated excitement will help in achieving extra airflow, as when exclaiming: *"Wow, what a wonderful day!"*

Exercise 2-3 READING A TEXT ALOUD DRAMATICALLY

Using a dramatic approach, read selected texts aloud, such as the short, three-stanza text from the group song, "Viva L'amour" (p. 126)—"Let every good fellow now join in a song, viva le compagnie! Success to each other and pass it along, viva le compagnie!" Each student in the class can speak a verse, using an exaggerated, oratorical characterization similar to that voiced by Shakespearean actors. Eventually this technique can be expanded to *speaking-singing,* a hybrid voice form characterized by an *atonal* or declamatory style, which is often referred to in German as Sprechstimme or Sprechgesang. This approach can also be applied when singing the more tonal, speech-like singing form known as *recitative.* This exercise provides an opportunity to experience the more vitalized, full-toned potential of the speaking voice that was mentioned in the preface to Exercise 2-2.

Exercise 2-4 SPEECH-TO-SINGING ROUTINE

The preceding exercises can be integrated by experimenting with this speech-to-singing routine. For example, repeat a short phrase, "Oh, what a beautiful mornin'," (see song of same title, page 275) at four levels of increasingly higher dynamics, progressing from normal speech to full-fledged singing. Use the following progression of voice levels:

1. **Conversational.** This is normal speech of a casual nature, similar to what you would use in a quiet, small room with low background noise. The dynamic level ranges from *piano* (*p,* or soft) to *mezzo piano* (*mp* or moderately soft).

2. **Elevated.** This level is used with a small- to moderate-sized audience, as in an average classroom with some background noise. This level of speech will probably suffice when you speak in voice class, such as making introductions and comments prior to performing and when you recite song texts. The dynamic level averages out at approximately a *mezzo forte* (*mf,* or moderately loud) level.

3. **Declamatory.** This is an oratorical manner of delivery you might use in a large room or an outdoor space with large audiences present, the same as used with Shakespearean dialogue or evangelistic preaching. The dynamic level averages out at approximately a *forte* (*f,* or loud) level.

4. **Speech-singing (Recitative)** This is an exaggerated, operaticlike speech form or singing style based on either tonal (recitative) or atonal (speaking-singing or Sprechstimme) pitch organization. The dynamic level ranges anywhere from *mezzo piano* to *forte* (moderately soft to loud), depending on the nature and mood of the text.

Getting Started with Physical/Vocal Exercises

Because many vocal warm-up exercise routines begin with vocalized tone based on the **lip-buzz** technique, it's important to learn how to produce it correctly. Simply put, the lip-buzz is produced with vibrating lips when air is blown through them, similar to the imitation of a powerful motorcycle engine revving up or the energetic sound you make when exclaiming "B-b-b-b-um, it's cold outside." For a variety of reasons, some people are unable to perform a lip-buzz, in which case the rolled *r* may be substituted; the "br-r-r-r-r" sound is common to many languages, notably Italian. Usually, students who at first have difficulty producing lip-buzzes and the rolled *r* are able to develop them in good time with regular, effective practice. Here are some suggestions for producing both the lip-buzz and the rolled *r*, both of which require vigorous breath action to keep the lips or tongue vibrating in sounding a full-voiced tone.

- To produce a lip-buzz, first relax the lips, perhaps by placing the index finger of each hand on both sides/edges of the mouth to avoid tensing. Next, voice "brup-brup-brup-brup" as quickly as possible to facilitate looser lip action.

- To produce a rolled *r*, begin by relaxing the tongue, with the tip touching the upper dental ridge. Next, voice "tuh-duh-tuh-duh" or "dah-dah-dah-dah" in quick succession (as fast as possible) to loosen and make the tongue more flexible.

Now you are ready to work on fundamental vocal technique. The following exercises are distilled and condensed from more detailed directions included in later chapters and are designed to get you started quickly and safely on your way to singing. *NOTE: Please consult the AIS Web site for a video demonstration of a warm-up routine that includes most of the exercises discussed in this section.*

Exercise 2-5   UPWARD STRETCH AND FULL CIRCLE DRAW

Reach upward, first with one hand, then the other, stretching up on tiptoes. While stretching your arms upward and drawing broad circles in the air, simultaneously emit random, rising and falling pitches using a lip-buzz ("b-b-b-b—um") or a hum, with a chewing action to loosen the jaw and tongue. Next, with hands remaining together in upstretched position and feet spaced approximately two feet apart, slowly draw a large circle from left to right in vertical relationship to the floor. Start at the top position and, on a high pitch, sing with a lip-buzz from high to low to high (or low to high) as you draw a full circle. Now repeat the exercise in reverse, drawing a right-to-left circle. In drawing the full circle, you will bend over at the hips as your hands almost touch the floor.

Exercise 2-6   RAG DOLL STRETCH

This technique is useful in achieving a state of relaxation and a full body stretch and alignment.

1. Begin by lifting and stretching your hands overhead while taking a deep, relaxed breath.

2. Let your arms swing gently forward and downward, leading your head and upper body into a bent-over position at the hips, with your arms and head dangling loosely and knees bent. While falling, let the air escape quickly with a lip-buzz.

3. While bent over and dangling loosely, hum *m-m-m-m* as though expressing great delight over a yummy meal. Notice the head vibrations resulting from the hum in the upside-down positioning of your head.

4. Gradually and slowly start to straighten up, beginning with the knees (but not locking them), then the buttocks, up the spinal column to the shoulders, neck, and head, finally lifting the arms upward as though you're reaching for the sky. When you reach a full-stretched position, observe the position of your chest, with a high breastbone (**sternum**), but not too artificially high, as it may create muscular tensions.

5. Drop your arms while keeping your elevated chest position. The feeling you should aim for is an upward, buoyant stretch, with a head that moves freely, as though bobbling on top of the spinal column. At the same time, your feet should be firmly planted on the floor approximately 8 to 12 inches apart, and your knees should remain flexibly unlocked.

If all has gone well up to this point, you should have a correctly aligned body for singing (see chapter 4 for a more detailed body alignment routine). Congratulations—you're looking like a confident singer!

Exercises for Coordinating Breath, Phonation, and Resonation

At this early point we want to establish initial awareness of (1) a complete breath connection (respiration), (2) a clean vibration of the vocal folds (phonation), and (3) coordinated resonators (resonance). It should be noted that not all accomplished singers concur on the kinds of sensations experienced when singing. But, generally speaking, when these three steps of the vocal process are effectively coordinated, most experienced singers report similar sensations, including (1) a full body connection, from the low abdominal area to the chest and climaxing in the area surrounding the eyes; (2) a relaxed, "open" egg-shaped throat position; (3) a well-focused, nonpressured tone, without harsh or breathy qualities at the vocal-fold level; and (4) head vibrations centered mostly around the eyes and bridge of the nose.

After these three elements are in place, you will be ready to build a voice based on healthy, efficient vocal technique. Though the coordination of these three elements is the goal, each needs to be considered separately. Again, for supplementary voice guidance, please consult the Web site (www.mhhe.com/ais4).

Exercise 2-7 BREATHING CHECK

1. Begin by standing in the tall, stretched position achieved at the end of the "Rag Doll Stretch" (Ex. 2-6), with a comfortably lifted chest and expanded rib cage. Place your right hand open on your lower abdominal area (gut) with the thumb tip located on your navel. Experts who work with relaxation techniques speak of "centering" oneself by concentrating on a point approximately 2 inches below the navel. This is approximately where the focus of your breath expansion and energy should be felt when singing or expelling air.

2. Place your left hand flat, with fingers slightly spaced, on your upper abdominal area (stomach area or **epigastrium**) between the navel and the breastbone, with the left thumb on the tip of your breastbone and the little finger touching your navel. Place your right hand on the lower abdominal area, with your thumb touching your navel and the little finger touching the lower abdominal wall. In this position you will be able to

experience the effects of relaxed, full breathing. Note that most of the movement upon inhalation and exhalation should occur in the upper abdominal area.

3. Let the jaw go slack, as if dumbstruck or surprised in reacting to something unbelievable, with lips slightly parted, approximately one finger wide. Blow out as much air as possible, to the point of needing air. Hold this position for 4 to 5 seconds before taking a full, deep breath through your nose (with mouth still in dumbstruck-surprise position), as though smelling a wonderful aroma. Allow the rushing intake of air to fill your lungs completely in a downward and outward manner. If you are doing this exercise correctly, you will observe your hands moving outward as a result of the air moving in. Caution: It is important to relax the lower abdominal wall rather than hold it with tense muscles.

4. To experience how the breathing system works in singing, begin by blowing out air. Then, using the dumbstruck-surprised attitude to induce a totally relaxed jaw, (1) close your teeth together gently, but let the lips remain slightly parted, (2) slowly suck air in (4–5 counts), (3) hold it in suspension (1–2 counts), and (4) hiss it out slowly (10 or more counts) until most of the air is depleted. Finally, allow the breath to be sucked in, filling the lungs with air. Observe that when exhaling or blowing out, the action of the abdominal muscles is inward and upward, the opposite of when inhaling. If everything is working correctly, you should be ready to explore the connection of breath to vocal tone.

A *focused tone* is largely the result of efficient vocal-fold vibration that is produced by the vocal folds coming together (**adduction**) their full length when air passes through them. (The opposite of adduction is **abduction,** the term used to indicate open vocal folds, as occurs when breathing.) Any opening in the folds when speaking or singing will result in air escaping, and the resulting tone will sound "breathy." Conversely, too much pressure on the folds will result in a "pressed" or "tight" voice production. Therefore, the goal is to allow the vocal folds to vibrate naturally in response to airflow.

The lip-buzz technique discussed earlier illustrates the phonation principle very well. When one blows air in conjunction with humming ("b-b-b-b-um," the sound of a motorcycle revving), the results are similar to what occurs when air moves through the vocal folds, causing them to vibrate. This exercise is best accomplished with full-flowing breath and loose articulating organs. Use a very contented, high-placed (imagine air filtering through your eyes), exaggerated sigh on the vowel "ah" and/or "oh" in a medium-high to medium-low pitch range on an interval of a fifth or an octave (see Exs. 2-8a and b).

Exercise 2-8 LIP-BUZZ AND SIGH GLIDE

Another technique similar to the lip-buzz is a "sigh-glide." Use plenty of airflow to vocalize a descending pattern, such as an interval of a fifth or an octave. This technique is initiated with an "h" as occurs when voicing such words as "*where*" or "*what.*" When singing the following exercises (Exs. 2-8a, b), bear in mind the suggestions made previously regarding the dumbstruck-surprise attitude to achieve a relaxed jaw, articulating organs, and throat throughout the action of breathing and singing. Use the imagery of releasing breath through the region of the eyes, rather than the mouth or throat, with the understanding that the entire vocal tract is used in achieving a fully resonated tone that is characterized by having both "ring" or brilliance (high overtones) and warmth (low overtones).

Exercise 2-8a

B-b-b-b-um
Hah __
Hwee _
Hwoo _

Exercise 2-8b

B-b-b-b-um
Hah __
Hwee _
Hwoo _

Exercise 2-9   MOANING AND WHINING

After setting all previously discussed mental and physical conditions for singing, you can experiment with using a relaxed, let-go, moderately loud "moan" or even a slight "whine" to create a clean vocal-fold vibration. Avoid pressing or tightening the tone and use adequate airflow (without breathiness), and you should experience a more clearly focused vocal tone. In addition to random, natural-sounding moaning and whining pitches, the intervals in Exercises 2-8a,b can be used.

Though it's not possible to place the voice in any one spot of the vocal mechanism, the term *tone placement* is often used to refer to physical sensations experienced by singers when the tone seems to be produced freely and easily. The most important aspect of tone placement is that it must be associated primarily with *head* sensations experienced above the roof of the mouth, rather than in the mouth or throat. This is not to say that one does not use the mouth and throat for resonance when singing, for they are involved in allowing a fully resonated tone. However, one must not try to *make* things happen in the mouth and throat, for the tendency will be to create unnecessary tensions that will interfere with freeing the voice.

Listening critically to many singers, both amateur and professional, can provide a deeper awareness of types of voice production, particularly in observing how tone quality is related to resonance produced in the vocal tract (throat, mouth, head). The lateral, wide-open mouth position associated with "spread" or "white tone" quality often heard with most pop and musical theater singers indicates a predominance of mouth resonance, with plenty of high overtones but minimal low overtones. Conversely, the artificially dark tone production often heard in some classical singers, particularly the low male voices, indicates exaggerated use of throat resonance, with lots of low overtones but lacking in high overtones. Based on this artist-teacher's experience, most singers, pop and classical, tend to err on the side of using too much mouth resonance and not enough balanced resonance, a phenomenon attributed to "over-trying" or excessive manipulation of the articulating organs in attempts to *make* a beautiful tone. Of course, there are other explanations, mostly associated with psycho-emotional and social factors, which are addressed in subsequent chapters.

So how can one achieve balanced resonance? Depending on an individual's unique vocal experiences and perspectives, certain voice productions are often mistakenly interpreted. For instance, singers preferring warm, soft-sounding voices may interpret any nasal-sounding tones as being ugly or harsh sounding, whereas singers preferring bright, loud tones will consider any tones sensed more in the head as "hooty" or weak sounding. Most singers and teachers agree that sensations of vibrations should be sensed primarily in the facial mask—the region surrounding the eyes and the bridge of the nose between both eyes.

A popular approach achieving more head or nasal resonance involves the use of *nasal consonants*, particularly "m" and "n." Humming is commonly used as a helpful vocal technique because of the nasal consonant "m." In addition to the hum, singers often use "ng," the phoneme found in such words as si*ng* and so*ng* and hu*ng*. Although both sounds are useful for helping induce nasal resonance, the "ng" is usually preferable. Of course, you must learn how to vocalize these consonants correctly, for it is easy to misuse them by dropping the jaw too far or tensing the articulators (tongue, jaw, etc.) Because *there is no such thing as a foolproof vocal exercise*, students must depend on the listening ability and expertise of a qualified listener (teacher) for giving proper feedback.

When striving to produce a freely placed, fully resonated tone, *never attempt to drive, force, or "stick" the tone in the head*. Simply *allow* it to be there. As mentioned throughout this text, it is essential that you learn to let go totally of control mechanisms (tongue, jaw, throat muscles) when using these exercises. In other words, assume the attitude of being surprised, spellbound, or dumbstruck. Furthermore, avoid monitoring or adjusting the tone according to your hearing. Instead, trust the process and allow it to happen.

Exercise 2-10   DEVELOPING NASAL RESONANCE

Before vocalizing, check that the top blade of your tongue is loosely touching the hard palate (the bony ridge on the front portion of the roof of the mouth), not the soft palate (back portion of hard palate that connects to the *uvula,* the fleshy part that hangs down. Also, be sure the tongue is in an arched position, similar to the position used for an "ee" vowel. Now begin by saying "uh-huh," somewhat like "hum-um," but with your tongue in the position of "ng" rather than "m" to form the nasal consonant "ng." Next, intone the "ng" slowly on a descending sliding interval of a third, fourth, fifth, and an octave (Ex. 2-10a). Now try the "ng" on specific pitches such as 5–4–3–2–1 (Ex. 2-10b). Finally, sing it on a 1–5–4–3–2–1 (Ex. 2-10c) pattern, taking care to connect the 1 to 5 interval with a slight sliding pitch, or **portamento,** upward. All the while, maintain a high-arched inhaling gesture. In addition, sing the phoneme "nyam," which helps produce a balanced tone, with loose articulators and a speechlike "ah" vowel.

Exercise 2-10a

Ng ____   Ng ____
Nyam   Nyam

Exercise 2-10b

Ng _____
Nyam ____ Nyam ____ Nyam

Exercise 2-10c

Ng _____
Nya_____m, Nyam_____Nyam

When you have achieved a well-focused tone both in head resonance and at the vocal folds, you should automatically have a good breath connection as well. That's why many teachers prefer to concentrate initial efforts on phonation and resonation before spending much time on "breath hook-up." The main thing to remember is that the voice is carried on a *flowing air stream* (without breathiness), and you must always be aware of using sufficient airflow as the foundational support for the voice.

Getting Started with Learning and Performing a Song

Because students will probably begin learning and performing songs at the outset of vocal study, the following brief introduction to learning and performing a song is provided. (More information can be found in chapter 11.) Also, for students with limited music-reading skills, chapter 12 provides an overview introduction to the fundamentals of music. In tandem with voice study, a formal course in music fundamentals is highly recommended. Some very good ones are available as software programs that allow learners to study independently at a comfortable individual pace.

Song Study

The first step in learning a song is to find one suitable to your present talent and experience. The Song Anthology, found in this book, provides a wide range of possibilities from which you and your teacher can make an appropriate selection. It helps the learning process if you are enthusiastic about the song selected, so try to find one that will challenge and inspire you when working on it.

Most beginners will benefit from selecting a simple song, either from the group or folksong collections. For instance, "Vocalizing Fun" (p. 129) is easy to learn and allows the student to concentrate on various technical issues when singing, because each verse addresses a specific technical concern. Several folk songs work well, although it might be wise to avoid any song already familiar to the singer, such as "Amazing Grace" (p. 134), a song that has been performed by many well-known singers using a wide range of styles. When singing songs in one's native language that are very familiar, novice singers tend to use old vocal habits. For this reason, many voice teachers assign simple songs in Italian, a singable language that can be sung more objectively. Several simple Italian songs are located in the song anthology, notably "Non lo diro" by Handel (p. 218) and "E l'uccellino" by Puccini (p. 188).

Because hearing others perform a particular song is a good way to become more familiar with it, try to listen to a recording of the song performed by a reputable vocal artist. Of course, this suggestion applies mostly to students performing some of the popular art songs, most of which have been recorded. Another listening exercise involves having class members sing through it in unison as a song-study project. "Vocalizing Fun" and "Viva L'amour" are two group songs that can also be used by individuals as solo projects. The latter song also allows the class to join in singing the rousing chorus part. It's easy to understand that learning a song is greatly facilitated when more than one person is studying and performing the same song in class. Increased exposure and instructive comments by the teacher and classmates serve to enhance and hasten learning.

Students with limited keyboard skills are strongly encouraged to use the supplemental CD to gain greater familiarity with the song. Better yet, record the song when it is performed (solo or group) in class.

The most efficient strategy for learning a song requires separating the song into specific components, each of which can be mastered independently before integrating them into a final memorized product. This approach will require (1) studying and reading aloud the text for meaning and clear pronunciation of all words, (2) learning the melody and rhythm accurately, as well as becoming familiar with the harmonic structure, (3) using appropriate dynamics (soft, loud, accents), (4) making decisions on phrasing and breathing points, and (5) interpreting and communicating the song's meaning or intent.

Song Performance

In vocal performance, the singer assumes an acting role, with the responsibility to present a song's musical and dramatic content as intended by both the composer and the textual source (poet, author). This means that your presentation should mask, to some extent, your own personality as you become the person interpreting the song's special meaning.

With your entire body language (bearing, gestures, attire, grooming, attitude, etc.), you are expected to command attention upon entering the performance area, normally from stage right, with your accompanist following slightly behind. Walk directly to the "crook" area of a grand piano or to the side of an upright piano, which should be angled so that the accompanist can observe you, usually with the accompanist's back slightly sideways to the audience. Upon reaching the performing area, recognize the audience and their applause with a sincere "thank-you" bow. Calmly, slowly, and firmly introduce yourself, the title of your song, the composer (and textual source), and your accompanist. Before singing, take a moment to relax and release any tensions, breathe deeply, and collect your thoughts. Although you will have many technical things to think about, such as breathing, tone quality, words, pitches, rhythm, and dynamics, your primary artistic responsibility is to concentrate on delivering the song's meaning.

After the mood is established, subtle signals such as posture, breath, and focus will let your accompanist know you are ready to begin. Throughout the song your entire body should appear relaxed, particularly fingers, hands, and arms, although your concentration should remain constant, especially during piano interludes. Remain consistently focused on your performance until the *final note* of the song. Depending on the nature and the mood of the song, pace your "return to reality" by keeping your concentration for a few seconds following the last note of the song. When the applause begins, graciously take a solo bow—hands loosely by your side, bending slightly at the waist with the top of your head pointed toward the audience—followed by a duo bow with your accompanist. Exit stage right followed by the accompanist. For more information, see chapter 12.

Visual Physical Assessment

Self-Observation. It helps greatly to practice while viewing yourself, using a large mirror (preferably full length) and a video camera. Using a mirror provides instant subjective biofeedback, which can be distracting in the initial stages of mirror observation because individuals tend to be very self-conscious when viewing themselves.

Video Observation. In addition, using a video camera to record your practice sessions will allow you to go through your normal practice routine with fewer concerns about how you look or sound. Afterward, it will be easier to view your practice session more objectively, warts and all. Depending on your stage of study, be sure to include both technical exercises and singing of songs, preferably using the recorded keyboard accompaniments. While practicing, ask yourself, "Do I have any peculiar mannerisms: eye blinking, brow furrowing, finger twitching, hand and arm conducting, body swaying, or chest heaving?" Experience teaches us that the more these viewing learning tools are used, the more comfortable singers become in using them for self-evaluation; consequently, singers improve faster.

Go to www.mhhe.com/ais4 to learn about additional Web-based resources that supplement the content of this chapter.

CHAPTER 3

Expanding the Mind

You may be wondering why an entire chapter is devoted to exploring facets of our psycho-emotional selves. Most books on singing touch on the subject superficially, if at all, but it is this author's educated opinion that the way we think and feel about ourselves—as well as how we approach learning new information and skills—has a firm footing in the psycho-emotional realm. Indeed, *the process of singing begins in the mind*, with mind-body communication occurring through cognition and volition. Experienced voice teachers are well aware of this vital issue, as they are constantly confronted with voice problems that appear rooted in the psycho-emotional dimension of their students' lives. One prominent voice teacher, Pearl Wormhoudt, recognized a need for addressing the psycho-emotional aspects of singing, so she produced a book appropriately titled, *With a Song in My Psyche: On the Psychology of Singing and Teaching Singing* (2002). So now that you understand the rationale for this chapter, let's begin exploring your vocal roots.

The Roots of Your Vocal Self-Image

Learning to sing, like any worthwhile endeavor, occurs first in our *imagination*—a mental faculty that perceives, previews, or images future experience and guides us as we bring it into being. But imagination cannot work alone. Because emotion and thought precede action, our *attitudes* also determine *how* we interpret what we see and experience in undertaking any activity. For example, persons holding negative attitudes will tend to see a half-filled glass as being half empty, whereas those with positive dispositions will perceive it as being half full.

Imagination and attitudes are filed away in our memory, providing us with the ability to recall past experiences, including scenes, words, sensations, tastes, and smells. These three ingredients—imagination, attitudes, and memory—form the basis for "possibility thinking," the ability to create a mental idea of a positive future outcome. For example, to become successful singers, we must first believe in the possibility and then commit to a vision that will inevitably become clearer as experience and expertise is gained. Thus, we begin our vocal journey by using our inner resources to explore aspects of imagination, attitudes, and memory.

Part of what we bring to voice study is our vast storehouse of memories and conditioned responses called *habits*, which are largely influenced by others. If we were to pinpoint the major influences on our vocal personality, we would list parents, relatives, friends, colleagues, media figures (including singers and entertainers), teachers, and other significant personalities. Generally speaking, our voices reflect our origins—cultural, social, and familial.

In exploring your vocal roots, for instance, you'll probably find a striking resemblance between your own vocal mannerisms and those of your parents or siblings. By listening attentively to them, you will probably hear echoes of yourself. Moreover, by listening to or recalling the voices of childhood and teenage friends, you may hear speech patterns and vocal characteristics that you have assimilated. Males, in particular, mimic voice mannerisms of their peers, especially during adolescence when the voice pitch changes from high to low and their new rumbling masculine voices emerge, sometimes seemingly overnight. Young female voices change more slowly, almost imperceptibly. But as their chest (lower) voices gradually develop, they too enjoy exploring their increasing vocal powers. The vocal habits of a lifetime often stem from this period of intense youthful experimentation and exploration.

For better or worse, it is during the impressionable years of adolescence that we are likely to develop a taste for a particular vocal style, usually of a popular genre. Pop singers, although exemplary in some ways, may be less than ideal models of healthy, efficient voice use. Generally speaking, professional pop singers and particularly "hard rockers" lack adequate vocal resources and training, yet remain very influential as vocal role models. Young singers enamored of certain classical singers can also run into problems, as when trying to emulate the developed voice production of mature artists, particularly the lower-voice types with large voices. Without having a complete understanding of how model classical singers produce such powerful sounding tones, young singers can get into vocal trouble by trying to mimic mature singers' tone quality. Thus, some young singers must take deliberate steps to unlearn the strong influences that model singers have impressed on their vocal personality.

As a way of appreciating the impact of voice apart from visual effects, let us look at some realistic situations in which a person's voice is a major factor in determining how others perceive him or her. For example, how often have you had telephone conversations with people you have never seen before and formed impressions of them based solely on their speaking voices? When listening to people on a radio call-in show, do you visualize callers according to their voices? Usually, we tend to match particular voice qualities (high, low, soft, loud, smooth, rough) with faces and personalities we think suit the people to whom we are listening or speaking. Frequently, when we eventually make first-time visual contact, we are surprised that the mental image we've fashioned bears little resemblance to their actual physical appearance.

Indeed, it's not only *what* we say, but also *how* we say it that determines the perception others have of us. To continue exploring your vocal image, ask yourself these questions: (1) "What do I think of my voice?" (2) "What do I think others think about my voice?" (3) "Are my impressions compatible with others' views?" (4) "Am I aware of voice changes associated with the state of my general health or mental attitude?" After giving careful thought to answering these questions, it should be apparent that you are recognized and judged by your speaking voice—its tone quality, dynamics, expressiveness, and general state of health. Dr. Morton Cooper, well known in the Los Angeles area as "voice doctor to the stars," writes in his popular book *Change Your Voice, Change Your Life*:

> Though your voice image is probably a new concept to you, it is one of the most vital, pervasive, meaningful, and controlling factors in your life. It pertains to sound and persona. It designates the way you perceive your own

sound and the way you perceive others' sounds, as well as the interpretive judgments you apply to those sounds (Cooper, 1984, p. 5).

We are entering an area of discussion that will involve delving into psycho-emotional issues and, more specifically, into the role of the mind and its constantly interacting relationship with the body. Although we will not pursue this subject in depth, we will take a cursory look at some topics related to the mind/body connection.

Personal Voice Perceptions

Because we receive and transmit information about the world through our senses, voice study can be approached on several sensory levels. One level is *visual* (seeing), or imaging a mental picture to create, interpret, or project an idea, a thought, or an emotion through our voices. A second level is *aural* (hearing), which affords immediate feedback on our tone quality or verbal communication. For singers, hearing is perhaps the most readily accessible monitoring device, but unfortunately it is not always the most dependable. A third level is *kinesthetic* (feeling), or developing awareness of physical sensations associated with any form of body movement (standing, walking, sitting, gesturing, etc.), the tensing and relaxation of muscles, and even sensing vibrations of acoustical energy generated by vocal responses. A fourth level, which relies on the three previous sensory levels, is based on an *analytical* (thinking) approach—for example, learning cognitively how the voice functions physiologically and acoustically.

Because of how the human body is constructed, it is physically impossible for us to hear our voices as others do. Upon hearing our recorded voice for the first time, we often react to the vocal sound in disoriented disbelief. "That can't be me, I don't sound like that!" is a typical response. Developing an ear for our true vocal sound and hearing ourselves as others do requires the assistance of a good-quality audio recorder. Without feedback from an impartial listening source, we hear our voices primarily through internal head-bone conduction and reflected external sound waves, which presents a distorted impression at best.

Paradoxically, the individual's perception of his or her sound is often somewhat different from the way it is externally perceived by others. Since the phenomenon of *inverted imagery* applies in all areas of singing, it must be kept in mind constantly if a singer wants to make steady progress. For this reason, the voice student must have confidence in the teacher's assessment, and diligently execute all reasonable instructions.

The relevance of the inverted image, and an expanded concept known as the *integration of opposites*, can be further explained by viewing an illustration of the "pendulum analogy" (Figure 3-1). The pendulum at rest (center) illustrates a co-

Figure 3-1
The Pendulum Analogy

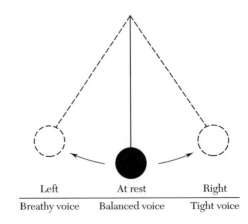

Left	At rest	Right
Breathy voice	Balanced voice	Tight voice

ordinated vocal process; the polarities or opposites of movement represent the singer's shifting vocal quality in varying degrees to the right and left of center. For example, a singer who is tight voiced (extreme right) might be well advised to work toward the other extreme, namely vocal relaxation or breathiness (extreme left), to counteract tightness caused by excessive muscle tension. It is possible such a singer may believe his or her voice is full and resonant, when in fact it is tight and tense. By thinking and working for a more breathy quality, the singer will probably make a vocal compromise, with the tone becoming more balanced in the middle of the two extremes.

Opposites: Coping with Contradiction

One perplexing issue students confront is the necessity of coping with seemingly contradictory concepts or instructions. For example, in the process of learning to sing, the student needs to reconcile contrasting vocal characteristics, such as brilliance and warmth, lightness and heaviness, intensity and relaxation, words and tone, vowels and consonants, releasing and focusing. To be instructed to do something that conflicts with previous instruction can be confusing: for example, when first encouraged to "relax and let go," but later told to "energize and intensify."

A philosophical explanation for this paradoxical phenomenon is that opposites represent the extremes of reality, which must be integrated and balanced in everything we do. Extremes or opposites of thought and action are manifested in a multitude of ways: between **classicism** (rationalism) and **romanticism** (emotionalism) in Western philosophy and its counterpart of "yang" (active, positive) and "yin" (passive, negative) in Eastern philosophy. Other significant examples include the opposites of science and art, form and content, idealism and realism, and product (ends) and process (means). Rather than reacting with distress when coping with opposites, we must simply accept their existence and then strive to reconcile and integrate them throughout the learning process. As English jurist, philosopher, and reformer Jeremy Bentham (1748–1832) said, "The mark of a first-rate mind is that it can maintain two contradictory ideas at one time."

The Two-Part Brain and Two Intelligences

Perhaps we are capable of reconciling opposites because the human brain is naturally equipped to handle such a complex task. Since the early 1960s, brain research has shown that two distinct regions of the cerebral cortex function independently by processing information differently. Theoretically speaking, the two hemispheres in the brain help us understand how we are able to learn and perform complex physical and mental skills, including singing.

The two lobes of the human brain are normally referred to as the left and right hemispheres. In general terms, the *left hemisphere* processes information by sorting and ordering individual components and is dominant in analytical/rational functions, such as speaking, reading, timing and rhythm, logical thinking, conscious mind processes, and controlling the right side of the body. The *right hemisphere* perceives stimuli holistically, contextually, and intuitively and is dominant in controlling visual-spatial relationships, pitch discrimination, imagination, creativity, expressiveness, and the left side of the body. Although the brain is composed of two equally important hemispheres, most tasks require collaboration between the two. This is especially the case with dynamic singing, which requires coordinated use of complicated intellectual, verbal, muscular, and vocal skills.

Closely related to the right/left brain connection are two types of intelligence, both of which are important in learning and executing tasks. The familiar type of intelligence is associated with "smartness" and is typically measured by traditional IQ (intelligence quotient) tests. Goleman (1995) has labeled the other *emotional intelligence*, which is measured by such personal qualities as self-awareness, self-motivation, persistence, empathy, social deftness, altruism, and compassion. Such emotional qualities play a predominant role in determining how people of moderate IQ are capable of achieving outstanding accomplishments, all the while coping effectively with life's normal ups and downs.

The Two Aspects of Self

Another illustration of opposites can be found in comparing our external lives with our internal lives. Our *external life* involves what we do in the world, the way we present ourselves to others through our looks and behavior, and how we interact with our environment. In contrast, our *internal life* involves our psycho-emotional selves—the way we think and feel about everything we experience. One way to view these two realms is as "game boards" on which we play continuously.

In external games, we work to overcome obstacles that interfere with external goals—for example, doing whatever is necessary to perform well and gain success. In internal games, we struggle with inner obstacles that block our goals—for example, gaining self-confidence by overcoming self-doubt and fear. By eliminating or minimizing internal obstacles, we can more easily achieve external goals, effectively reconciling and integrating these two opposites.

In the realm of vocal performance, the external game is to overcome all external obstacles associated with the performance of a prepared vocal work. The internal game is to overcome the mental and emotional obstacles we might encounter through the learning and performing process, including the anxiety known as stage fright or performance anxiety. As with most activities requiring complex skills, the main way to reduce anxiety is to reconcile and balance it by focusing our mind on the external goal or task at hand (an expressive rendition of the song's message for the benefit of listeners) rather than self-conscious concerns ("What are people thinking?" or "How do I look?" or "Am I singing well?"). In this as in other situations, our thoughts govern our actions. Because stage fright is associated with high levels of stress, we will discuss this topic again in the next chapter, along with offering some proven stress-reduction strategies.

Extending the analogy further, the game of opposites can be described as a contest between two aspects of self: the *external/nurtured self* and the *internal/natural self*. The former represents all that we have become through the influences of civilization. And the latter represents the innate, instinctive, spontaneous, childlike self.

Personality integration requires connecting our internal and external selves, the states of *being* and *doing*. In the ideal world, people nurtured from birth to adulthood within a creatively stimulating learning environment develop the requisite knowledge and skills to play both external and internal "life games" effectively. In the real world, personal growth without negative influences is rare indeed, perhaps even impossible.

For additional information, see *The Inner Game of Music* (1986) by Barry Green with Timothy Galwey and *A Soprano on Her Head* (1982) by Eloise Ristad; both are highly recommended books for delving into these topics.

Learning Modes

Of course *how* we learn is just as important as *what* we learn. Research within the past two decades has increased our understanding of individual differences in how people select, comprehend, absorb, and use the raw data of experience. This subject, mentioned earlier from the viewpoint of sensory modes, is fully addressed in numerous publications, including Wesley Balk's *Performing Power* (1986) and Dawna Markova's *The Art of the Possible* (1991). Only a brief summary of the major learning/expressive modes—visual, auditory, kinesthetic, and analytical—is presented here.

- **Visual mode.** The visual learner receives input through the eyes and the inner window of the mind's eye. Experiences are processed through sight and visual images, such as visual details, colors, visions, maps, lines, lists, views, perspectives, drawings, doodlings, writings, graphical images, diagrams, charts, movies, television, photographs, and wardrobe. Visual output involves transferring ideas to visible form, as in writings, paintings, or film.

- **Auditory mode.** The auditory learner receives input through the ears, and experience is processed through sounds and words, by means of conversations, innuendo, vocal tones and inflections, music, spoken meanings, poems, stories, debates, speeches, noise, radios, audio recorders, and lectures. Auditory output involves using sounds and words to express consciousness. As might be expected, singers tend to be well developed in this mode.

- **Kinesthetic mode.** The kinesthetic learner receives input through hands, skin, and muscles. Experiences are collected in smell, movements, actions, touch, feelings, textures, awareness of physical space, temperature, pressure, use of energy, and internal images of feeling and movement. Kinesthetic output involves activity using the hands and body—running, walking, dancing, playing, working, and so forth.

- **Analytical mode.** In addition to the three principal learning/expressive modes, some psychologists refer to a fourth mode, analytical, which is associated with reason, logic, analysis, ideas, and abstract thought. People who are deep thinkers will use these rational tools both in receiving input and for expressing output.

Whether three modes or four, it is relevant for singers to be aware of the role each mode plays in learning and expression. Can you identify your primary learning/expressive mode from the preceding descriptions? Although most people have a dominant mode, all people use all three modes with varying degrees of competency. Even though it is a rarity to be equally proficient in all three modes, such proficiency would be ideal for singers, who must be equally skilled in imagination (visual), voice (auditory), and acting (kinesthetic) ability in order to become consummate vocal artists.

The Goal and the Journey as One

As with any challenging long-term task, the road that leads to success for a singer will be more interesting and rewarding if the focus is on *process* (means) rather than *product* (end). Focus on process means that our energy is concentrated on the entire journey rather than merely reaching a predetermined destination. There is very good reason for such an emphasis on the journey/process. To paraphrase Eloise Ristad (1982), if we single-mindedly concentrate all our energies on reaching a desired destination or goal, we risk missing out on some rewarding views, opportunities, and experiences along the way.

One of the major impediments on the road to learning is *impatience*. Because of eagerness to reach the destination, beginning students are often tempted to look

> When it comes to art, the real competition should be within yourself, with your potential: the struggle to draw the best from your spiritual, intellectual, and emotional wealth. Ultimately, there is only one competition in life, and that is the race with time [throughout life's journey] to realize your potential in only one lifetime.
>
> —James Conlon, conductor

for shortcuts or quick results, without applying the requisite disciplined mental and physical effort expected of elite singers. Experience suggests that when we learn to enjoy the journey—that is, the process of learning with the detailed routine of practice—real progress begins. In place of an instant-voice mentality, the cultivation of a long-term perspective will help prepare the learner for slower but steadier development.

Be forewarned that even the most patient, enjoy-the-process approach inevitably will include *learning plateaus*, those indefinite periods when little or no growth is apparent. In such situations frustration can be avoided and long-lasting results achieved by using learning plateaus as opportunities for consolidating and internalizing mind/body responses through purposeful, repetitious practice. By waiting patiently and continuing to plug away, the next growth spurt will probably take you by surprise.

Being process-oriented also means being continuously aware of your feeling state in the present moment. Consciousness of body/mind status helps you to focus attention on what's happening in the present rather than the past or future. This intense state of concentration, often referred to as *flow*, is easily acquired when you are deeply involved in an enjoyable activity that results in an optimal experience. Frequently, under such ideal conditions, your absorption in a challenging activity is so intense that nothing else seems to matter and time appears to stand still, an experience similar to the meditative results reported by yoga practitioners. When thinking of the activities you most enjoy, you surely will recall similar sensations associated with intensely experienced accomplishments. Wouldn't vocal study be more rewarding if you were to truly enjoy the many hours spent in preparation for performances?

By now it should be clear that learning to sing well, technically and artistically, takes considerable effort and time. Although learning cannot be rushed, you can certainly enhance the process by consciously working to make singing an enjoyable long-term pursuit. George Leonard, instructor in the martial art of aikido and author of a compelling little book, *Mastery: The Keys to Success and Long-Term Fulfillment*, addresses this topic with these words of wisdom: "We fail to realize that mastery is not about perfection. It's about a process, a journey. The master is the one who stays on the path day after day, year after year. The master is the one who is willing to try, and fail, and try again, for as long as he or she lives" (Leonard, 1992, p. 140).

To summarize some of the major points made thus far, effective learning requires willingness to make constructive personal changes. To make consistent, steady progress, the serious learner must give attention to the three "Ps" of personal growth: PRACTICE, PERSISTENCE, and PATIENCE.

The Singer as Risk Taker

Although conscientious singers must be willing to take calculated risks in their pursuit of excellence, they also must allow room for the possibility of imperfection or failure. The typical perfectionist struggles constantly in the pursuit of challenging goals, often driven by a subconscious *fear of failure* that can lead to procrastinating or shirking responsibilities. In stark contrast to the fear of failure, there is also the *fear of success*. It's difficult to understand why some people unconsciously

> I enjoy taking risks when I sing . . . I need to test my limits, to see how far I can go . . . I always make an effort to bring something new to the part instead of singing the same way night after night; there is always something I want to try out, something to analyze.
>
> —Ramon Vargas, tenor

sabotage their own efforts, but it might be attributable to an individual's inability to handle the high expectations associated with success. If either of these tendencies suit your personality profile, this might be the time to recognize the condition, accept it, and move forward with taking constructive measures to correct it.

The achievement of any worthwhile endeavor requires the investment of time and energy and a willingness to take some calculated risks, as the old saw, "Nothing ventured, nothing gained" aptly suggests. Participants in all kinds of competitive performance venues, notably sports, dance, and music, are typically strong, individualistic people with a high degree of risk tolerance. The risk-taking thrills sought by singers are usually connected with the major challenges of learning and performing extremely difficult vocal repertoire, such as full-length song recitals or major opera roles.

Process-oriented risk takers are continuously aware of their psycho-emotional states, a constant mind body awareness that focuses attention on the present rather than the past or future. Under ideal conditions this enjoyable state of intense concentration (flow) becomes so intense that time may appear to stand still. Singers, for example, frequently report being so caught up in performances that "it was over before I knew what happened."

One of the most impressive books on this subject is *Flow: The Psychology of Optimal Experience* (1990) by Milhaly Csikszentmihalyi of the University of Chicago. The author describes individuals who have self-contained goals, are seldom anxious, never bored, intensely involved with what is happening in the present, and capable of turning potentially threatening situations into enjoyable challenges. His rules for developing characteristics of a self-directed person (similar to those of the risk taker) are the following:

- **Set challenging yet realistic goals,** based on inner decisions rather than external sources, and plan a course of action to accomplish them effectively.

- **Seek a judicious balance** between your level of expertise and the opportunities any activity offers for self-expansion and improvement.

- **Concentrate fully on the activity** and you will lose self-consciousness (associated with stage fright) in the process of gaining an increased ability to sustain intense long-term involvement in rewarding activities.

Voice/Movement Improvisation Exercises

What follows are voice/movement exercises that involve making a vocal sound in conjunction with a corresponding physical movement. For example, a voice/movement event occurs when a person exclaims, "Oh!" in a surprised manner, simultaneously clasping his or her cheeks with both hands, or cheering "Yea!" accompanied by upraised fists when the home team scores a point.

The primary purpose behind these physical/vocal exercises is to explore uninhibited vocal expression, which whole-person actions require as synchronized mind/body coordination. As a strategy for developing spontaneous expression, mind/body exercises help free us from negative thoughts, or the "inner judges" we harbor. So when experimenting with sound/movement exercises, it helps to adopt a neutral attitude regarding right or wrong action. Instead, maintain an open-minded attitude, with the idea that whatever happens spontaneously in the act of connecting one's voice with body movement is perfectly acceptable. In performing these exercises, you are strongly encouraged to enjoy making a fool of yourself, in a playful spirit.

Exercise 3-1   MIRRORING

This exercise can be used in at least three situations: (1) as an individual working in front of a mirror; (2) as a couple, with each person taking turns leading; or (3) in a group with a selected leader, such as the instructor. In all cases, the idea is for someone to take the initiative in producing a unique motion exercise that is mimicked by the other. All the while, everyone simultaneously sings a mutually agreed upon vocal phrase. To keep the exercise uncomplicated, the phrase might be limited to simple vocal exercises (as found in Exs. 3-1a,b). These phrases may be sung on short phrases, such as "How are you today?" or "We/You are going home?", using progressively higher keys.

Exercise 3-1a

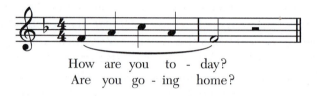

How are you to - day?
Are you go - ing home?

Exercise 3-1b

How __ are you __ to - day?
Are __ you go - ing home?

Exercise 3-2   PASSING AN OBJECT

This exercise is best done with the group standing in a circle. Someone describes an imaginary object, which is then passed from one person to another, simultaneously using voice and movement, until the exercise has come full circle. For vocal reasons, it helps to describe objects that require a healthy use of the mid-to-high-voice mechanism. For example, something described as "small, round, and lightweight" will elicit a higher, lighter voice than something described as "heavy and sticky." Each person is free to experiment vocally and physically, as long as the action reflects a genuine response to the imaginary object.

Exercise 3-3   TWO-PART VOICE/MOTION

The group again forms a circle. Each person performs a two-part maneuver: the first part when moving two or three steps into the middle of the circle and the second part when returning to the original position. Each consists of a different voice/movement exercise: *part one,* an inward voice/motion, and *part two,* returning using a contrasting voice/motion. After each person finishes, everyone mimics the entire voice/movement exercise in unison. Try

Adventures in Singing

not to plan ahead as to what you will do. The fun of the exercise is in experiencing the freedom of unconscious, spontaneous action. Don't think—do! Just go with the flow!

Exercise 3-4   PASSING ENERGY

Form a circle and act out passing "energy" (like a slow-moving electrical current) throughout the group from one person to the next. The energy enters each person at the point of physical contact and then passes to the next person through contact with any part of the body (finger, elbow, knee, foot, toe, head, hip). The energy source can be slow, fast, or variable, but it must be profoundly felt and vocally expressed as it progresses through the body.

Exercise 3-5   GIBBERISH

Gibberish is a form of made-up speech that can mimic any language but usually sounds more like a form of eastern European languages (Russian, Slavic) with all vowels and consonants in colorful combinations. (In other words, avoid voicing a few nonsense syllables repeatedly, like "lah-bah-doo-buh") To add an extra improvisational dimension, it can be applied to any of the preceding exercises. Making up a story in gibberish requires a bit more skill, but it provides a big challenge for those willing to work at it. Begin by sketching out a scenario. For example, a young man and woman get into an escalating argument that becomes even more aggravated as innocent bystanders join in the fracas, with the outcome left to chance. You can also create a skit around some object—a chair, a book, a coat, and so on. Now, if you really want to complicate the exercise, sing it! Speaking and singing in nonsense gibberish can be great fun, especially if you're a daring and skillful performer.

Voice and Self-Assessment

The following personal assessment exercises are questions that you can answer either mentally or in writing. You can also choose to answer them singularly or in a more general journal format.

Your Vocal Image.   Assuming that your singing is in a developing stage, what image do you have of your basic singing voice? Is it pleasing and satisfactory to you? Do you wish it were more like someone else's? If so, whose? What feedback have you received from others regarding your singing? Have you ever been discouraged from singing because of anyone's criticism? Do you have an idea of what you'd like your voice to sound like? What are some vocal qualities or characteristics you desire as long-term goals? In terms of the pendulum analogy, does your voice tend toward one of the extremes (breathy or tight) or more toward the balanced center?

Your Vocal Roots.   To explore your vocal roots, make a recording of yourself reading a text (poem, article, quotes) aloud using your normal speaking voice. Repeat the experiment with grandparents, parents, siblings, other relatives, and friends. In each case, describe the speaker's mannerisms as related to inflection, accent, pitch level, rate of speed, and phrasing. Make observations regarding both similarities and dissimilarities of your voice characteristics with those voices you have studied. What conclusions have you reached?

Your Ability to Cope with Change and Contradictions.   Can you think of some opposites other than those discussed in the text? If so, can you relate them to the process of learning how to sing? Do you consider yourself open-minded, or are you reticent to accept new information? Are you really willing to make changes in your vocal technique, or do you feel set in your ways? Can you make some differentiation between both your external and internal games and your external and internal self using concrete examples? Are you aware of the external forces or influences that helped shape your personality and who is ultimately in charge of your life?

Your Mental Attitude and Singing Personality. Which of the learning modes (kinesthetic, visual, auditory) do you perceive as your dominant mode? Which mode or modes need developing? Do you truly enjoy most of the activities you undertake or do you tend to be bored? Which activities do you most enjoy, and why? Do you think of yourself more as one who works only toward reaching a goal, or as one who also enjoys the process leading to the goal? Do you really like to sing because it's fun or because you think you should because of external pressure—parents, friends, teacher? Are you a person who plays it safe, or are you willing to take calculated risks in order to have a meaningful personal growth experience? Are you willing to share your inner thoughts and emotions ("bare your soul") with others as a communicative vocal artist?

Go to www.mhhe.com/ais4 to learn about additional Web-based resources that supplement the content of this chapter.

4

Energizing the Body

The Vocal Athlete

Like an athlete's body, a singer's body (his/her vocal instrument) needs comprehensive conditioning for managing challenging performance requirements, as well as providing protection against illnesses that aggravate voice problems. It's no wonder that serious-minded singers often think of themselves as "vocal athletes" in training.

> I try to do the "right" things by eating well, exercising regularly, and keeping in touch with my friends and family to keep myself balanced.
>
> —Elizabeth Futral, soprano

The mind/body coordination of an accomplished vocal athlete can be compared to that of an expert figure skater. Most operatic sopranos, for example, are capable of performing challenging opera arias, some climaxing with demanding musical passages containing a string of fast-moving notes rising to extremely high notes. In similar fashion, most well-trained figure skaters are skilled at executing double- and triple-axel leaps. To be sure, each uses different muscle groups, but the degree of achievement in each case is comparable. In both cases, performance expectations are extremely high, so exemplary results require (1) setting specific goals and objectives—short, medium, and long range, (2) setting high standards of excellence for technique and artistry, (3) committing to regular, self-disciplined effort and training, and (4) consistently producing a high level of physical energy for any given task.

> Singing is very athletic . . . When one stops doing it on a regular basis, one gets out of shape physically.
>
> —Patricia Craig, soprano

Admittedly, your motivation to study singing may not correspond to that of an "Olympic-level singer," but your level of energy is one measure of how far you will be able to go on your vocal journey. What is energy and how do you get it? Charles T. Kuntzleman offers a composite definition in his book, *Maximum Personal Energy:*

> Energy is your zest for working, playing, loving—living. It is the biological power or force within you—your physical capacity for living and your mental attitude toward your capacity for living. In practical terms, you have "energy" if you can get through your working day with enough resources to meet unexpected demands, and still enjoy life (Kuntzleman, 1981, p. ix).

Because energy is so crucial in athletic singing, we will discuss the energy building blocks of (1) fitness and exercise, (2) diet and nutrition, and (3) rest and relaxation. Then we will look at some strategies and exercises to build and maintain reservoirs of energy for dynamic singing.

Fitness and Exercise

Anyone trying out for a school-organized sport knows that getting in shape is expected. Because our bodies were designed by nature to be efficient, energy-producing mechanisms, we must engage in various kinds of physical activity regularly to develop peak performance.

The danger of a sedentary lifestyle is that prolonged physical inactivity leads to body weakness—inefficient lungs, a weaker heart, less-pliable blood vessels, and loss of muscle tone. With the body's capacity for delivering oxygen lessened, an overall weakened condition leaves the body vulnerable to illness and disease. Fortunately, sleeping, resting, and avoiding negative, artificial stimulants such as caffeine can help alleviate symptoms indicative of low energy levels and physical fatigue.

> I like to do power walking as often as I can. I work out a bit, sometimes at the gym. I lift weights, but I'm careful not to overdo it.
>
> —Samuel Ramey, bass

According to medical experts, the best type of physical conditioning for overall fitness is aerobic exercise. *Aerobic*, which literally means "with oxygen," is any activity that causes the participant to maintain a pulse rate in excess of 100 beats per minute for 20 minutes or more. Because oxygen economy is the key to physical endurance, the main benefit of aerobic exercise is the creation of a strong system of support for oxygen transport throughout the body. Exercise is virtually the only way to ensure that every cell in the body is furnished life-producing oxygen and that impurities are flushed out.

The *minimum* weekly exercise requirement for achieving optimum aerobic effect is 20 to 30 minutes of exercise at least three times per week, preferably on alternate days. An even better guide is to cover a distance of approximately two miles of variable terrain during each exercise session (or 8 to 10 miles if cycling). The safest and most sensible form of outdoor aerobic exercise is brisk walking for more than 20 minutes. Other popular forms of aerobic exercise include jogging, swimming, and cross-country skiing. Also, as part of a goal to adopt a physically active lifestyle, regular household tasks (cleaning, lawn mowing, leaf raking, snow shoveling) can be incorporated into an overall exercise plan. One hour of *accumulated* daily exercise (all types of physical activity) is highly recommended, and a half hour is a minimum. Whenever possible, develop a habit of walking rather than driving, taking stairs instead of elevators, fidgeting and moving about in place of spending many sedentary hours daily sitting at a desk, using a computer, playing video games, or watching TV. In other words, try to be more active.

In addition to aerobic exercising, everyone can benefit from judicious application of muscle stretching, calisthenic, and weight-lifting exercises to build muscle flexibility, strength, and tone. Other highly recommended mind/body exercise programs include the gentler forms of (1) yoga, a series of held postures or poses combined with breathing, (2) Tai Chi, a martial art form based on graceful movement and breathing, (3) Chi Gung, a combined form of breathing, movement, and meditation, and (4) Pilates, an exercise-based program for body balancing and alignment, with an emphasis on strengthening torso muscles. In addition, the Alexander Technique and the Feldenkreis Method are programs of self-discovery in moving with optimal efficiency. Each of these forms is represented by a variety of approaches, from gentle to more strenuous forms. Just be sure to do adequate research before settling on a program or an instructor.

Before undertaking any vigorous exercise program, it is important to have a thorough physical exam by a physician, which includes blood pressure monitoring and an electrocardiogram (EKG). It is usually recommended to begin an exercise routine cautiously, perhaps with muscle stretching and short walks, gradually increasing activity when the body is ready. Here is a rule for exercise as well as singing: *Always listen to your body*, and it will tell you what you are able to handle at any given time. The goal is to make physical conditioning a lifelong priority. Getting the most out of life—and your voice—begins with a serious commitment to maintaining a healthy mind and body.

Diet and Nutrition

The word *diet* in this discussion refers to a program designed to gain and maintain energy levels by means of ingesting nutritious food and liquids. Hence, although weight control is a very worthwhile benefit, especially as a measure for aiding long-term health, it is not the primary objective.

Fad diets—for example, high-protein/low-carbohydrate diets that emphasize one or two specific food sources—can be dangerous and should be avoided. In contrast, a well-balanced intake of all major food groups on a daily basis will satisfy normal nutritional needs. A healthy diet is based on a variety of the major groups: vegetables, fruits, grains, and meats. Although vegetables and fruits are nutritionally superior when fresh, canned foods are acceptable when packed in natural juices (or water) and free of excessive preservatives. As a general guideline for nutrition, seek out the natural state of any food source (e.g., fresh apples versus applesauce).

> Since then [being released from an opera contract because of her size] I've lost 45 pounds. Let's say I'm determined to lose more with [the assistance of] my personal trainer, with a combination of nutrition and workouts. I'm actually lifting weights!
>
> —Deborah Voigt, dramatic soprano

One of the most respected nutrition authorities is Walter C. Willett, M.D., chairman of the Department of Nutrition at the Harvard School of Public Health. In his popular book, *Eat, Drink, and Be Healthy: The Harvard Medical School Guide to Healthy Eating* (2001, p. 179), he summarizes his Healthy Eating Pyramid, which includes (in order of importance):

- Maintaining a stable, healthy level of weight for one's age.

- Replacing saturated and trans fats with unsaturated fats.

- Choosing healthier sources of proteins by trading red meat for nuts, beans, chicken, and fish.

- Eating plenty of vegetables and fruits.

- Using alcohol in moderation.

- Taking a multivitamin for insurance.

Dean Ornish, M.D., whose professional work focuses on the roles of exercise and diet in achieving and maintaining optimal health, offers another excellent resource with his well-known book, *Eat More, Weigh Less* (Harpertorch, 2001). The guidelines of his "Life Choice Diet" are very similar to Willett's.

Rest, Relaxation, and Recreation

A typical student's daily schedule is often irregular and intense, filled with a multitude of activities, including heavy academic loads, part-time jobs, extracurricular activities, and socializing. Such hectic schedules often lead to accumulated stress, leaving little or no time to catch up when getting sick or falling behind in meeting obligations. The result can be an occasional "crash" or "burnout," when the body says, "I've had enough" and shuts down for a day or longer. What can be done under such circumstances?

First, set priorities based on what is truly important in your life, with good health quality ranked at the top. Then be sensible in applying yourself so that you can accomplish realistic goals. A "mission statement" can help you define fundamental principles that will in turn help you clarify goals and objectives. Stephen R. Covey, author of the book *The Seven Habits of Highly Effective People* (1990), provides guidelines in a workbook format.

Everyone needs time to rest and recharge the body's "energy batteries," particularly during stressful periods when energy levels are low. The most significant rest period is the customary seven to eight hours (or more) of sleep that's needed by most people, especially young adults. Studies have shown that the more regular and peaceful the sleeping period, the more the body is revitalized. Because sleep requirements vary considerably among individuals, each person needs to learn how much sleep is required for optimum functioning. Whatever the amount of sleep, it should be scheduled into a daily time-management program.

For most people, relaxation (quiet time) and recreation (play time) are prerequisites for a sense of wholeness. Any activity that diverts the mind from other stressful activities and sets the stage for regeneration is salutary. Rather than waiting for a "crash time," consider scheduling regular recreational or hobby pursuits.

Assuming one has tended to all the health promoting guidelines discussed thus far—exercising regularly, ingesting nutritious food and drink, and getting sufficient rest and recreation—there still remain some helpful strategies for handling the considerable stress levels that singers encounter. Fortunately, there are several helpful stress-reducing strategies that can be used to calm and focus the mind, as well as relaxing and tuning the body for optimal neuromuscular responses.

Though muscle tension is largely determined by one's emotional state, relaxation techniques often begin with breathing and releasing muscle tensions. There are several proven methods for achieving more awareness of tensions associated with some common ailments, such as headaches, muscle spasms, and general aches. The three exercises that follow may help you to relax physically and calm your mind.

According to Jon Kabat-Zinn, a prominent expert in stress reduction, one of the most common relaxation techniques is *meditation*, an approach to living with awareness by paying attention to what is being experienced. He further describes meditation as a discipline for training the mind for the purpose of developing greater calm, which can be used to bring penetrative insight into our own present experience. It's a way of slowing down, allowing us to get in touch with ourselves, so we can inform our doing with a greater level of awareness and consciousness (Moyers, 1993).

An effective and easy way to achieve what is known as the *relaxation response* is to combine meditation with *progressive relaxation* techniques, by concentrating on relaxing certain muscle groups while moving thoughts slowly and methodically throughout the entire body. The technique begins with tightening muscles, followed by releasing tensions and observing the difference in sensations. Though it is possible to learn *biofeedback* techniques using the latest high-tech laboratory research equipment (such as electromyography) with expert medical supervision, one also can learn how to relax using the following very low-tech relaxation and meditation routine (Ex. 4-1).

34

Exercise 4-1   RELAXATION AND MEDITATION ROUTINE

This routine takes only a few minutes and is worth trying. To begin with, if surrounding noise is distracting, use earplugs, white background noise, or relaxing recordings of music. Wear comfortable loose-fitting clothes and close your eyes to shut out visual distractions. In addition to coping with normal stress, this exercise can be especially helpful in calming and centering oneself before a performance.

1. **Sitting position.** Sit in a comfortable straight-back chair in an erect, upright posture on the front edge—shoulders squared, chest elevated, and head stretched upward comfortably with a feeling of lift at the back of the neck. Knees should be separated approximately 8 to 12 inches and legs slanted forward with knees angled slightly more than 90 degrees. Hands and arms can hang loosely at your sides.

2. **Rag doll.** From this sitting posture, collapse over and downward like a loose rag doll—head forward, spine rounded, arms hanging, and chest coming to rest on the knees. While in this relaxed position, use autogenic phrases (self-talk) such as "I'm feeling calm, my right arm is heavy, my left arm is heavy, my fingers and hands are heavy," and so on. After about 20 to 30 seconds, straighten up slowly to a sitting position while taking a slow, full, deep breath. When attaining full upright posture, exhale the breath in a deep, peaceful sigh.

3. **Tension/release body scan.** In sitting position, with hands in any comfortable lap position, mentally scan (X-ray) the entire body from toes to head, first tensing muscles and then relaxing them. Start with the muscles of the feet by flexing and contracting toes and arches; then slowly move to the calves, thighs, hips and pelvis, lower abdomen (briefly observe breathing), stomach, back, chest, shoulders, arms, neck, and face. Facial muscles can be tightly drawn toward the center of the face and released; next, they can be expanded outward using a terrified expression (think of the boy—Macaulay Culkin—in the movie *Home Alone*) and then relaxed. In place of deliberate muscle tensing, it will also work well to mentally scan the body slowly from toe to head for existing muscle tensions, releasing tensions at will.

4. **Breathing concentration.** While seated, observe normal breathing characteristics for a few moments. If the rate of breathing is fast, allow it to slow down. If it is shallow and high, allow it to feel deeper. It is possible at this point to coordinate a "focus word" with the rise and fall of the breath, in the manner of safely floating in a rubber raft on gently rising and falling ocean waves. The focus word can either be voiced mentally on the exhalation cycle of the breath or according to personal preferences. Whenever the mind wanders, calmly bring it back to the breathing. Continue for at least 5 minutes or more.

Exercise 4-2   GUIDED FANTASY ROUTINE

This relaxation technique involves actively imagining personal situations that help you find deeper relaxation. A very simple technique is to close your eyes and imagine a peaceful scene, such as sitting on a sunny beach, viewing and listening to the surf, or sitting on a rocky ledge, viewing a panoramic mountain vista on a beautiful, temperate day. Think of memorable places and times in your life and select a few you can recall at any time for meditative and relaxation purposes. Whatever the imagery, the idea is to feel as though you are actually there with all your senses (hearing, seeing, feeling, smelling) tuned in to the occasion.

Exercise 4-3   CALMING RESPONSE

This brief technique, which is similar to the guided fantasy routine, can help break negative concentration or defuse a frustrating situation. Simply envision someone or something you care about. Then smile inwardly to yourself and say, "My body is calm, and I am at peace." You then inhale a little deeper than normal, and as you exhale allow your jaw, tongue, and shoulders to relax and drop a bit.

Care of the Singer's Instrument: Voice and Hearing

Although the first line of defense for warding off vocal problems is to maintain overall good health, you can still become ill and develop voice problems. Most singers have been vocally incapacitated at one time or another due to fatigue, illness, voice misuse, and abusive behaviors. Mild bouts of vocal fatigue are common among active voice users, especially when undergoing stresses that lead to a general run-down condition.

Susceptibility to vocal fatigue is a highly individual matter, closely related to your emotional, mental, and physical health. For this reason it is difficult to draw clear-cut guidelines applicable to all vocalists. For example, almost everyone has observed some "iron-voice" singers who are capable of sustained aggressive vocalism in spite of consistent mistreatment of their bodies and voices. On the other hand, some singers abide by all the rules of vocal health and yet are unable to ward off vocal problems. For whatever reasons (genetics, lifestyle, personality), some people tolerate stress better than others. Fortunately, by recognizing strengths and weaknesses and developing effective coping strategies, you can partially compensate for both natural and acquired limitations.

How does a singer know when there's a voice problem needing attention? In most cases, the problem comes about after a short-term upper respiratory illness, such as a cold or flu, or following excessive or abusive voice use. Some telltale vocal symptoms to listen for are marked disturbance in high pitches and soft-toned singing, intonation problems, particularly flat pitches in register transitions, "breaks" or sudden jumps from the upper end of the middle register into the head register, and less resonance and "ring" in the tonal quality. In addition, singers might also experience a lowering of pitch in the speaking voice, difficulty with singing in the middle-to-upper vocal ranges, a hoarse tonal quality marked by roughness and difficulty with phonation, and a need to remove a perceived obstruction from the throat by constantly clearing and coughing.

It's well documented that dehydration leads to unhealthy vocal conditions (including increased, thickened mucous flow) and precipitates infections. Because the human body is composed primarily of water, with up to a quart per day excreted in mucous alone, we need to drink 7 to 9 glasses of liquids daily to replenish reserves and maintain adequate hydration. Noncaffeinated drinks are recommended, but 1 to 2 cups or glasses of caffeinated drinks (coffee, tea, soft drinks) are usually acceptable. Moreover, it's essential to maintain a humid living environment (40 to 50 percent humidity), so when your indoor home environment becomes very dry, consider using a properly functioning steam humidifier or vaporizer, taking care to keep it free of mildew, mold, and bacteria.

Though most people err on the side of not drinking sufficient amounts of liquids, there are others who drink too much, constantly sipping or gulping. The ubiquitous water bottle has increasingly become a common site among singers, and there are indications that overdrinking is rather common. Some medical experts are now speaking out about the hazards of consuming too much liquid too quickly, or more than .7 of a liter per hour, the amount the kidneys can process. In extreme cases the result is "water intoxication," with body cells becoming overloaded and swelling like sponges. All body organs are negatively affected by swelling tissue, including the brain and vocal folds, and a "rebound effect" causes excessive mucous flow, the bane of singers. Also, the admonition to "pee pale," presumably an indication of adequate hydration, is now being questioned by some experts. In sum, when unsure of what to do, always let moderation be your guide, and stay abreast of the latest medical research.

Of course, everyone—singers in particular—is strongly advised to avoid ingesting or inhaling any harmful substances, including excessive amounts of alcohol, tobacco products of any kind, or any recreational drugs (too many to list). Singers who fail to abstain from harmful substances are taking uncalculated risks with their physical and vocal health and stunting their vocal progress in the process. In sum, the risks associated with using mind/body-altering drugs are too great for any singer to experiment with them. Using any potentially addictive substances can be condoned only under special medical conditions, such as when undergoing treatment for serious illnesses under the supervision of a qualified physician.

It's possible that when first experimenting with new vocal techniques, a singer might experience some peculiar throat or neck soreness and pain. In some cases the problem may be attributed to using certain muscles that have not been exercised regularly. But if the problem persists for more than a few days, it may be time to reevaluate your vocal exercises and how you're executing them. In any case, when any vocal problems arise, whether due to illness (colds, allergies, etc.), misuse, or abuse, professional advice is needed, beginning with your teacher. After hearing you, he or she will probably recommend that you see a vocal specialist known as an *otolaryngologist*. After performing a thorough examination of your throat and larynx, the physician will offer a diagnosis, and possibly prescribe medication. Or perhaps you will be referred to another medical specialist, such as a *speech-language pathologist*, one who assists with rehabilitating injured voices. Because singers use their voices in a more high-powered way than the average person suffering a voice disability, some research is needed to find a voice doctor experienced in working with singers.

The most common vocal problems that singers encounter are upper-respiratory ailments caused by allergies, asthma, colds, bronchitis, sinusitis, flu, and the like. Remedies generally include the standard treatment—getting sufficient sleep, vocal rest, ingesting healthy liquids, and taking appropriate medications. The list of treatments varies according to who's prescribing, but most medical experts caution against using all-purpose over-the-counter medications, such as decongestants or menthol-based lozenges that cause dehydration. Seemingly everyone has a "miracle pill" to recommend (zinc, vitamin C, various herbs, etc.), but it's best to observe common-sense guidelines (see "The Do's and Don'ts of Vocal Health") and avoid taking any scientifically unproven substances. Even aspirin has its downside when used in excess, with its function of blood thinning, which has been linked to rare cases of vocal-fold hemorrhaging.

Other notable voice disorders include (1) *Temporomandibular* dysfunction (TMD), which can create a variety of painful symptoms throughout the facial, neck, and shoulder areas; (2) *gastroesophageal reflux disorder* (GERD), the backup of stomach acids into the upper airways and larynx; (3) *hormonal conditions*, such as menstruation, menopause, etc.; (4) *vocal nodules*, which may be the combined result of misuse, abuse, chronic gastric reflux, or other causes; and (5) a variety of severe disorders that directly affect the vocal folds, such as contact ulcers, polyps, cysts, and blood vessel hemorrhaging. All the preceding disorders require more information than the scope of this book allows, but more information is easily available on several medical Web sites.

Because singers rely on their hearing for feedback and for fine-tuning the voice, being aware of aural health and knowing how to prevent excessive hearing loss are important. The Environmental Protection Agency estimates that more than 20 million people are exposed to injurious noise levels every day, and 16 million suffer impaired hearing due to genetic damage, disease, or excessive loud noise. No age group is immune to "noise pollution," and there is growing evidence that young people today are experiencing greater hearing loss than previous generations. The growing addiction to using various types of listening devices—cell phones, music-listening devices, computer and TV earphones—is contributing to an increase in dysfunctional hearing, particularly among youth who have grown up using them. The main problem is that many users plug these devices into their ears for hours daily, not only for their listening pleasure and to communicate with others, but partially as a way of masking environmental noise. Unfortunately, the tendency is to turn the volume so high that, over time, hearing can become damaged.

To protect against hearing loss, try to (1) reduce the number of hours per week of exposure to loud noises (90 decibels or more for extended periods), including music; (2) wear ear protection whenever possible (plugs or muffs); (3) have a periodic examination by an audiologist or otologist if hearing damage is suspected; and (4) if hearing loss is severe, consider being fitted with one of the latest-model hearing devices, which are greatly improved in comparison with the older models.

General guidelines for maintaining a healthy vocal instrument are summarized succinctly in the box titled "The Do's and Don'ts of Vocal Health." These pointers should prove very helpful in safeguarding your voice, hearing, and overall health.

The Do's and Don'ts of Vocal Health

Do

- Consume a variety of nutritious foods, beverages, and vitamins.

- Attain and maintain physical fitness with regular aerobic and muscle-toning workouts.

- Obtain sufficient rest, sleep, and recreation.

- Maintain a humid living environment (40–50 percent humidity).

- Maintain body hydration by drinking 7 to 9 glasses of liquids daily.

- Use efficient vocal technique in speech and singing.

- Use the voice judiciously.

- Wash hands frequently.

Physical/Vocal Exercises

One of the perplexing "opposites" issues confronting singers is that of tension and relaxation. Every physical function involving muscle use is dependent on **muscular antagonism,** a balance of muscle tension and relaxation between **agonist** (prime mover muscle group) and **antagonist** (opposing muscle group). This may be confusing if we are accustomed to thinking of relaxation as a positive term and tension as a negative one. Muscular antagonism refers to the natural muscle opposition that occurs in physical activity, as when one set or group of muscles contracts while an opposing group relaxes. For our purposes, we will think of *relaxing* as a state of releasing negative, interfering muscular activity and *tensing* as a state of increasing muscular activity. Our objective will be to find acceptable ways to release those excessive tensions that often block mental, physical, and emotional energies.

The warm-up techniques are designed to assist you with a systematic approach for developing a balance between relaxation and tension. Whenever possible, a full-length mirror (or video camera/playback equipment) should be used to aid self-observation when doing these exercises.

Warm-Up Exercise Routine

Begin by reviewing the general exercises listed in chapter 2: Exercise 2-5, "Upward Stretch and Full Circle Draw," using the lip-buzz on sliding, random pitches; and Exercise 2-6, "Rag Doll Stretch." Begin with these exercises in preparation for the specific exercises that follow.

Exercise 4-4   TENSION/RELEASE

As though lifting a heavy weight, stretch arms and hands out in front of you; tighten and release. Spread arms straight out to both sides; tighten and release. Pull shoulders up to ears; tighten and release. Make a distorted, tense facial expression and release.

Exercise 4-5   SHOULDERS

Lift shoulders to ears; hold, and drop. Rotate forward, then backward two full turns. Notice the expanded rib cage and the elevated chest position that result when shoulders rotate to a backward position.

Exercise 4-6 NECK AND HEAD

Stretch gently and slowly to the left and right by looking over your shoulder, each time holding the position 4 to 5 counts. Then, while looking straight ahead, tip your head toward your left shoulder, then toward your right shoulder, and then forward for 4 to 5 counts per position. Create a "dumb-jaw" effect by letting the jaw drop open when you lean your head left and right.

Exercise 4-7 JAW

Begin with the dumb-jaw look, feeling absolutely no facial expression other than stupidity. (For most singing, notably in the speaking ranges, jaw drop should not be exaggerated. However, for high-note singing, there must be a considerable jaw drop.) Sigh contentedly with the jaw stretched comfortably. Chew slowly and with exaggeration. Check under the chin (from chin to larynx) for muscle tension. Move the jaw from side to side (with the tongue following the jaw's motion). These exercises will help you discover tensions and create flexible, articulating organs. (Note: Grinding and clicking sensations in the jaw should be checked by a physician, especially if there is any pain.)

Exercise 4-8 TONGUE FLEXING

Stick the tongue out as far as possible. Roll it around, then side to side, and finally up and down. While gently holding the chin in a relaxed, downward position with your index finger, sing the vocal exercises (Exs. 4-8a, b) 1–2–3–4–5–4–3–2–1 and 1–3–5–8–5–3–1 on the syllable "yah," with the tongue sticking out on the first, highest, and last pitches.

Exercise 4-8a

```
Yah _   yah _    yah _  yah _   yah
Lah _   lah _    lah _  lah _   lah
```

Exercise 4-8b

```
Yah ____   yah ____   yah.
Lah ____   lah ____   lah.
```

Now sing "lah" on the same exercises, this time allowing the tongue to act as a valve cover for the mouth. In other words, extend the tongue up to initiate "l" and then down to lie relaxed in the mouth, lolling out on the upper lip. Roll an "r" as in "r-r-rah."

People who are tongue-tied may experience some minor difficulty with these exercises. This condition can be determined by examining the connecting membrane underneath the visible part of the tongue, from the bottom of the tongue blade to the bottom of your lower dental ridge. If the membrane extends more than halfway up the full extension of the tongue, you may have to adjust the way you articulate certain consonants, such as "l," "t," and "d," especially in high-range singing.

Allow the tongue to lie as relaxed as possible, with the rounded tip slightly touching the back side of the lower dental ridge and teeth. The tip of the tongue should never be pointed, pushed back, or curled up when sustaining vowel sounds, as any extraneous tension in the tongue will be felt and heard in the vocal tone, especially if the back of the tongue is tense. In general, the entire articulating mechanism should be flexible and agile for producing fast and crisp articulation.

Efficient Body Alignment

Appropriate alignment of the body is extremely important in setting up the right conditions for coordinating the vocal process. Physical carriage reveals much of your personality through "body language," and movement courses, such as modern dance, provide excellent training for the vocalist who desires to move with an attractive, graceful physical appearance. Valuable insight into proper body alignment may also be gained by investigating yoga, Tai Chi, Pilates, The Feldenkreis Method, and the Alexander Technique, a body-awareness method using principles of efficient body movement. A reprint of F. M. Alexander's book *The Use of the Self* (Centerline Press, 1984) is a prime source of information. Although we have worked on body alignment in earlier exercises, the following suggestions will further help you in developing a flexible, dynamic posture.

Exercise 4-9   NINE STEPS FOR ESTABLISHING EFFICIENT BODY ALIGNMENT

This exercise will take you through 9 steps to help align your body for optimal singing.

1. Start with the "Rag-Doll Stretch" (Ex. 2-6) to create a spinal stretch from the bottom to the top of the body. Beginning at the feet, slowly straighten up from the bottom upward: first to the knees, second to the buttocks and waist, then vertebra by vertebra upward to the top of the neck and head.

2. Assume the stance of an athlete ready for action: vital and balanced with feet planted firmly on the floor. You should feel anchored to the floor, yet buoyant.

3. Place feet 6 to 12 inches apart with one foot slightly in front of the other for total balance.

4. Keep the knees flexible and unlocked, and tuck the posterior slightly to avoid a swayback and to balance the pelvic area.

5. The abdominal area remains relaxed on inhalation and the lower abdominal area remains firm (but not tight) on exhalation.

6. The chest remains comfortably high, but *not* pushed out and upward in the manner of a soldier at attention (see Fig. 4-1).

7. The shoulders hang loosely and relaxed with arms dangling loosely at the sides of the body.

8. The neck is held in an erect position, but not rigidly.

9. The head is balanced on top of the spinal column so that it can roll easily in any direction. A good analogy of this flexible balance is a bowl turned upside down and balanced on the tip of a short stick.

Figure 4-1
Incorrect and Correct
Body Alignment

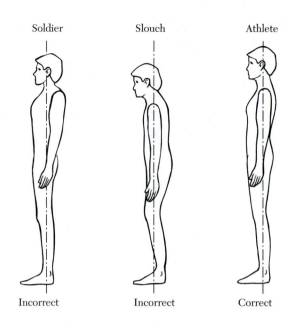

Soldier   Slouch   Athlete

Incorrect   Incorrect   Correct

Vocal Athlete Assessment

Caring for Your Voice. How do you feel about your genetic endowment? What physical limitations have you observed or have been pointed out to you by others that might have a bearing on your vocalism? Have you experienced any vocal disorder because of illness or misuse and abuse? If so, how have you dealt with the problem? If you have an ongoing affliction—for example, allergies, asthma, temporomandibular joint (jaw hinge-joint) problems, gastric reflux, or hormonal imbalance—does it affect or incapacitate you as a singer? Do you recall any major changes in your voice that occurred because of physical growth and aging, such as the typical voice change that occurs during adolescence? If so, do you recall your thoughts and feelings about the change and how you used your voice? Is your daily professional activity "voice intensive?" If so, do you take care to use your voice according to techniques discussed in this book? Are you frequently exposed to loud noise or sound? Do you take precautions to protect your hearing?

Caring for Your Body. How would you classify your eating and drinking habits? Do you eat balanced meals (major food groups) regularly, primarily for nourishment and nutrition? Have you ever dieted to lose or gain weight? Is your present weight normal for your height, body type, age, and sex? How would you classify the physical activity quotient of your life? Are you sedentary, somewhat active, moderately active, or very active? As a vocal athlete, are you a spectator, a "bench warmer," a sandlot player, an amateur player, or an aspiring professional? What type of physical activity do you do on a regular basis? Does your exercise program include a variety of physical activities, including aerobics and muscle stretching, toning, and strengthening? Are you aware of your posture and the way you "carry yourself" throughout each day? How do you visualize your health in 5, 10, 20, and 30 years? Are you satisfied with the way you treat the vehicle in which you will journey the rest of your life?

Go to www.mhhe.com/ais4 to learn about additional Web-based resources that supplement the content of this chapter.

CHAPTER

5

Managing Breath

The Role and Benefits of Breathing

Depending on an individual's level of activity, a typical adult completes approximately 20,000 to 25,000 breath cycles daily, in the process exchanging 10,000 or more liters of air. For healthy adults, the normal involuntary at-rest inspiration-expiration cycle lasts about four to five seconds, with inspiration taking approximately one second and expiration averaging about three seconds.

Although breathing is, for most purposes an automatic subconscious function, we are able to exercise some degree of voluntary control. Yoga practitioners are able to regulate their pulse rate, metabolism, and brain activity through direct control over their breathing. Athletes, particularly swimmers, weight lifters, and long-distance runners, rely on their aerobic training and breath control to accomplish feats requiring physical strength and stamina. Because vocal athletes are also highly dependent on their respiratory capacity, they, too, must learn how to optimize their ability for taking in air and managing it effectively.

Some of the potential benefits of conscious, self-regulated breathing include increased physical strength, heightened awareness, acute concentration, and total relaxation. One special benefit of a singer's deep-breathing practice is an increased output of *endorphins*, the same hormones released in aerobic exercise that produce a relaxation response.

An understanding of the respiratory mechanism and its functioning will help you develop and maximize your breathing in all facets of life, including speaking and singing.

The Anatomy and Physiology of the Respiratory System

For study purposes, the anatomical structure of this highly efficient "breathing machine" can be organized into four principal components: (1) skeletal framework, (2) head airways and larynx, (3) sublaryngeal system (trachea, bronchi, lungs, diaphragm, and rib cage), and (4) musculature.

Skeletal Framework

The underlying structure of the respiratory system consists primarily of the *torso* (body trunk), except the head airways. The *spine*, or backbone (Figs. 2-1 and 5-2), is the main pillar of the breathing mechanism and is composed of 24 *vertebrae*, graduated in size from the smallest in the neck to the largest in the small of the back. The 12 ribs (Fig. 5-2), or *costae*, are somewhat semicircular, and the upper

43

seven of them connect with the breastbone (sternum) in front, forming an imperfect circle. Because they do not reach the sternum, the very short eleventh and twelfth ribs are known as "floating ribs." Ribs 8, 9, and 10 show the most movement during inspiration and expiration. The *rib cage* serves as the housing for the lungs and diaphragm. The importance of keeping the rib cage comfortably raised in singing will become more evident as we proceed.

Head Airways and Larynx

The source of energy or fuel used in respiration is the very air we breathe, and the two head airways are in the nose (nasal cavity) and mouth (oral cavity). The passage of air into the body begins in the nose and mouth (Fig. 5-1) and continues through the **pharynx** (throat), the larynx, the trachea, and the bronchi, into the lungs.

For quick breaths and exhalations—as during heavy physical exertion and fast, loud, singing—mouth breathing is more efficient than nose breathing. When done properly, the advantages of mouth breathing are that (1) volumes of air can be inhaled more quickly and (2) more interior space is formed by lifting and arching the soft palate, relaxing the articulating organs (tongue and jaw), and lowering the larynx. The combined result is a vocal tract effectively prepared and aligned for singing. Because the nasal passages are equipped to filter, moisten, and warm the air as it enters the body, singers should try to breathe through the nose whenever feasible, especially when the pacing or mood of a song permits slower breathing. The sensation of correct mouth inhalation is a "cool spot" high in the back of the throat at the level of the soft palate. After achieving this initial breathing position, the singer simply maintains the established "sensation of breathing" throughout the singing process.

The valving action of the larynx allows for the movement of air in and out of the lungs, with the opening and closing of the vocal folds. When the folds are open, air is allowed to pass in either direction—in or out. When the folds close during such acts as holding one's breath (swimming underwater), the air is effectively "dammed" by the folds' closure. This valved adjustment of the folds during singing retains and slows the exit of air at a pace partially determined by technical facility, dynamic levels, vocal range, and length of musical phrases. (The role of the larynx is more fully discussed in the next chapter.)

Sublaryngeal System

Air movement from the larynx to the lungs passes first via the **trachea** (windpipe), a flexible, cylindrical, cartilaginous pipe resembling a vacuum hose, to the two

Figure 5-1
The Breathing Mechanism

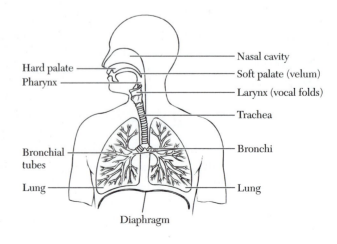

Hard palate
Pharynx
Bronchial tubes
Lung
Nasal cavity
Soft palate (velum)
Larynx (vocal folds)
Trachea
Bronchi
Lung
Diaphragm

bronchi (branches) within the lungs. From there, the bronchi further subdivide into millions of ever narrowing **bronchiole** that terminate in approximately 3 to 7 million *alveoli* (air cells), where carbon dioxide and oxygen are exchanged.

The *lungs* (air sacs) function somewhat like rubber balloons filled with air. Because of their elasticity and spongelike characteristics, the lungs gradually expand as air is inhaled. When the lungs are filled, the accumulated air pressure exerts a recoil force upon exhalation that reduces them to their preinhalation state. So the volume of expired air is directly proportionate to the amount of air inhaled, the body's way of equalizing inside and outside air pressure. You can observe this phenomenon by inhaling and exhaling a series of increasingly larger breaths, each time noting the proportionately larger volume of air expelled with the increasingly larger breath intakes. The volume of air moved in and out of the lungs depends on an individual's air requirements at any given moment.

Respiratory Musculature

The **diaphragm** (Figs. 5-1 and 5-2), the second-largest muscle in the body and the single-most important muscle in the process of inhalation, is responsible for 60 to 80 percent of increased air volume. Separating the **thorax** (chest cavity) from the **viscera** (abdominal cavity), the diaphragm serves as both the floor of the chest cavity and the ceiling of the abdominal cavity. Unlike most skeletal muscles (which exist in pairs, one for each side of the body), the diaphragm is a single muscle that spans the entire thoracic cavity. During inhalation, the diaphragm flattens to resemble the shape of an inverted salad plate, forcing the abdominal organs downward and outward, distending the abdominal wall, and creating a bulge in the epigastrium—the triangular part of the abdomen located at the base of the sternum, directly below the ribs. At rest the diaphragm resembles an inverted salad bowl with two irregular domes (Fig. 5-1), the right side of which is slightly higher than the left.

Two muscle groups called **intercostals** (Fig. 5-2) attach to the ribs, filling the gaps between the ribs with muscles and membranes. Their main purpose is to aid in inhalation and exhalation and to help create a constant air pressure below the

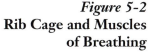

Figure 5-2
**Rib Cage and Muscles
of Breathing**

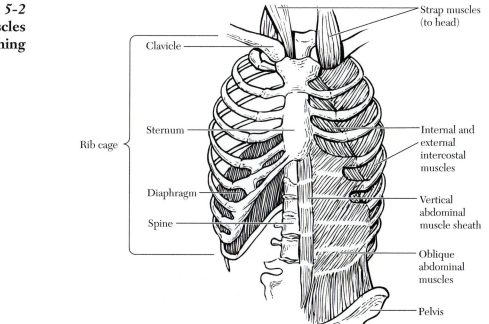

Strap muscles
(to head)

Clavicle

Rib cage

Sternum

Internal and
external
intercostal
muscles

Diaphragm

Vertical
abdominal
muscle sheath

Spine

Oblique
abdominal
muscles

Pelvis

vocal folds for voice use, which is accomplished by coordinating and balancing the action of the muscles involved in inspiration and expiration.

The external intercostal muscles raise the ribs, which are attached to the spine and sternum, and the width of the thoracic cavity increases. When we inhale, contraction of the external intercostals causes the rib cage to expand simultaneously vertically (up and down), horizontally (side to side), and anteriorly-posteriorly (front to back).

In contrast, the internal intercostal muscles, which are responsible for expelling air from the lungs, use a contracting, recoiling muscle action to lower the ribs, effectively causing the rib cage to collapse and decrease in size vertically, horizontally, and anteriorly-posteriorly. Singers try to resist this collapsing process by maintaining a comfortably high chest position.

The abdominal wall ("belly") muscles (Fig. 5-2) are used for expiration and to support or steady the tone when speaking and singing. They help achieve a coordinated balance of inspiration and expiration for voice use by providing opposition to the recoil forces of the lungs and diaphragm during expiration. These powerful vertical and oblique muscles cover the entire upper and lower abdominal region, including both sides. You will experience these muscles' opposing and balancing actions when using the breathing and singing exercises introduced at the end of this chapter.

Summary of Respiratory Action

During "normal, at-rest breathing," the action of the diaphragm and abdominal muscles during a complete inspiration-expiration cycle can be described in four phases: inspiration, suspension, expiration, and recovery (Fig. 5-3).

1. **Inspiration** (Fig. 5-3a). The in-down-out actions of inspiration consist of the following steps: (1) when oxygen is needed, the diaphragm contracts and rib cage volume is increased, assisted by the external intercostal muscles; (2) inhaled air enters through the mouth or nose, passes through the pharynx, larynx, trachea, and bronchi, filling and expanding the lungs; (3) the diaphragm descends; and (4) the chest and middle/lower torso area expands, particularly around the waist, including the sides and back. At rest, the inspiratory process takes approximately one second.

Figure 5-3
Air Movement during Inspiration and Expiration

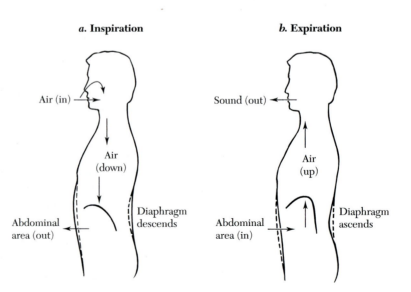

2. **Suspension.** A "brief" suspension period occurs when recoil forces overcome the muscular forces of rib-cage expansion, and the process reverses direction. This usually lasts less than a second but could last considerably longer if the muscles of inspiration (mainly the external intercostals) are held in a contracted state to check the recoil forces. However, there is seldom any need to suspend breath in speech or singing for longer than one second, because muscle tensions can occur throughout the breathing mechanism, creating a "locked" (static, held) position.

3. **Expiration** (Fig. 5-3b). The "breath release" cycle follows the reverse action of inspiration and consists of the following in-up-out actions: (1) the lungs recoil inward, drawing the rib cage with them; (2) the abdominal muscles and viscera (internal organs) begin returning to their resting state; (3) the diaphragm recoils upward; and (4) air is expelled from the lungs, first through the trachea and then through the larynx and vocal tract, either silently or with vocalized tone. The length of the expiration phase lasts approximately 1 to 5 seconds for normal speech, and 15 to 20 seconds for singing.

4. **Recovery.** Finally, there is a moment of relaxation for all muscles involved in the breathing process before the breath cycle begins anew.

Methods of Breathing

We can breathe three principal ways: high torso, middle torso, and low torso. The majority of singers concur that the most efficient approach involves both the middle and low torso. We will discuss these three approaches, from the least to the most desirable.

- **High torso breathing** involves shoulders and upper chest. This is the "breath of exhaustion" and is observed, for example, in sprinters who have just run 1,000 meters at top speed. In this type of breathing, the shoulders and chest pump violently to move air quickly in and out of the respiratory system. The breath of exhaustion is definitely not conducive to effective vocalism, as it leads to tensions in neck and throat muscles and unsteady tone production.

- **Middle torso breathing** involves expansion of the ribs (primarily sideways and partly forward), but neglects lower abdominal breath-related action. This "corseted" manner of breath control tends to create an overly pressurized, tense breathing system that restrains airflow, which in turn hinders voice production, especially in high-range singing. This Victorian manner of breathing was encouraged by a voice culture that used the admonition "hold in those tummy muscles," particularly when working with young women.

- **Low torso breathing** involves greater use of low abdominal muscles. In this method the diaphragm fully descends for a relaxed and complete breath. In middle torso breathing the lower abdomen is pulled in, whereas in low torso breathing these muscles relax and release. Low torso breathing is widely practiced in disciplines of meditation and concentration, such as yoga. Another low torso breathing method overemphasizes forced breathing activity in the lower abdominal area. Although deep breathing is beneficial for singers, excessive "pushing-down-and-out" muscular effort should be avoided.

- **Middle/low torso breathing** involves a combined use of the **costal** (rib) and abdominal muscles. This is the best possible breathing technique for singing and is achieved through a combination of middle and low torso expansion, which includes a comfortably elevated chest/rib cage to provide space for full lung expansion, and relaxed abdominal muscles that expand (primarily around the waist at the bottom of the rib cage) in response to diaphragmatic distension and downward lung expansion upon inhalation. The sensation of expansion is experienced around the entire waistline, including in the back, as most of the exercises below will demonstrate.

All three types of breathing are used at various times for specific purposes, but the middle/low torso combination is best suited for most physical activities. It helps to bear in mind that because breathing is a very natural process, most people tend to breathe adequately in most circumstances. However, in stressful situations—as often occurs in vocal performance—breathing can become shallow and labored. Also, because the act of singing is generally conceptualized as a superhuman achievement, novice singers tend to work too hard at breathing, often using gasping and pumping maneuvers. The purpose of the following exercises is to help you discover or rediscover the most naturally efficient way to breathe.

> You either breathe or you don't! I'm not a big one for focusing on that. People are going to read this and say, "What's she saying?" I think it [breathing for singing] should be natural.
>
> —Renée Fleming, soprano

Breathing and Breath Management Exercises

Many of the following exercises are most effective when done with the assistance of a full-length mirror. When performing these exercises, gain awareness of how your body works in breathing. First, try placing your hands (thumbs backward and fingers forward) on both sides of your waist, below the rib cage to sense expansion all around the waist. Next, place one hand over the upper abdominal area (epigastrium) and the other over the lower abdominal area to feel muscular actions. The lower abdominal area lies below the navel, which can be considered the center of the entire abdominal area.

Exercise 5-1 BLOWING OUT

In the standing "singer's posture"— upward stretched, chest uplifted, and feet evenly spaced—begin by blowing out (exhaling) as much air as possible. When air is expelled, hold for 5 to 6 seconds, or until you feel a strong need to breathe. Then, using the dumbstruck-surprise attitude, let the air rush in, comfortably filling the lungs. Observe the physical sensations associated with performing this exercise.

Exercise 5-2 LYING DOWN

Lie flat on the floor on your back and place both open hands over your entire abdominal area. It helps to place either pillows or rolled up towels under your neck and knees to better align the spine and reduce spinal stress. Breathe in and out in a slow, relaxed manner, observing the rise and fall of your abdominal area with each breath you take. Continue the exercise with the addition of a weight (such as a large book) placed on the upper abdominal area. Next, try lying on your stomach while breathing slowly and deeply, and observe what happens.

Exercise 5-3 PANTING

Pant like a dog at rates varying from fast to slow, and notice the outward and inward action of the high-middle-low abdominal area. Let your tongue rest loosely on your bottom lip with the jaw dropped comfortably.

Exercise 5-4 SITTING AND LEANING

Sit erect on the edge of a chair with your legs spread comfortably and rest your feet flat on the floor. Lean over slightly and place your elbows on your knees. You should be facing the floor at about a 45-degree angle. Take slow and relaxed breaths at first; then pant at various rates while observing the sensations experienced with lower-torso muscle action.

Exercise 5-5 STANDING AND LEANING

Stand erect with your legs spread as far apart as possible and with your hands on your waist in reversed position (thumbs forward). Affecting the mechanical manner of a "toy water bird," bend over slowly at a 45-degree angle from a fulcrum point at the bottom of the pelvic area (not at the waist). Breathe slowly, gradually increasing the breathing tempo as you pay attention to the action of the breathing mechanism.

Exercise 5-6 BENDING

Spread your feet slightly, stand erect, and then bend over at a 90-degree angle, placing your hands on your ankles. Breathe as described in the previous exercises, but be particularly aware of expanding when taking a full breath, which will be sensed as tightness in the back below the ribs. This exercise can also be done by placing your forehead on your hands at the edge of a table while bending over at a 90-degree angle.

Exercise 5-7 BENDING AND BLOWING OUT AN INTENSE FLAME

Assume the same position as in Exercise 5-6. Hold your right (or left) index finger approximately 4 to 5 inches from your mouth and pretend you are attempting to blow out an intense flame emanating from your fingertip. Use a vigorous breath for three to four seconds. Observe the action of the abdominal area and rib cage.

Exercise 5-8 SNIFFING AND HISSING

Begin by exhaling air from the lungs. Then inhale slowly through the nose for 3 to 4 seconds, until you reach a comfortable lung capacity. Next, while maintaining the sensation of inhaling, release the breath on a vigorous hiss through closed teeth (but relaxed jaw and articulators) for approximately 10 counts, releasing any pent-up air at the end. Observe the muscular responses that occur while hissing, as the abdominal muscles firm up and move inward throughout the exhalation cycle.

Breath Coordination and Management

Most singers are concerned about having enough air to complete long, difficult phrases. (In many cases inadequate breath in singing can be attributed partially to inefficiencies in vocal-fold vibration and resonation, topics to be addressed in subsequent chapters.) To compensate for running out of breath, some singers crowd the lungs with more air than needed, causing bottled-up, high-pressure sensations. Advanced-level singers plan and rehearse taking appropriately measured breaths to complete each phrase of a song without running out of breath. Occasionally, it may not be possible to make it through an extended phrase, in which case singers have the option of taking additional breaths at opportune moments. Only on rare occasions should one take a breath in the middle of a word—for instance, in some early music when sustaining extended vocal lines are set to a single word. An example of this occurs in the aria "Oh Sleep, Why Dost Thou Leave Me" by Handel at measure 19, page 200, on the word "wandering," where an optional **catch breath** is indicated. Such judicious catch breaths will usually not harm the phrasing, as long as the singer concentrates on the musical/textual intent of the phrase—that is, "carrying over" or "connecting" the textual and musical idea.

Frequently, the excitement and "performance jitters" of a performance cause a singer to burn more oxygen than normal, resulting in an inexplicable loss of breath. If you have difficulty getting through a specific phrase during rehearsals, it might be prudent to consider "working in" some extra breaths as a safeguard.

Relaxed breathing involves the rhythmic expansion and relaxation of the upper abdomen/epigastrium. Two muscle groups work in opposition to one another (the principle of muscular antagonism), with the lower abdominal muscles being active and the diaphragm remaining relatively passive. Airflow rate varies, depending on the demands of the spoken or sung phrase and the resistance of the vibrating vocal folds at the laryngeal level.

It usually works best for beginning students to concentrate first on acquiring a relaxed, yet energetic, flow of breath, although the eventual goal is to find a "balanced pressure" between inhalation and exhalation when sustaining tone. One way to get an image of balanced muscular coordination is to place the back of one hand into the palm of the other and applying a gentle but firm equalized pressure with both hands. Then allow one hand to slightly overcome the other, similar to the way abdominal muscles pull inward gradually during singing, as air is slowly expelled. The sniffing-hissing exercise (5-8) also demonstrates this principle very well.

When using abdominal muscle support, be aware of the tendency to tighten muscles rigidly. At all times the abdominal muscles must be flexible enough to respond to external manipulation. To demonstrate this, sing a sustained tone on "Ah," and press your fist inward on the epigastrium area (2–3 inches below the sternum) with regular pulses. You should hear and feel the tone changing from a soft to a loud (**marcato**) dynamic each time you press inward (see Fig. 5-3b, expiration).

Be aware that coordinating exhalation muscles requires contradictory muscle actions. For example, when the lower abdominal muscles firm up and move inward to expel air during exhalation, the epigastrium area (under the sternum and lower ribs) bulges outward; the degree of "bulging" is determined by how aggressively the lower abdominals thrust. This partially helps explain the controversial issue of whether one "supports" by "pushing out" or "pulling in." In reality, both pushing and pulling occur simultaneously, for when the lower abdominals are activated inwardly, the epigastrium automatically reacts by distending. (Please be cautioned that any in-or-out muscle movements should be the result of natural action, not artificially contrived efforts to push out or pull in abdominal muscles.) Though it is possible for a singer to achieve similar results by using either a pull-in or push-out technique, the preferred approach is to allow an inward movement of the lower abdominals when singing. These muscular actions can be experienced while singing marcato (stressed notes) exercises (see Exs. 5-14a,b).

Breath-Tone Coordination Exercises

Up to this point we've been working on exercises that aid in taking relaxed, comfortably full breaths. Now we turn our attention to techniques that assist in connecting breath with vocalized tone, in a coordinated action that involves using breath to activate vocal-fold vibration, in turn engaging the vocal tract resonators. With the exception of using an unvoiced hissing release of breath for the first exercise (Ex. 5-9), the remaining exercises require vocalized tone.

Exercise 5-9   DEEP BREATHING WITH TONE

Use the deep breathing exercises presented earlier, especially Exercises 5-1, 5-2, and 5-3, this time with normal vocalization. As described earlier (Ex. 2-7,1), place hands on the abdominal area to feel the breathing action.

Exercise 5-10   ABDOMINAL MUSCULAR RESPONSE

Establish the proper sense of muscular support by softly grunting, sobbing, laughing lustily, or calling out "Hey" or "Hi" as if to someone across the street, using the higher pitches of the head voice. Be aware that occasionally the natural response of these muscles is the opposite of the singing response. For example, they might go "down and out," not "in and up" as in healthy singing. Because these same muscles are used for evacuation of body wastes and other natural functions, singers must train them to work in an opposite movement but with the same intensity.

Exercise 5-11   BREATHE-SING

Place hands on your abdominal area, assume the correct posture, and relax. Perform the following exercises in an exaggerated panting manner (breathe—movement out; singing tone—movement in). Do this on a comfortable pitch and in moderately slow tempo, first with grace notes and then without them.

Exercise 5-11a

Hah _   hah _   hah _   hah _   hah _

Exercise 5-12   HOOK-UP MANIPULATION

Spread both hands over the middle-lower abdominal area and sing **vocalises** and phrases from songs that place sufficient demands on your breathing. Feel the outward action on inhalation as well as the inward and upward action when singing. Help the breath connection or "hook-up" by hand manipulation if necessary. If there is a pulling or sucking sensation when the breath releases during singing, it is probably a good indication that airflow is free. At the beginning it is fairly normal to experience a need for more breath. This sensation will change gradually as a balanced coordination of the vocal process is achieved. In any case, avoid pushing downward or outward during exhalation.

Exercise 5-13   BOUNCE-JIGGLE

Take a normal breath, and while vocalizing on a sustained pitch, bounce or jiggle your entire body by repeatedly rising on the balls of your feet (lifting and then dropping your heels). A more vigorous and rapid bounce will exaggerate the effect, demonstrating how the bouncing action causes breath to be forced from the lungs due to natural muscle responses.

Exercise 5-14 PULSATING AND STACCATO

Pulsating and staccato exercises will enable you to notice and develop a proper sensation of support in the coordination of breath and tone. The action of both the lower abdominal and back musculature will also be experienced when you do these exercises. Various combinations of rhythmic patterns and keys may be used in addition to the ones illustrated next. The idea is to move from slow to faster pulses as your technique allows.

The following pulsating and staccato exercises are to be sung on "ah" and other vowels, with marcato [>] and staccato [•]. Marcato requires a stressed, strong emphasis, whereas **staccato** requires a light, detached execution. The contrasts between slow, vigorous, loud laughter and faster, lighter, higher-pitched laughter will give you an idea of these two types of singing. In addition, you can sing the first verse of "Vocalizing Fun" (p. 129), which also provides an opportunity to sing some marcato and/or staccato notes on the nonsense word "hi-ho."

Exercise 5-14a

ah   ah   (etc.)

Exercise 5-14b

As we wind down this chapter on breathing and breath management, remember that *when you are breathing correctly, there is no gasping for air, and no distracting, stressful-looking movements in the head, neck, shoulders, and chest.* The best way to overcome these mannerisms is to be aware of them, and this will require observing yourself, using either a full-length mirror or a video camera. Think of the exaggerated posture of the traditional red-coated British royal guards at the entrance to Buckingham Palace, standing for long periods at rapt attention, as though frozen in place. Of course, there's no need to stand rigid like a palace guard. But you do need to know how to remain still, breathe, and sing with a steady visual and emotional focus that isn't broken by noticeable body movement, because no one enjoys viewing performers who exhibit superfluous body movements or unnatural facial grimaces. An exercise calling for lying on the floor (Ex. 5-2) can help you achieve a more poised way of breathing. So take a relaxed, full breath, and sing!

Breath Management Assessment

Breathing.   Have you had respiratory problems such as asthma, allergies, or bronchitis? If so, what effect did illness have on your voice? Are you ever conscious of your breathing during activities such as sleeping, public speaking, walking, jogging, and singing? Normally, do you breathe low and full, or high and shallow? How do you breathe when you are under physical or mental stress? Are you aware of your posture, chest, and rib cage positions throughout the day? Do you understand the physiology of breathing as discussed in this chapter? Do you think your body type affects your breathing habits? What sensations do you have when breathing deeply and fully? How would you describe your sensations when breathing during singing? Are these sensations different from those you experience when you are speaking?

Breath Coordination and Management.   Can you perform all the exercises listed according to the muscular responses discussed—the outward and downward movement upon inhalation and the inward and upward movement upon exhalation? Do your muscles respond immediately when singing staccato or marcato exercises, or is there sluggishness in muscular response? Are you aware of your body's energy level during singing? How long can you sustain a specific pitch at a moderately loud dynamic level? Do you have trouble singing complete musical phrases without taking frequent breaths? Do you take most of your singing breaths through your mouth, your nose, or a combination of mouth and nose? Can you perform the pulsating exercises (Exs. 5-14a,b) with relative ease, or are they somewhat difficult to execute?

Go to www.mhhe.com/ais4 to learn about additional Web-based resources that supplement the content of this chapter.

CHAPTER

6

Producing Tone

Characteristics of Vocal Tone Production

Phonation, or laryngeal vocal-fold vibration, is the result of complex interactions of the vocal folds' muscular and elastic properties working in combination with airflow to produce tone. Three conditions occur simultaneously in phonation: (1) recoil of the lungs and diaphragm, sometimes combined with action by the intercostal and abdominal muscles, causes air to flow through the space between the two vocal folds; (2) muscular forces within the larynx draw the vocal folds close together; and (3) airflow through the narrowed space causes the vocal folds to vibrate together very rapidly, anywhere from 50 to 2,000 vibrations or cycles per second (pitches or **frequencies** G1 to B6).

When breath is expelled from the lungs and passes through the vocal folds, the folds part slightly, allowing a tiny puff of air to escape. The folds immediately close, then reopen, allowing another puff of air to escape in a continuously repeating cycle. Airflow at fast speed in these cycles produces high pitches, and airflow at slow speed produces low pitches. For example, 440 vibrations per second of the folds produce the pitch A4, whereas 880 vibrations produce A5, an octave higher. Vocal-fold adjustments of length and thickness also play an important role in producing pitch. Commonly referred to as "hook-up," this coordination of airflow and vibrator is an interaction that occurs in all wind instruments.

The following exercises will give you a better idea of how the vocal folds vibrate:

> Singing is also a question of the development of the voice, and it involves a set of muscles that must constantly be exercised . . . That's how you acquire a solid technique. You can't become a singer in the space of one year. It takes a long time, you must develop slowly.
>
> —Maria Bayo, soprano

Exercise 6-1   PAPER BLOWING

Hold two sheets of notebook paper in a vertical position in front of your mouth and blow forcefully between them. You will observe that, contrary to what you might expect, the sheets of paper do not separate perceptibly as air passes between them. Instead, they vibrate together in much the same manner as the vocal folds vibrate when air passes between them.

Exercise 6-2   LIP-BUZZ

Next, blow air through your lips as though you are exclaiming, "B-b-b-b-uh, it's cold today." Better yet, use the rumbling, revving Harley-Davidson motorcycle sound ("B-b-b-b-uh-m-m-m") used earlier. As you become adept at using this exercise, you will likely discover that it is possible to emit a tone throughout your full vocal range, provided your lips are loose and breath flow is adequate. This particular exercise is a visible illustration of what occurs when the vocal folds vibrate. It is also an excellent general vocalise for enhancing vocal development, establishing at least five helpful objectives: (1) consistent breath flow; (2) freedom of the jaw, tongue, and lips; (3) efficient humming; (4) full vocal tract (head) resonance sensations; and (5) range extension.

Exercise 6-3 TRUMPET MIMICKING

Perhaps you have experimented with mimicking trumpet sounds by tightening your lips and blowing through them, just as real trumpeters do. If so, you are aware that the lips become more tightened and airflow increases as pitch rises. Conversely, as lower pitches are sounded, the less air pressure and lip tightening is used. A brass instrumentalist uses this technique, adding to the final effect by adding a mouthpiece and full instrument (resonance chamber) to enhance the quality and volume of tone. You can experiment, first by using your hand to create a makeshift mouthpiece, with your fist shaped into an "oo" position. Then, to simulate a larger instrument, scroll a sheet of paper into a cone shape that's small on one end and large on the other. Place the small end on your lips and use your trumpet-player lips to create a fundamental buzzing tone that is acoustically enhanced by your improvised cone-shaped resonance chamber—the result being a louder, more musical tone quality.

Anatomy and Physiology of the Larynx

The **larynx,** a cartilaginous framework situated at the top of the trachea, serves as a housing for the vocal folds. Its three primary functions are to (1) keep food and other foreign matter from entering the lungs through the trachea by closing the epiglottis, (2) retain the inhaled air to provide back pressure (torque), known as *thoracic fixation*, for such activities as lifting heavy objects, giving birth, or defecating, and (3) produce vocal tone.

Larynges of humans and animals are extremely diverse, and in all cases, laryngeal dimensions greatly determine the overall characteristics of any vocal instrument, including its basic volume level (small, large, etc.), comfortable tessitura (ease of singing in low, medium, or high vocal ranges), and performable vocal range (from low to high). For example, the human male larynx is approximately 20 percent larger than the female's. Although all healthy human larynges share general anatomical characteristics, each larynx will be as uniquely formed as an individual's facial features.

The basic framework of the larynx (Fig. 6-1) consists of three major parts: (1) hyoid bone, (2) thyroid cartilage, and (3) cricoid cartilage. During childhood and youth, the horseshoe-shaped **hyoid bone** is the only true bone in the larynx; but with increasing age, both the thyroid and cricoid cartilages gradually **ossify** (become more bonelike). The **thyroid cartilage,** shaped like a shield, is commonly thought of as the **Adam's apple.** It is more prominent in males because of its larger size and its increased protrusion at the front of the cartilage. The **cricoid cartilage,** which resembles a signet ring, connects to the thyroid above and the trachea below. You can actually explore the dimensions and shape of your own vocal instrument by using your fingers to gently feel your larynx. Begin at the very top with the hyoid bone and slowly work downward to the thyroid cartilage, the cricoid cartilage, and finally the trachea at the very bottom.

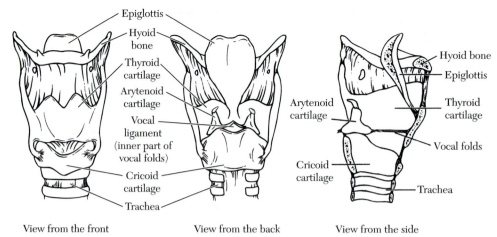

Figure 6-1
The Larynx Viewed from the Front, Back, and Left Side

View from the front   View from the back   View from the side

Two bilateral, pyramid-shaped **arytenoid cartilages** (Fig. 6-2) are located at the top portion of the cricoid cartilage. The arytenoids are the attachments for muscles whose functions are to open and close the **glottis** (the space between the vocal folds) during breathing and phonation and to assist in adjusting both pitch and loudness. The arytenoids are capable of a number of movement patterns, depending on which muscles are contracting. The degree of vocal-fold closure determines the quality of voice that is produced—from the extreme of whispering (breathiness) on one end of the vocal spectrum to the extreme of phonation that is tight, pinched, or pressed on the opposite end.

Attached to the inside of the thyroid notch is the **epiglottis**, a leaf-shaped cartilage that functions as a cover for the glottis. It folds over the vocal folds during swallowing to protect the folds and keep the lungs from ingesting foreign matter.

The musculature associated with activity of the larynx can be divided into two parts: (1) the **intrinsic** (internal) muscles that have points of origination and connection to points of attachment on or within the framework of the larynx and (2) the **extrinsic** (external) muscles that originate from a point on or within the larynx and connect to another part of the body, such as the jaw or sternum.

Intrinsic bilateral muscles adjust the vocal folds and cartilages for four basic movements: (1) abductors for opening, (2) adductors for closing, (3) tensors for lengthening and thinning, and (3) relaxers for shortening and thickening. The extrinsic bilateral muscle system, commonly referred to as **strap muscles,** stabilizes and anchors the larynx in a suspended position within the neck and throat. In addition, intrinsic tongue muscles connecting to the larynx and hyoid bone are also capable of affecting laryngeal adjustments. It is easy to understand why undue tensions in any of these muscles can adversely affect the quality of vocal tone.

The action of the vocal folds can best be viewed from an overhead view. Figure 6-2 shows the inner structure of the vocal folds, with both illustrations (open and closed) split down the middle to show a fleshlike representation on the left and a schematic representation on the right. Figure 6-3 reveals the vocal folds as viewed with a laryngeal mirror. Both figures present the folds in open position (illustrations on right) and closed position (illustrations on left). In this normal overhead view, the false folds lie above the true folds. These false folds are activated only by severe vocal utterances, such as harsh coughs or gagging reflexes, which protect the airway to the lungs. (The rough-voiced production of renowned jazz trumpeter/singer Louis "Satchmo" Armstrong is a good example of the sound created by engaging the false folds in singing.) Separating the true folds from the false folds is a **ventricle** (cavity or open space), which is difficult to see from

56

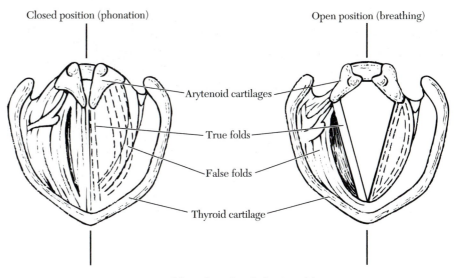

Figure 6-2
**The Physical Structure
of the Vocal Folds
Viewed from Above**

Closed position (phonation)　　　　　　　Open position (breathing)

Arytenoid cartilages

True folds

False folds

Thyroid cartilage

Front of thyroid cartilage (Adam's apple)

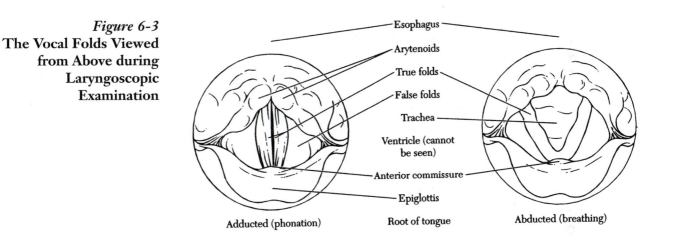

Figure 6-3
**The Vocal Folds Viewed
from Above during
Laryngoscopic
Examination**

Esophagus

Arytenoids

True folds

False folds

Trachea

Ventricle (cannot
be seen)

Anterior commissure

Epiglottis

Adducted (phonation)　　　Root of tongue　　　Abducted (breathing)

an overhead viewing. (A video of a human larynx, with vibrating folds, is provided on the supporting Web site.)

Three Types of Tone Production

In addition to innate reflex systems, singers must learn to control vocal tone production through voluntary "prephonatory tuning," which is based on *proprioceptive memory*, the ability to mentally image, sense, or hear a desired tonal result in advance. In other words, the kind of vocal tone produced is the direct result of the singer's intentions. For this reason, student singers of both pop and classical orientations will tend to sing any vocalise or song using a production modeled on familiar tonal images.

From the extreme of breathiness—such as whispering—on one end of the vocal spectrum, to the other extreme—tight, pinched, or pressed phonation—on the opposite end, the type of tone production is the product of both the force and the duration of vocal-fold closure during each vibratory cycle. There are essentially three types of normal phonation: (1) aspirate (lax, breathy), (2) pressed (tense, tight), and (3) coordinated (balanced, blended). In addition, there are abnormal types that are the result of physical abnormalities or vocal misuse and abuse.

The three types of sustained phonation that characterize a person's general vocal production are briefly summarized next.

- **Aspirate (lax) phonation.** This hypofunctional (low energy) vocal production uses variable airflow combined with a weak adductory force of the vocal folds. The perceived result is a "breathy voice," characterized by noisy airflow and flutelike tone quality.

- **Pressed (tense) phonation.** This hyperfunctional (high energy) vocal production uses high subglottal breath pressure combined with a strong adductory force of the vocal folds. The perceived result is a "tight voice" characterized by a stressful-sounding tone production, including "crackling."

- **Coordinated (balanced) phonation.** This balanced vocal production, known as "flow phonation," uses moderate levels of subglottic pressure and vocal-fold adductory force. This optimal pattern of vibration allows a moderately large airflow with little air turbulence or interference. Flow phonation also allows a rather large amplitude of vocal-fold vibration, resulting in ample loudness, yet with greatest efficiency of energy use.

Singing with balanced phonation is often referred to as singing "on the breath" or on the "sensation of inhalation." When the singer maintains a sensation of inhaling throughout the act of vocalization, the throat remains in a comfortably open and stretched position. As the throat opens, the soft palate (velum) is lifted and creates what is often referred to as the "arched tone," a sensation of vertical stretch that enlarges the throat (pharynx) and lowers the larynx to create a larger resonance chamber. One should imagine initiating singing with a light stroke on the thin edges of the folds, avoiding a heavy, pressed use of the full body of the folds. Another way of approaching the coordinated onset is to image the breath releasing in the high-arched position, all the while forming vowels in a natural speechlike pattern.

Three Types of Vocal Onset

Closely related to the three types of sustained phonation are three corresponding ways to initiate and release tone. Thus, hypofunctional (breathy) singers will tend to use aspirate onsets, whereas hyperfunctional (pressed-tone) singers will tend to use glottal onsets. Singers with efficiently produced voices will generally use a balanced approach for both onsets and sustained phonation.

In singing, the manner in which a tone is initiated often depends upon technical, stylistic, textual, and dramatic considerations. For example, when initiating tone on a vowel, one may choose to use an **aspirate** (soft) onset for relaxed expressions or a **glottal** (hard) onset for explosive expressions. For example, the exclamation "Oh" can be used either in a breathless, surprised way, as in "Oh, how beautiful it is" (aspirate), or in a tense, angry way, as in "Oh, you don't say" (glottal). In most of our vocal expressions, the healthiest, most efficient vocal onset will require a medium approach, or coordinated (balanced) onset. These three primary ways of initiating (**onset**) and releasing vocal tone are explained next.

- **Aspirate (soft) onset.** Anytime one uses an "h" to initiate a tone, an aspirate onset results, as when speaking such phrases as "*H*ow are you?; *H*e is here; and *Wh*o are you? This form of onset can relax the larynx and encourage an easier vocal production. William Vennard (1967) actually suggests singing with an imaginary "h" to encourage an easily flowing vocal tone.

- **Glottal (hard) onset.** The glottal onset is created when breath pressure builds up below strongly adducted vocal folds and explodes them apart upon initiating a sound. A light glottal onset (hiatus) is normal for clear articulation of many initial vowels in words and is especially needed in certain languages, such as English and German. In contrast, the Italian and French languages minimize the use of glottals. Frequent use of glottal onsets tends to encourage pressed phonation.

- **Coordinated (balanced) onset.** As in flow phonation, balanced onset is an ideal combination of airflow and vocal-fold adduction, which depends upon dynamic adjustments of the inspiratory-expiratory muscles, vocal folds, and resonators.

Three Types of Vocal Release

Because the way a tone ends influences the onset of any tone that follows, learning how to best release or end a tone is also very important. The three ways to release a tone correspond to the three vocal onsets: (1) aspirate (soft) release, (2) glottal (hard) release, and (3) coordinated (balanced) release.

- **Aspirate (soft) release.** An aspirate release occurs when the vocal folds do not close completely during each glottal cycle, resulting in a breathy tone quality. Usually caused by the collapse of the breathing mechanism and a subsequent loss of "hook-up," the soft release lacks intensity and is often very weak.

- **Glottal (hard) release.** Glottal release is epitomized by the "terminal grunt" one hears when large-voiced opera singers end a loud high note. Although it has its place as a dramatic device in performance situations, the glottal (hard) release is out of place in soft to moderately loud dynamic levels and in low-to-medium pitch ranges.

- **Coordinated (balanced) release.** Accomplished singers strive to end most phrases with the same consistent tone quality sustained throughout the phrase. This requires a coordinated or balanced release, with the vocal folds under neither too much tension nor too little. To experience a coordinated (balanced) release, laugh in a relaxed, hearty manner.

Characteristics of Efficient Vocal Tone

How can we know if a tone is well produced? Aside from our gut instincts—the emotional response to certain singers we enjoy hearing—we can evaluate what we hear using some guidelines that describe the characteristic properties of efficiently produced vocal tone. Aesthetics of tone quality vary from expert to expert, but most agree that a good tone will include the following:

- A unique vocal quality that seems natural to the person producing it; artificiality or unnatural tendencies are usually sensed by the listener.

- Freedom from observable extrinsic and intrinsic muscular strain and tensions in the face, neck, limbs, and torso.

- Tonal clarity and accuracy; out-of-tune singing is one of the best indications that something is not right.

- A self-starting and self-stopping elasticity, with the ability to sing varying dynamic levels on a sustained tone.

- Ample volume level with a ringing, forward-in-the-mask focus, particularly when increasing airflow for louder dynamic levels.

- A timbre best described as having both bright and dark tonal characteristics (**chiaroscuro**); that is, brilliance and ring plus warmth and richness.

- Flexibility and agility in slow-fast movements, in soft-loud dynamics, and in low-high range.

- A vibrato pattern of 6 to 8 pulses per second.

Exercises for Developing Efficient Phonation

The objective in phonation is to synchronize breath pressure with vocal-fold vibration. This is accomplished by fine-tuned adjustments of the vocal mechanism to avoid excesses in either breath pressure or vocal-fold tension. Efficient phonation includes a sensation of "singing on the breath." The following exercises are sequenced to allow a dynamic vocal adjustment to occur.

Exercise 6-4   BREATHING AND HOOK-UP REVIEW

Begin by reviewing the breathing exercises in chapter 5, especially Exercises 5-3 and 5-13, with emphasis on the outward and inward movements of inhalation and exhalation in conjunction with tone production.

Exercise 6-5   UNVOICED SIGH OF CONTENTMENT

Begin by setting up the appropriate conditions in the vocal tract—relaxed articulators and throat muscles and a sense of inner lift—by sensing an incipient sneeze or of inhaling a pleasant aroma. Next, take a relaxed breath through your nose (high-arched nasal passage) and release it using a non-voiced "H-h-h-h-h" in a contented sighing manner, gently directing breath toward the hard palate area, as well as allowing it to filter through the nasal passage. The sensation of allowing breath to filter through the facial mask or eyes may be helpful.

Exercise 6-6   VOICED SIGH OF CONTENTMENT

Repeat the preceding exercise, this time adding a vocalized tone to the relaxed, comfortable, and contented sigh on a descending one-octave sliding-pitch scale. At this point don't be too concerned about pitch accuracy.

Example 6-6a

Hah _____
Hwee _____
Hoo _____

Exercise 6-7   DESCENDING VOCALISES

Having established the "contented sigh" technique, you can experiment with various modifications. The following vocalises (vocal exercises) employ descending musical patterns for developing the head voice and are especially helpful in countering tight-voiced (pressed) production. These exercises should be sung lightly, but fully engaged in an enthusiastic manner, with a vibrant, nonbreathy intensity. Begin in the speaking range and gradually move into the upper range. As you progress in coordinating phonation, the "h" sounds may be minimized or eliminated altogether.

Exercice 6-7a

Hi ___ there!
Hel - lo!
Hwee ___
Hoo ___

Exercice 6-7b

How _ are you?
He _ is here!
Hwee _____
Hoo _____

Exercice 6-7c

How _ are _ you?
Who _ are _ you?
Hwee _____
Hoo _____

The vocal hook-up effect is achieved by the following staccato (•) and marcato (<>) exercises, which require coordinated control of the respiratory and phonatory systems. Here you need to vigorously apply breath energy at both soft and loud dynamic levels. But be careful not to push, blow, or force air through the folds when doing these exercises. Feel free to raise or lower the keys throughout your comfortable singing range. Start by reviewing the breath-sing exercise (Ex. 5-12). This exercise should be practiced at first with softer dynamics (*mp*), gradually increasing to louder dynamic levels (*mf*).

Exercise 6-8   STACCATO EXERCISES

Sing some light staccato exercises on five-note scales and octave **arpeggios,** raising the key higher with each repeating **scale** and arpeggio. Although "ah" is the preferred vowel, you are encouraged to use the other major vowels "ee," "ay," "ah," "oh," and "oo," either singly or in combination, according to your proficiency level.

Exercise 6-9   MARCATO ATTACK

Be sure to begin with a dumbfounded, surprised emotional expression and breath intake to relax the articulators and throat muscles. Next, sing the same five-note scales and octave arpeggios using marcato pulses, this time perhaps at a slower pace to accommodate the extra stress of each note. This will necessitate a more energetic use of the breath and greater activation of the supporting respiratory musculature. After these simple exercises are mastered, you might be ready to experiment with more extended vocalises that incorporate both staccato and marcato onsets in various combinations of tempo, range, dynamic levels, and rhythmic/melodic patterns.

Exercise 6-10 NASAL CONSONANTS

Nasal consonants such as "m," "n," and "ng" are very helpful in establishing a clean vocal-fold vibration, especially when the articulators are relaxed. In addition to Exercises 8-1 and 8-2, the lip-buzz is an excellent exercise for balanced phonation. Students who tend toward breathy tone will benefit from exercises that encourage more vocal-fold closure—for example, "whining," "moaning," and sirenlike tonal qualities that aid efficient vocal-fold vibration. Because the voice works best as a coordinated unit, most exercises will achieve more than a single objective. Hence, an exercise using "ng" that is performed correctly will help coordinate breath, vocal-fold vibration, and resonators into a single positive response. This is achieved primarily by stimulating tonal sensations experienced in the head, notably in the nose, facial mask, and upper mouth (hard and soft palate region).

> Solidifying my technique took me 10 years. To be a successful singer, one has to start with a natural instrument. But some of us have to really take an enormous amount of time and effort to get the whole mechanism functioning.
>
> —Renée Fleming, soprano

Phonation Assessment

Principles and Physiology. What is your understanding of phonation? What are the primary functions of the larynx? Do you understand how the vocal folds vibrate, and can you demonstrate this by means of the two exercises mentioned at the beginning of this chapter? Do you have a fundamental understanding of the major parts of the larynx and how they function?

Vocal Tone. Can you name and demonstrate the three ways of initiating and releasing vocal tone? Are you aware of vocal onset and release as you sing? Is your tonal quality affected by the way you initiate and sustain vocal tone? What are the properties of a well-produced vocal tone? How does your voice measure up to these characteristics? Are you able to sing staccato exercises clearly and accurately?

Go to www.mhhe.com/ais4 to learn about additional Web-based resources that supplement the content of this chapter.

CHAPTER 7

Connecting Voice Levels

Explanation and Description of Vocal Registers

Everyone experiences changes in voice quality when speaking or yelling at various pitch levels. This is particularly noticeable when we have laryngitis or when we are singing from our lowest to highest vocal ranges. These high and low vocal ranges and their peculiar tonal characteristics are called **registers,** a word developed hundreds of years ago to serve the design and construction of church organs.

The smoother a voice sounds throughout its range and the more ease with which it moves through various dynamic levels, the less aware we are of vocal registers. On the other hand, the more unskilled the singer, the more likely we are to detect contrasts in registers, such as obvious voice "shifts" or "breaks" with sudden changes in tone quality and volume.

A useful analogy is to compare register changes with the gears of an automobile. The low-gear mechanism of the automobile helps negotiate slow driving speeds, and the low-voice mechanism helps negotiate low pitches. When the automobile's low gear—and the singer's low-voice mechanism—reaches its upper limits of intended use, it must give way to other mechanisms that permit extended operation. For example, the automobile's higher gears facilitate increased speed and reduce stress on mechanical parts, and the voice's higher "vocal gears" facilitate access to higher pitches with less strain on structures of the vocal mechanism.

Anyone familiar with driving motor vehicles equipped with either manual-shift or automatic transmissions has experienced differences in smoothness and comfort. Although a driver's manual shifting may be skillful, an automatic transmission is normally much smoother, especially when acceleration is moderate. It is easy to imagine the smoothness of a luxury automobile equipped with automatic transmission compared to that of a multigeared semitrailer ("18 wheeler") as both take off from a stoplight at moderate

> I really believe in vertical singing all the way up through the low and the middle. Then, on the very top, it can get a little bit lifted. But, for the most part, it is really a very vertical, cylindrical kind of approach.
>
> —Patricia Craig, soprano
>
> I think of my voice as an hourglass. The bottom has breadth and width and a color that is deeper and darker. As I go up through the passaggio . . . I must imagine a sound that is narrow, like the waist of an hourglass . . . slim and focused, and no pressure or weight . . . As the voice moves into the top of the hourglass, the sound can open up and blossom.
>
> —Renée Fleming, soprano

63

speeds. Voices are capable of behaving in similar fashions—easily and smoothly, or sluggishly and unevenly.

Voice Register Theories

There are several current theories or descriptions of vocal registers, each with enthusiastic proponents. Most voice experts subscribe to one of the following three positions:

One-Register Theory

Proponents of this idealistic theory argue that when the voice is functioning correctly, there is a seamless vocal quality throughout the vocal range. They may also argue that it is nonproductive to discuss registers with singers because it tends to confuse them—the less said, the better. Although the one-register viewpoint has merit, most students do, in fact, benefit from learning about the components of the voice and how they interrelate in speaking and singing.

Two-Registers Theory

The theory of chest and head registers seems to adequately explain what is evident when listening to the average unskilled singer.

Chest register, modal, or heavy mechanism is typically the speaking and yelling voice. It is called **chest voice** because physical sensations (vibrations) are experienced in the chest cavity when one vocalizes in that register, usually in the lower two-thirds of one's vocal range and sometimes at louder dynamic levels. The primary muscles of the vocal folds (*thyroarytenoids*) are the predominant vocal muscles used in chest voice production. When chest voice is used in a healthy way, with proper airflow and sensations of resonance in the head, it can add strength and vitality to the speaking and singing voice.

Unfortunately, some singers, particularly pop and music-theater female vocalists, often overuse and abuse their chest registers by using an unhealthy **belting** technique. The real danger comes when forcing raw chest register tones into high range. Most belters are able to carry chest voice up to about C5, a practice even some operatic tenors use when belting full-volume "high Cs." Teachers who understand and work on "legitimate" belting technique recognize the difference between healthy and unhealthy approaches. The healthy method encourages giving more attention to proper breath use, relaxation of articulators, head-dominant resonance (above the roof of the mouth), and increasingly mixing more head register in ascending notes.

Head register, loft, or light mechanism is the higher and softer-voiced mechanism we use when speaking in a soft-spoken, "heady," animated conversational voice. The *cricothyroids* are the primary vocal-fold muscles used in head voice production. The term *head voice* is derived from the physical sensations experienced when singing in head register, which normally encompasses the upper two-thirds of the vocal range. Female pop singers commonly sing with strong chest voices and weak head voices, with the familiar yodeling sound that occurs when moving abruptly between chest and head registers. In contrast, female classical singers make great use of head register, mixing it with chest when needed to achieve a smooth connection throughout their vocal range. Thus, contrary to what most beginning-level singers think about head voice ("it's weak," "too high in range"), this often-neglected mechanism has much dynamic vocal potential.

When developed, it usually becomes quite powerful, particularly in the higher singing range.

Three-Registers Theory

The three-registers theory incorporates the chest and head registers plus an additional one called the **mixed** or **middle register** (the middle range of the voice). The mixed register is the result of blending the qualities of chest and head registers (heavy and light mechanisms) in the middle range of the voice, approximately the middle one-third of the entire vocal range. Female singers make great use of mixed registration, and classically trained male singers use it primarily in the upper part of their pitch range. An important identifying mark of "middle voice" is that it bridges the chest and head registers without noticeable disturbances. Singers seem to experience increased head vibrations when singing in middle voice and, because the voice is not locked into a particular register, there is a greater sense of vocal security.

The three-registers theory also recognizes that the entire vocal instrument is quite flexible and capable of greater or lesser adjustments of any one mechanism. For example, using more chest mechanism can create a belt tone when carried up into the higher range. Conversely, when the head voice is carried lower, a softer, sweeter quality results—although the tone may sometimes be weaker, depending on such factors as airflow, intensity, tonal placement, and vowels. When singing in the middle register, the singer has greater possibilities of mixing registers according to dynamic and expressive objectives.

The three-registers theory helps explain how accomplished singers are able to smoothly connect chest and head registers. Supported by current research and practice, the theory appears to be the most widely used concept in teaching vocal registration.

Auxiliary Registers

In addition to the three major registers—chest, head and mixed—there are two identifiable high-voice auxiliary registers: falsetto and flute/whistle, at least one of which is common in most voices. In addition, there are two rare types of low-voice male registers that may be of interest, especially to young basses. Known as *Strohbass* (straw bass) and *Schnarrbass* (growl bass), these somewhat stressful productions, used mostly by eastern European choral basses, are not recommended for young basses.

Falsetto Register

Once believed to be produced by the false vocal folds in the larynx, the falsetto register is actually caused by the thin, long, stiff, bow-shaped true vocal folds vibrating only at the marginal edges. Although falsetto occurs in both sexes, it is primarily associated with male voices. Perceived as "effeminate" in character, falsetto is characterized by a "hooty," breathy tone quality, the result of the vocal folds not fully resisting the breath stream during phonation, unlike head voice production, when the vocal folds are adducted. Inefficient vocal-fold closure means lower intensity, making it virtually impossible for a singer in falsetto register to **crescendo** (get louder) or **decrescendo** (get softer) on a sustained pitch without an obvious "break." As a technical device, falsetto may be particularly useful for helping hyperfunctional male singers gain more ease in accessing upper-middle and high notes.

Flute/Whistle Register

The flute/whistle register is the high-range extension of the female voice occurring approximately above the pitch C6 (the sixth C from the bottom of the keyboard). This extended high register creates overtones that produce a floating, disembodied sound, often clearly focused, "squeaky," and resembling a penetrating whistle tone, as demonstrated by loud, high-pitched female screaming. Many women feel an aversion to the flute/whistle register and often resist exploring high-voice **coloratura** potential, even though it provides opportunities for expanding vocal range, as well as dramatic expression.

In physiological terms, flute/whistle registration results when (1) the vocal folds vibrate at a high rate of lengthwise tension (very thin), (2) the posterior (back) portion of the folds has considerable "damping" (diminishing amplitude in successive vibrations), (3) the vibrating mass of the folds is limited, and (4) the subglottic air pressure and airflow are high (Miller, 1986, p. 148).

The Function of the Larynx in Registration

Recall from chapter 6 that (1) larynges vary in size, shape, and other innate characteristics and that (2) the vocal folds can be lengthened, shortened, thinned, thickened, tensed, and relaxed by the action of the intrinsic laryngeal muscles and, to a lesser degree, by the extrinsic laryngeal muscles. Individuals can therefore produce a range of pitches (frequencies of vibration) determined by the innate characteristics of their own larynges and vocal folds and by the vocal-fold muscular adjustments they can achieve. Moreover, for each individual, there is a fairly wide range of pitches that can be produced with a variety of different vocal-fold configurations, determined by various adjustments of the intrinsic laryngeal muscles. It is the different degrees of contraction of the intrinsic laryngeal muscles that determine (in large part) which vocal register is used at any time.

Because singers must learn to make smooth adjustments between chest and head registrations, a simple explanation of how these mechanisms work should be helpful. In the chest register, or heavy mechanism, the vocal folds (thyroarytenoid muscles) are active, thickened, and shortened while longitudinal tension is lessened. In the head register, or light mechanism, the folds are more passive while other muscles (cricothyroids) are more actively thinning and elongating, another example of muscular antagonism. To sing in head voice registration, the singer's larynx must tilt or rock forward, in effect stretching and thinning the vocal folds, as Figure 7-1 illustrates. You can experience this forward (and upward) movement by placing a finger in the notch of the thyroid cartilage of your larynx (see Fig. 6-1), and vocalizing an octave interval leap three or more times in a yodeling manner

Figure 7-1
Laryngeal Adjustments to Facilitate Registration Changes

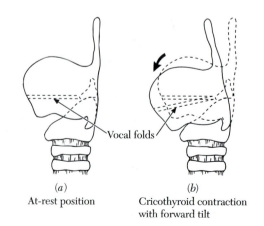

(a)
At-rest position

(b)
Cricothyroid contraction
with forward tilt

(1–8–1–8–1–8–1), using a moderately high key. In moving from the lowest note to an octave above, you can feel the bobbing movement of your larynx each time the high note is sounded.

Under the best of circumstances, the opposing muscle actions of thyroarytenoid (chest voice) and cricothyroid (head voice) muscles must be coordinated when singing from low to high or high to low range to achieve a unified, consistent vocal tone. However, the untrained singer may occasionally experience an abrupt shift or audible break from one register to another. When the mixed/middle register is developed, the chances for such dramatic register changes diminish.

The following experiment will demonstrate the principles by which the vocal folds and laryngeal muscles operate to produce various adjustments of pitches throughout the vocal range. Because this exercise requires the ability to mimic a brass instrument by using your lips to create a lip-buzz tone, you may find it difficult to perform. If so, perhaps someone in the class (a brass instrument player) will be able to demonstrate it effectively.

Exercise 7-1 PITCH AND REGISTRATION EXPERIMENT USING TRUMPET MIMICKING

Beginning on the pitch C5, initiate a buzzing tone with your lips very tightly closed, making sure that only the lips produce the tone, not the vocal folds. If this pitch is too high for you, start at a lower pitch. Descend the C Major scale stepwise at a moderate speed for three octaves to C2. As you descend, pay close attention to the adjustments in your lips and the corresponding changes in tone quality and pitch. Now produce octave portamenti (slides) from C5 to C4 to C3 to C2 at a moderately slow tempo. You will observe during your descent that certain series of pitches are produced by specific adjustments and degrees of lip tension and breath pressure. For example, the adjustment for high pitches is characteristically very tight and for the lowest pitches very loose, primarily to facilitate the frequency of vibration. Some pitches seem to be most easily produced with a specific *embouchure* (mouth, lips, tongue adjustments) whereas others can be produced with a tighter (pressed) or looser (breathy) adjustment. This action is similar to the way singers create pressed or breathy vocal tones by varying vocal-fold tension and breath pressure.

Regarding the use of chest and head mechanisms according to gender and traditional vocal training, men sing primarily in chest voice, blending gradually into mixed and head voice for the upper-middle and higher notes. In contrast, with the exception of pop-oriented vocalists, women sing primarily in head voice, blending gradually into chest voice as they descend into the lower third of their vocal range. This octave separation in pitch is caused by the disparity in size between male and female larynges. Adult males have larger larynges (15–20 millimeters) than adult females (9–15 millimeters), with correspondingly longer vocal folds (Sundberg, 1977).

Negotiating Register Transitions

Register transitions occur at rather predictable points in the voice. Registration is considered smooth when it is coordinated; that is, when (1) the body and vocal tract are properly aligned, (2) all interfering tensions are eliminated (lips, jaw, tongue, soft palate, larynx, and neck muscles, etc.), (3) adequate breath flow is provided, and (4) the release of breath and tone is experienced predominantly at and above the roof of the mouth. When transitions are rough, the symptoms and causes are usually the result of faulty registration in voices that may be untrained, misused, or abused.

Most singers tend to experience register transitions when moving between low and high singing ranges or chest and head registers, depending primarily on the dynamic level and type of voice production used. One common problem is the tendency to carry excessive vocal weight (overuse of thyroarytenoid muscles) too high in chest voice, as when belting, effectively prolonging the desired register change into head voice. In cases when production is overstressed, the tone will usually sound strained, perhaps even under pitch (flat), with limited upside potential.

The transition from chest register to head register is called the **passage zone (zona di passaggio)**, and it tends to occur between D4 and F4 for both male and female singers. Sopranos, for example, experience this transition in their low range when moving between chest and head voice. Tenors, meanwhile, experience the same register shift in their upper-middle range, on the same pitches, when moving between chest and head registers. This octave difference between the sexes helps explain why women sing mostly in head voice while men sing mostly in chest (Titze, 1994). Moreover, among both male and female singers, the passage zones will vary according to the size and weight of the individual voice, which is largely determined by physical proportions, including dimensions of the larynx and resonating cavities. For instance, a heavier-voiced dramatic tenor or soprano will have a lower passage zone than a lighter-voiced lyric tenor or soprano.

Although most singers will experience registration events occurring throughout the passage zone, the most troublesome transition actually encompasses an upper **pivotal zone** of only two to three pitches. For example, when the vocal technique is insecure, a lyric tenor will normally experience some difficulty at E–F♯4 (fourth from bottom of keyboard); a lyric soprano at F–F♭5; a lyric mezzo-soprano at E–F5; and a lyric baritone at E–E♯4. Finally, it must be pointed out that the female voice must usually learn how to deal with the chest voice's lower pivotal zone around E–E♭4 for soprano and F4 for mezzo-soprano. Learning how to negotiate the use of chest and head mixture—in the lower voice for all females and the upper voice for males—is a goal of all singers. For more detailed coverage of registration events, the reader is referred to Richard Miller's book *The Structure of Singing* (1986).

If the lower mechanism, or chest voice, is forced upward until an abrupt change in the voice occurs, one experiences the rigid muscular activity associated with a *static adjustment* of the laryngeal mechanism. Straight-tone singing is also a result of this type of adjustment. On the other hand, a *dynamic adjustment* facilitates responsive muscular action, which in turn encourages natural register changes, accompanied by vibrato in the tone. Normally, when approaching a register transition, an extra surge of breath energy is required, all the while maintaining high-placed head sensations (above the roof of the mouth and in the area surrounding the eyes).

The fine-tuning essential for a dynamic balance between the lower and higher mechanisms can be further explained in relation to how we perceive pitch, loudness, and timbre:

- **Pitch.** Vocal pitch (frequency) is determined by heavier adjustments (chest voice) in the lower part of the voice and lighter adjustments (head voice) when ascending into the higher range.

- **Loudness.** Tonal loudness on any given pitch is determined by a lighter vocal production (without breathiness) in softer singing and a heavier vocal production (without pressing) in louder singing.

- **Timbre.** The heavy mechanism produces a stronger tone quality, and the lighter mechanism produces a sweeter tone quality.

68

Exercises for Coordinating Voice Registers

One registration goal in singing is to produce an even scale, a series of notes in which registers blend, vowels match, and dynamics merge, so that the differences shade into each other with no perceptible line of demarcation: every tone from lowest to highest matches as closely as possible in quality and is passed smoothly from one to another—homogenized, so to speak. The two meanings and pronunciations of the term should be noted: homo*gene*ous (of the same or similar nature) and ho*mog*eneous (diverse elements blended into a uniform mixture). Both meanings apply in describing an even scale. Exercises 7-2, 7-3, and 7-4 are designed to help equalize registration.

Exercise 7-2 SLIDING PITCHES

One way to connect the registers smoothly is to slide from low to high pitches in the manner of a siren, using sliding pitches (portamenti) from low-to-high and high-to-low randomly; that is, without regard for specific pitches or keys. Use the lip-buzz exercise, first humming and then using random vowels, particularly the French nasal vowels [ɛ̃], [ɑ̃] and [ɔ̃] (see Fig. 9-3), which will help establish efficient vocal-fold adduction and high-placed mask sensations that promote a ringing, full tone. Imitating a sirenlike tone quality using the French vowels may be particularly helpful. The same approach can also be used when singing other intervals, such as a fifth, an octave, or random pitches. While vocalizing, be aware of extraneous tensions in the jaw, tongue, soft palate, neck, and shoulders. Stay loose but energized.

Exercise 7-2a

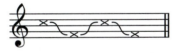

Exercise 7-2b

Exercise 7-2c

Exercise 7-3 ASCENDING/DESCENDING SCALES

Allow the voice to change by "lifting on the breath" to a lighter, headier quality when ascending in pitch. To experience this, it usually works best to sing lightly and easily, but firmly, on an ascending and descending scale. While singing the following exercises (Exs. 7-3a,b), hold the jaw down lightly with a finger placed horizontally in the groove between lower lip and chin. Sing each "lah" with the tongue reaching up to the upper lip and dental ridge for the articulation of the "l" and subsequently falling to the bottom lip and dental ridge to complete the "ah" vowel. These exercises help relax the articulating organs and aid in registration adjustments as the voice ascends. They may also be sung on various vowels and/or combinations of vowels at varying dynamic levels and tempi to help blend and equalize the registers.

Exercise 7-3a

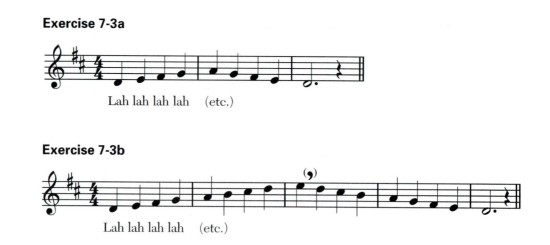

Lah lah lah lah   (etc.)

Exercise 7-3b

Lah lah lah lah   (etc.)

Occasionally, some students will have difficulty with these scale exercises (Exs. 7-3a,b), especially if their tongues are "tied." The connecting membrane beneath the tongue varies considerably among individuals, resulting in diction-related tensions, particularly in high-range singing. If a professionally oriented vocal student appears to have such a problem, he or she should be referred to a medical specialist for an evaluation.

Exercise 7-4   YODELING EXERCISE

This exercise allows the freedom of moving between registers in a **yodeling** manner, allowing the voice to move quickly and smoothly between chest and head registers. It is important to allow the voice to make its own shifts at the appropriate pitches. Although your tendency might be to sing the yodeling exercise disconnected and jerkily, the goal is to sing it smoothly and connected so that the voice sounds unified and consistent throughout. Begin by using moderate keys and tempi, eventually expanding keys, dynamic levels, tempi, and vowel/consonant combinations (such as "nyah") as your competency increases.

Exercise 7-4a

Nyah _____

Exercise 7-5   CRESCENDO/DECRESCENDO

Traditionally, the technical vocal exercise favored for blending heavy and light registers on a sustained crescendo/decrescendo pitch is the **messa di voce** (soft-to-loud-to-soft). When mastered throughout the entire singing range, this exercise indicates a well-trained singer. Because this exercise requires the utmost in mental concentration and physical control over the voice, it should first be mastered at low-to-moderate pitches before moving into upper register transition pitches. Although in most cases the "ah" vowel will be the easiest to sing, you should eventually sing the messa di voce on all vowels, including the French nasal vowels [ɛ̃], [ɑ̃], and [ɔ̃].

Exercise 7-5a

Voice Registration Assessment

Assessing Others. Are you able to discern when singers are using different registers, such as head voice and chest voice? Can you tell exactly when the change occurs as they move from chest to head or from head to chest? Can you differentiate between head voice and falsetto when hearing male singers sing in the high, soft voice range? Are you aware of the flute register when it occurs in the female voice, usually above C6? Have you ever heard a singer's voice "break"? Have you heard singers who sing smoothly throughout their vocal range with only slight modifications in their basic tonal quality? If so, what kind of vocal repertoire did they perform?

Assessing Yourself. Are you aware of obvious changes in your voice as you sing throughout your entire vocal range? If so, on which pitches do you experience noticeable changes? How often and under what conditions do you experience these changes? Can you sense the body and head vibrations that account for the popular use of "chest" and "head" in describing these two registers? Are you able to negotiate your registration shifts smoothly or do you hear and feel such changes when they occur? Do you have difficulty in sustaining a high tessitura, or vocal range, for several seconds? Can you crescendo, or swell from soft to loud, a tone on a sustained pitch, in your highest transition zones and decrescendo, (diminish) from loud to soft, the same pitch without a noticeable break or glitch in the voice?

Go to www.mhhe.com/ais4 to learn about additional Web-based resources that supplement the content of this chapter.

8 Optimizing Tone Quality

Acoustics—The Science of Sound

Every time we hear or produce a sound, we experience the phenomenon of acoustics. At some time you've probably experimented with creating various acoustical effects, such as (1) blowing air across the top of a narrow-necked pop bottle, (2) using a metal utensil to strike glasses that contain various quantities of water, (3) depressing the damper pedal after opening the top of a piano, then shouting into the piano to hear the response, or (4) producing and hearing echoes, reverberations of sound where the acoustical environment is responsive, as occurs in responsive outdoor and indoor environments. Each of these experiments demonstrates an aspect of acoustics referred to as **resonance,** the spontaneous amplification, reinforcement, or prolongation of vibration when another vibration of the same frequency is applied to it.

Many people find that singing in a shower stall is one place where exhilarating acoustical effects can be enjoyed. Other "acoustically alive" spaces include canyons, dome-shaped buildings (the Capitol Rotunda), and cathedral naves, where vocal sounds can be easily heard, even when whispering. Conversely, some environments absorb or dissipate sound—an insulated automobile interior, an open field, a thick forest, or a room heavily upholstered with carpets, curtains, and padded furniture. Each of these acoustical environments demonstrates acoustical principles that have both positive and negative effects for the singer. In general, singing in an "alive" acoustical space (with moderate reverberation) provides positive aural feedback, whereas performing in an acoustically "dead" space provides negative feedback.

A brief introduction to **acoustics**—the science of the production, propagation, and perception of sound waves—will lay the groundwork for understanding resonators, which are essential for optimizing tone quality. In scientific terms,

> In terms of placement, I believe you have to get into the middle of your optimal resonance. It usually is somewhere on the front side of the center of your hard palate. It could be anywhere from there to the middle of your front teeth.
>
> —Patricia Craig, soprano

> The use of mask resonance, as opposed to the natural tendency to speak with mouth and chest resonance, is crucial to every young singer's development, as it's the only way to project the voice to the back of the hall without strain. It's the "buzz," "hum," or squillo that develops the nascent shape of a tone into a full-blown operatic sound.
>
> —Renée Fleming, soprano

sound is a disturbance of air particles or variation in air pressure that impinges on the ear. Understanding how sound is created, enhanced, and perceived can help improve the overall quality of your singing.

Properties and Characteristics of Sound

As mentioned earlier, all instruments, including the voice, use three essential elements in producing sound: (1) an *actuator* (air)—the source of power, (2) a *vibrator* (vocal folds)—the energy activator of sound waves, and (3) a *resonator* (nasal, mouth, and throat cavities)—a secondary vibrator that increases the intensity of the vibrator's product, thereby improving its quality.

Sound is propagated by wave action, a common natural phenomenon; for example, the ripples caused by a rock thrown into a pond or the radiating shock tremors from an earthquake's epicenter. Whereas waves of water move primarily on the surface of the pond in a horizontal direction, **sound waves** expand outward from the sound source in *all* directions.

Air, which is composed of submicroscopic bits of matter known as *molecules*, explodes outward in all directions from the sound source when disturbed, somewhat like an expanding balloon. As sound waves move outward, molecules crowd close together, creating an area of higher pressure known as *compression*. When they return to their original position, the molecules become less dense, creating a lower pressure area known as a *rarefaction*. The continual cycling of **compression phase** and **rarefaction phase** is the sound wave, which expands outward as long as the sound source continues—a "balloon within a balloon" effect. Sound waves expand at approximately 1,130 feet (345 meters) per second, which is known as the *speed of sound.*

Regular, repeating sound waves create musical tone, whereas irregular patterns produce noise. Regular, repeating sound waves in singing are partially determined by vowels, whereas irregular patterns in speech and singing correspond to the use of consonants (see Chapter 9).

The four most significant properties of a musical tone are (1) frequency (pitch); (2) intensity (amplitude, loudness); (3) timbre (tone color), a combined product of frequency and intensity; and (4) duration. In addition, extraneous sound (noise) is also an integral property of musical sound.

Frequency. Frequency, the number of vibration cycles per second as measured in **Hertz (Hz),** is perceived as **pitch;** the faster the frequency of vibration, the higher the pitch. For example, the International Standards Association concert pitch of A4 will result in 440 vibrations or waves per second. The frequency range audible to the human ear is approximately 20 Hz to 16,000 Hz. In speaking and singing, pitch is determined by the frequency of vocal-fold vibration, which is varied by increasing tension or changing the mass of the vibrating vocal folds.

Intensity. Although **amplitude** is the actual attribute of vibration, it is more typically measured as **intensity,** the amount of pressure generated by the vibrator (vocal folds). This vibrator-generated pressure results in sound waves moving through the air, subsequently striking the ear's tympanic membrane. The standard unit of measurement for *sound pressure level* (SPL) is the **decibel** (dB), the number of decibels roughly corresponding to what is perceived by the listener as *loudness* (not intensity).

Timbre. The audible characteristics of sound are the result of harmonic **overtones,** acoustical frequencies created by a vibrator in conjunction with its connected air cavities or resonators. In the voice, timbre, or tone quality (the characteristics of a particular tone), consists of the **fundamental** (tone or pitch) of the vibrator (vocal folds), plus the harmonic overtones generated in the vocal tract, a very complex and variable resonator system. When overtones are in sync with the vibrator, the tone will be perceived as being in tune and pleasant to the ear. Each musical instrument produces a unique configuration of overtones that enables the human ear to distinguish one from another. In like fashion, each voice, and even each vowel, presents unique overtone configurations based on the properties of pitch, intensity, and timbre.

Duration. A sound's waveform has three durational characteristics: (1) the *attack* (onset)—the time it takes for the sound to reach its steady state, (2) the *steady state*, or relatively stable sustained quality, and (3) the *decay*—the time it takes for the sound to die away. For example, a xylophone tone has a sharp attack, no actual steady state, and an immediate decay. Conversely, when a gong is struck, the sound builds to its highest point, and then gradually decays. The vocal tone also has attack and decay, known as onset and offset, and a sustained portion, which may or may not be a steady state, depending on the singer's technical facility.

Vocal Resonators

A **resonator** can be considered any object through which a sound wave can be filtered, subsequently enhancing and modifying the final sound product. Resonators are usually thought of as hollow objects with air-filled cavities that have their own natural frequency of vibration.

The three important factors in determining tone quality and pitch produced by a resonator system are size, shape and openings, and texture. The larger the resonator, the less frequent the vibrations; the smaller the resonator, the more frequent. Moreover, the larger the resonating air cavity, the lower its pitch; and the smaller the cavity, the higher its pitch. Because resonator shapes and openings can determine pitch and tone quality, a spherical cavity with a large opening will produce a high pitch. However, if a neck is added to the spherical cavity, the pitch will be lower. For example, in striving to create a warmer, richer tone, some classically trained singers enlarge their resonators by rounding and extending their lips as a common practice. But the downside of this technique is the possibility of artificially darkening and stressing one's voice, especially if the voice production is not efficient.

Finally, the composition and surface of resonators can affect the tonal product by either encouraging or discouraging potential overtones. For example, metal and flesh will respond differently according to their composition. In general, hard surfaces will make a tone more brilliant by reflecting high overtones, and soft surfaces will absorb the rapid, short vibrations, resulting in more mellow, sweeter tones.

We continue our discussion of vocal resonators by looking at a diagram of the human resonating system (Fig. 8-1), followed by a discussion of each area.

Chest and subglottal airways. Because the lungs are filled with spongy, absorbent material, they are not considered viable resonating cavities. However, singers do experience vibratory sensations in their chests, particularly when singing in low range and at full voice. Such vibratory sensations are actually the result of forced sympathetic vibrations produced within the lungs and rib cage. The hard surfaces of the subglottal trachea and bronchial tubes also qualify them as resonators, but the

Figure 8-1
The Human
Resonating System

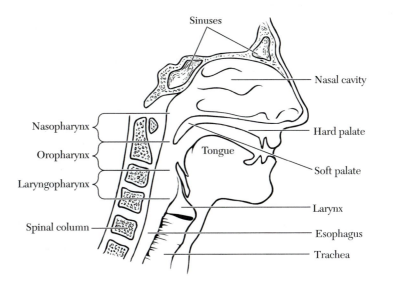

amount of resonance available to enhance the singing voice has not yet been scientifically confirmed.

Larynx.   Though the laryngeal cavity is small, the larynx may be classified as a small resonator and possibly even a very important one. Sundberg (1977) has made a strong case substantiating the possibility that resonance is generated in the **laryngeal collar,** a space just above the vocal folds and below the rim of the epiglottis. Scientists speculate that this space might be the source of the typical "ring" heard in the voices of professional singers.

Pharynx and oral cavity.   Together, the *laryngopharynx* and *oropharynx* form the largest resonating cavity and have the greatest effect on tonal quality. The laryngopharynx, extending from the base of the cricoid cartilage to the top of the epiglottis, also includes the laryngeal collar. The larger oropharynx extends from the top of the epiglottis to the soft palate. The "open throat" terminology used by many teachers refers to this combined spacious resonating cavity. In close juxtaposition to the pharynx, the mouth cavity is the most variable resonator, primarily because of constantly fluctuating tongue and jaw positions.

Nasal and sinus cavities.   The cavity immediately above the *velum* (soft palate) and extending to the base of the skull is the *nasopharynx.* The opening and closing of this **nasal cavity port** is primarily controlled by sphincter action of the velum (soft palate) and muscles connected to the velum. This action determines to a large extent the production of certain consonants as well as the tonal configuration of vowels. Although the amount and quality of resonance generated by the coupling of the nasal cavity is controversial, accomplished singers report experiencing sensations or illusions of sympathetic vibrations in the nasal cavities when they are singing well. The perceived sensations are often described in terms of *nasal* (head) *resonance,* sometimes referred to as "twang," or "ring," terms not meant to denote nasal singing, a less desirable tone quality requiring a lowered velum (soft palate). It should be duly noted that because the sinus cavities are small and practically inaccessible (because of their small apertures), they are thought to be unsuitable as resonators.

Finally, the coupling of all primary resonating cavities into a single, highly complex, and variable resonating system is often referred to as the *vocal tract.*

Maximizing Vocal Resonance

For maximum resonation, the vocal resonators must be optimally enlarged, primarily by intrinsic and extrinsic muscular adjustments in the vocal tract that control the positioning of specific vocal organs (larynx, velum, tongue, and jaw).

Larynx

The pharynx is enlarged when the larynx is lowered in a relaxed, nondepressed manner, primarily by the action of the strap muscles. This is achieved with the assistance of the swallowing muscles, which pull upward and backward toward the base of the skull, and the tongue muscles, which pull upward and forward toward the point of the jaw. The resonating chamber of the vocal tract can be enlarged naturally in four ways: (1) by chewing, as when slowly eating a tasty meal with an easy, loose chewing action, which helps relax the swallowing muscles; (2) by swallowing, and then feeling the relaxation of the swallowing muscles; (3) by inhaling through the nose or mouth, as when taking a surprise breath; and (4) by sighing with a feeling of pleasurable contentment. The sensation felt at the beginning of a sneeze can also help accomplish a similar natural adjustment of the resonators.

Tongue

The tongue is a very large muscle that, by the nature of its strategic position and functioning, has a significant influence on the shape and size of the vocal tract. Behind the chin and under the tongue are muscles that need to be free from tension to produce quality tone. Massage these muscles with your fingers during vocalization to help create a relaxed condition. The exact positioning of the tongue is determined chiefly by vowel shaping and consonant articulation. The important thought to bear in mind is that it should always be relaxed and never stiff, and the tip should be rounded and not pointed. Normally, the tongue tip is slightly touching the lower teeth and dental ridge, never curled up into the mouth or pulled back. Whether it is naturally grooved depends on your physiology. For example, on the vowel "ah," the tongue should lie relatively flat and rounded at the tip. Refer to tongue-training Exercises 4-8a,b for help in developing flexible tongue control.

Pharynx

The wall of the pharynx consists of muscle tissue, including the swallowing muscles, the pharyngeal pillars, and the velum (see Fig. 8-2). When the larynx is low and the soft palate high, these muscles create the inner stretch often referred to as *open throat*. A moderate sensation of this inner stretching will suffice and can be gained by creating the sensation of taking a breath with a dumbfounded surprise expression, which creates a sensation of an "inner smile." In addition to the laryngeal collar, this slight stretching of the pharyngeal wall is thought to enhance the ringing quality heard in all highly developed voices. Figure 8-2 illustrates the interior of an extremely exaggerated open mouth, including the relaxed flat tongue, the raised soft palate, and the two pairs of pharyngeal wall muscles known as the *anterior* and *posterior faucial pillars*. This is an extreme opening, but some singers might open nearly as wide when singing a full-voiced high note on the vowel "ah."

Figure 8-2
**Open Mouth:
Pharyngeal and
Tongue Positioning**

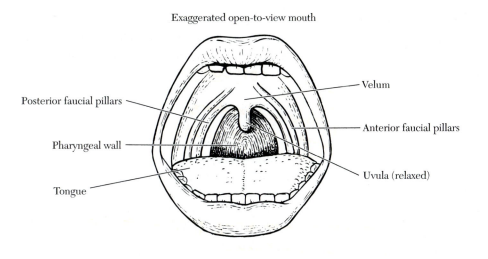

Exaggerated open-to-view mouth

Velum

Posterior faucial pillars

Anterior faucial pillars

Pharyngeal wall

Uvula (relaxed)

Tongue

Jaw

Because the jaw is so interconnected with the tongue and other vocal tract musculature, its role in singing is crucial. Apparently, we humans carry a lot of excess
tension in our jaws, as indicated by such descriptions as "clenched teeth," "gritted
teeth," and "tight jaw."

To begin with, singers are cautioned not to open the jaw too wide, no more
than a two-finger width for most persons. Of course, a singer's mouth size largely
determines the degree of mouth opening. In all cases, when opening the mouth, it
works best to allow the jaw to drop comfortably, using a dumbstruck, surprised expression, as described previously. The chin should not jut outward, nor should
there be any physical effort to create an overly large vocal-tract space. When taking a dumbstruck, surprise breath, the jaw releases properly, causing the larynx to
lower and the throat to feel relaxed and spacious. A gentle, incipient yawn is another technique that helps assist a relaxed jaw opening. Although the amount of
jaw drop will depend on such factors as individual anatomy, pitch levels, and vowels and consonants articulated, one should exercise moderation, especially in the
middle pitch range. Generally speaking, when the mouth is forced open beyond
the aforementioned two-finger width, excessive muscular tension can occur, particularly in the muscles under the jaw that connect to the larynx. A helpful guideline
for opening the jaw comfortably is to experience sensations of gentle stretching.

Another problem related to excessive manipulation is the "over-jawing" of
words in order to articulate more clearly. Aggressive jaw action needs to be minimized in most vocalization, especially in the low-to-middle vocal ranges, including the speaking voice range. Only at the low and high extremes of the vocal range
does the jaw need to be lowered to create an extended, yet comfortable opening.
To reiterate, articulation should be flexible, loose, and precise—never tense—
according to natural speechlike functioning.

Lips and Mouth

In general, lip use appears to be diminishing in the speech of most modern languages as people become more complacent in articulating consonants and shaping
vowels accurately (in part because of increasing reliance on electronic sound amplification). This trend is especially noticed with North Americans, who tend to
speak with lateral mouth positions and lax articulation. A role model of crisp,
clear, resonant, and expressive speech is male actor James Earl Jones, the Darth

Vader in *Star Wars*. Like Jones, most professional classically trained actors and singers are accustomed to using lip action in exaggerating all consonants in order to be heard in large performing spaces. In contrast, novice singers rarely use their lips actively in articulation, as it may seem a bit unnatural at first. With time and regular practice, however, lip action gradually improves.

The primary reason for rounding the lips is to shape "rounded vowels," such as "oo" and "oh." Acoustically, puckering to extend the oral cavity is similar to adding a neck to a resonating cavity, effectively muffling high overtones and augmenting low overtones. To the listener, the aural perception is one of a richer, lower-pitched tone. Most singers benefit from using a vertical mouth position in voicing most vowels, particularly the more brilliant "ee" and "ay" vowels. However, as a general approach for singing vowels, excessive puckering or rounding of the lips should be used with discretion, for reasons explained earlier.

In contrast to a more relaxed vertical mouth position, an exaggerated wide smiling mouth shape usually indicates tense muscles in the throat, jaw, tongue, and neck. Instead, the singer must learn to smile with the eyes instead of showing lots of teeth. Of course, because there are always exceptions to every rule, one must occasionally allow some latitude with this particular issue, particularly when performing certain character, Broadway, or popular music songs. Moreover, singers who tend to sing with too much throat space can sometimes benefit from adopting a smiling, upbeat attitude, a technique that helps release throat tensions and allows the tone to sound more natural or speechlike, with higher head sensations. To counteract any tendencies toward singing too laterally, that is, spread-toned or shrill, Exercise 8-1 should help establish a more relaxed vertical mouth/lip position.

Exercise 8-1   VERTICAL MOUTH/LIP SINGING POSITION

Place both hands vertically on both cheeks and the chin so that the jaw is slightly lowered and lips are relaxed and oval shaped, somewhat as when exclaiming in great surprise, "Oh, my!" While vocalizing on scales and arpeggios using all vowels, you should think of elongating more when singing into the higher range. This translates into an increased jaw drop and a more open vertical lip and mouth position. The important objective is to strive for a natural, forward-placed tonal focus that is balanced with a relaxed, vertical position. While doing this exercise, maintain the inner-smile position to counter a tendency toward "dead-panning" or a "hung jaw."

Tone Placement and Focus

Without getting too technical, it is important to know that overtones are involved in the perception of focus. In the sound spectrum of any instrument there exists clusters of energy frequencies known as **formants** that produce specific tonal characteristics. For instance, specific configurations of formants make it possible for us to discern the subtle or not-so-subtle differences between various instruments, voice types, or speech phonemes. Remarkably, the well-trained human voice is identifiable by the third formant, or "singer's formant," which ranges in frequencies from 2,500 to 3,200 Hz. Thanks to this special formant, a well-trained singer is capable of being heard when singing with a large orchestra.

The terms *tone placement* and *focus* are frequently used by advanced singers in describing their physical sensations, which are actually sympathetic vibrations emanating from the vocal resonators. In general, tone placement is more concerned with *where* the tone is sensed, and focus is more concerned with *how* the tone is produced. In other words, **placement** describes the localization of sensations within an appropriately aligned vocal tract, usually in the region around the eyes, and **focus** describes an efficiently produced vocal tone that maximizes vibration sensations, achieved by coordinating efficient vocal-fold vibration and breath flow. In vocal terms, while placing the sound in the head might result in a perceived tonal improvement, the quality might be fuzzy—unless it has focus. For this reason, most voice experts acknowledge two concepts of focus, both of which are necessary for a complete understanding of this phenomenon: (1) *phonation focus*, the result of efficient vocal-fold closure or onset that continues throughout the vocalized tone, and (2) *resonance focus*, which is based on vocal tract vibrations and sensations.

In addition to the dumbfounded surprise breath mentioned several times previously, some of the more popular suggestions for establishing vocal tract alignment are to imagine and imitate (1) taking a drink of water, (2) smelling a rose or something odorous, (3) smiling inwardly (suppressed smile), (4) beginning to sneeze, (5) beginning a pleasant yawn-sigh, and (6) holding your breath while swimming underwater. All these suggested images depict reflexive actions, and all help to align the musculature and organs of the vocal tract by subconsciously causing the soft palate to lift, the anterior-posterior faucial pillars to stretch (Fig. 8-2), and the larynx to lower. The objective of these stretching actions is to achieve both a relaxed throat and a desirable vocal tract alignment.

The imagery that the voice is actually initiated with the high-arched breath-release gesture may help to alleviate excessive efforts of throat muscles and articulating organs. However, caution should be exercised in the process of intense mental concentration. One must not force, push, stick, or drive the tone in attempting to "place" it in the head (above the roof of the mouth in the area surrounding the eyes). Instead, the tone should be allowed to "exist" or "hang" there, while simultaneously releasing all tensions, especially the tongue, jaw, and neck musculature.

This "height" of head-tone sensations may be said to lie approximately at the roof of the mouth, extending from the hard palate (at the front) to the soft palate (at the back), depending on the pitch or vowel vocalized. The focal area lies in the region surrounding the eyes, but sensations might also occur at the hard palate, predominantly when singing in the low to medium-low range. The direction of focus may appear to move gradually backward toward the soft palate as one ascends to the very top notes of the singing range. Some singers describe the sensation of singing very high pitches as coming from "out of the top of the head" or even occasionally from "back and down," ostensibly as the throat relaxes and full resonance is experienced. Other singers report that under right conditions, the illusion is that "the tone is singing itself, out in front of the mask." As these examples of singing terminology show, there are several ways of using imagery to describe tone placement, which are mostly determined by a singer's unique physiology.

Usually, when tone placement is right, the vocal folds vibrate efficiently. However, this is not always so, for one can still have either a pressed or breathy phonation in tandem with a high tone placement. In some cases, it may be necessary to concentrate on achieving an efficient focus at the vocal-fold level (see chapter 6). In addition to the yawn-sigh and the staccato and marcato exercises listed, vocal-fold closure (adduction) can also be achieved by humming and vocalizing on the nasal consonants "m," "n," and "ng" and the "nasty vowels" (see Chapter 9). Vocal exercises based on "moaning" and "whining" will also help induce a complete vocal-fold closure. More drastic measures might include mimicking the nasal twang of a hillbilly singer, the twang of an electric guitar, or the wickedly "twangy" laugh of the Penguin (Batman's nemesis)—under the supervision of a voice teacher. In all cases, one should be careful never to feel excessive muscular tensions in the soft palate, throat, tongue, and jaw.

Exercises 8-2 and 8-3 should be sung with a relaxed jaw and tongue and with a very forward, narrow (vertical) inner-smile sensation in the upper mouth area. (Again, singers should be guided in performing exercises correctly. If, for instance, the "ng" is produced with a tense tongue or a dark/backward concept, the tone will sound stressed.) The tonal concept should be that of a relaxed moan, whine, or siren. In addition to the "ng," the phoneme "nyam" is very helpful in producing a balanced tone, because it loosens articulators and facilitates speechlike vowels. Both exercises can be sung in all the keys encompassing a comfortable vocal range. The same techniques can also be used with any number of scales and arpeggios, especially the 1–3–5–3–1 and 1–3–5–8–5–3–1 arpeggios and the nine-tone scale.

Exercise 8-2

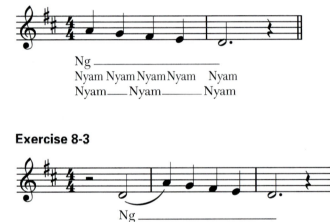

Exercise 8-3

Resonance Assessment

Acoustics. Are you aware of the acoustics of different kinds of spaces, as in a "live" or "dead" room? Do you have a practical understanding of the relationship between the science of sound and voice? Do you find acoustics irrelevant and boring, or interesting, stimulating, and informative? Do you think a knowledge of acoustics will make you a more informed and better singer? What are the three elements of any musical instrument? What are the properties and characteristics of sound and musical tone? Do you understand overtones and how they influence the quality of vocal tone?

Resonators. How do shapes and sizes of resonators affect the tone quality and pitch? Do surface and composition textures affect tone quality and pitch? What are the main resonators in the human vocal mechanism? Of what significance is the resonance created in the nose, chest, throat, mouth, and sinuses? What roles do the tongue, jaw, and other articulating organs play in resonance? What are the normal positions of the larynx, tongue, pharynx, jaw, and lips in singing?

Tone Placement.   What are the two kinds of focus? Do you sense vibrations in the mask when you sing? Do these sensations change as you sing from low-to-high range and from soft-to-loud dynamics? Are you conscious of letting go of extraneous tensions in the jaw and tongue when singing? How would you describe sensations you feel when singing is difficult and when it's easy?

Go to www.mhhe.com/ais4 to learn about additional Web-based resources that supplement the content of this chapter.

9

Voicing Vowels and Consonants

A visitor to any foreign country quickly discovers how not knowing the native tongue can hinder communication, proving that language greatly influences how people relate to one another and to the world at large. As the early twentieth-century Viennese philosopher Ludwig Wittgenstein succinctly stated: "The limits of my language stand for the limits of my world." On the singing journey, the singer whose artistic intent is to stir people's emotions learns that the value of being well grounded in all aspects of language opens up a more extensive, colorful palette of expressive means.

We have learned that every musical instrument has three essential elements in common. The violin, for example, has (1) an actuator (bow), (2) a vibrator (strings), and (3) a resonator (soundboard). In human voice production these three elements correspond to breath, vocal folds, and resonating cavities. But, in addition, the human voice has an articulator that uses movements and adjustments of the speech organs to form and produce an infinite variety of sounds. It is this particular function that makes the human voice unique compared to other musical instruments.

Linguistic Terminology

When discussing effective speech and language communication, the terms *articulation, enunciation, pronunciation,* and *diction* are sometimes used interchangeably, often without attention to precise technical denotation. As the following definitions demonstrate, however, each term represents a specific aspect of expressive linguistic communication.

- **Articulation** refers to the mechanics of producing speech sounds. Specifically, articulation includes the movements and adjustments of speech organs (lips, tongue, jaw, velum, cheeks, larynx) in pronouncing a particular speech sound, called a **phoneme,** in its entirety. For example, the sound "ng" requires an adjustment of the soft palate (velum), which directs the sound into the nasal passages, and the raising of the body of the tongue to the velum, effectively closing the passage into the mouth. More generally, articulation also includes connecting phonemes (vowels and consonants) to form words in the fluent and cohesive manner dictated by the language being spoken or sung.

- **Enunciation,** a less frequently used term, refers to the act or manner of pronouncing syllables, words, or sentences in a clear, distinct manner.

Enunciation is also associated with definitive statements, declarations, or proclamations.

- **Pronunciation** is the act or result of uttering phonemes, syllables, words, and phrases in a particular manner according to accepted standards. In American English, for example, the word "poor" is generally pronounced as "oo" throughout most of the United States; however, in certain regions it is pronounced "oh," as in "pore." In singing practice, the former ("oo") is accepted as standard pronunciation, although exceptions are found in folk and pop music where regional dialects are more common. Another more humorous mispronunciation occurs in the word "duty," which in some regions of the U.S. is pronounced "doody," while the more appropriate pronunciation is "dyooty," as spoken in the U.K. and much of the U.S.

- **Diction** is a general term that refers to using the prevailing standards of word usage and pronunciation in a comprehensible manner and style. For example, a singer is said to have excellent diction when a listener hears and understands every word and phrase of a song text presented expressively.

How words are uttered and expressed is largely determined by a particular language's general characteristics. Each language has its own peculiar sounds, expressions, and inflections that compose its identity. A language is often recognized by its unique pronunciations (generally referred to as "accent"). When speaking a foreign language, for instance, most people normally have difficulty disguising their "foreign accent" because of a lack of genuine, native pronunciation, word treatment, and expression.

Primary Singing Languages

Singing experts concur that the four languages in which English-speaking classical singers are expected to be proficient are English, Italian, German, and French. These four languages are considered the most vital because of the vast vocal repertoire composed over the past 300 years in the United States, Britain, Italy, Germany, and France. Note that the German and French phoneme symbols listed in the following brief observations about the major languages are explained later in this chapter.

> Dawn Upshaw knows some German, French, and Italian, but isn't fluent in any of those tongues. Whenever she sings in another language, she works with language and vocal coaches and people who speak the language to make sure she gets it right. *"Singers take their language very seriously,"* she says, but adds with a laugh, *"My absolute favorite is English."*
>
> —Dawn Upshaw, soprano

Native Language (English). Assuming one has good speech habits, the beginning student's native language usually affords the greatest ease and facility. Thus, the North American student is more comfortable singing in a general English dialect similar to that used by the typical national TV or radio newscaster. Except for occasions when a certain style and character of vocal dialect is required for authenticity, singers normally avoid such regional vocal mannerisms as southern drawl, eastern Brooklynese, and midwestern twang.

Italian, Latin, and Spanish. Novice singers usually begin foreign language singing with Italian or Latin because of their simplicity and ease of execution. Because Italian contains relatively few vowel and consonant phonemes and makes generous use of pure vowels, its simplicity encourages easier vocalism. Latin, the classic language from which contemporary Italian evolved, is used primarily in sacred texts, with either Italian or German pronunciations. Spanish is also quite similar to Italian and Latin in basic pronunciation, with some minor exceptions. Using these languages can challenge the student with fresh, uncomplicated concepts about phoneme formation, a practice that can circumvent incorrect habits in one's native language.

German. Though English is somewhat more complex than German—mostly because of derivations from several European languages—both languages employ a variety of consonants. The German *umlaut* vowels—[ø], [œ], [y], and [ʏ]—add color and warmth to the voice. German is stereotypically thought of as a guttural, harsh language, but this is not the case when it is spoken in a sophisticated, expressive manner.

French. The French language is noted for its fluidity, which results from the merging of vowels and consonants, flowing together to create a legato singing style. The plentiful use of the French nasal vowels—[ɛ̃], [ɑ̃], [ɔ̃] and [œ̃] help in adding nasal resonance to the voice. As in German, the "mixed vowels"—[ø], [œ], [y], and [ʏ]—also provide extra colors in the overall tonal spectrum.

> Languages always improve for me over the years, regardless of whether or not I use them very consistently, in much the same way as music. . . . The fact that music is as much a language as German or French is one aspect of learning that fascinates me.
>
> —Renée Fleming, soprano

Most European languages share the same basic vowels and consonants, with some notable exceptions. For example, the [i] vowel—as in the English word "lip"—is never used in Italian and Spanish, occasionally used in German, and rarely used in French. Also, some consonants are treated differently, such as [p] and [t] which are more imploded (less air) in Italian and French, but more exploded (more air) in English and German. Becoming aware of the differences in these languages will help a singer gain greater sophistication in foreign language diction.

Introduction to the IPA and Vowels

Up to this point, all vowels and consonants have been presented in their standard usage format ("ee," "ah," "oo," etc.). This chapter introduces the International Phonetic Alphabet (IPA), a worldwide standardized system for transliterating all speech sounds into phonetic symbols that can be read and translated back into uniform sounds of speech. All IPA symbols are included in a series of eight figures found in Appendix A, pp. 302–305. Most vowels and consonants are discussed throughout this chapter, but if you have any questions or concerns, please consult this appendix.

The figures in Appendix A illustrate all the IPA vowels and consonants used in English, Italian (I), French (F), and German (G). In most IPA figures, the phoneme illustrated in word samples is italicized; for example, "ee" is illustrated as "*seat*." In the text, IPA symbols are enclosed in brackets; for example, "ee" is symbolized as [i]. Figure A-1 contains all basic vowel symbols used in the primary singing languages.

As you read this chapter, bear in mind that IPA symbols are merely close approximate representations of phonemes used in all languages, and that there are subtle variations in how most phonemes are pronounced. As any North American knows, English is spoken in several regional and socio-cultural dialects, with some phonemes and words pronounced very differently. Though an initial exposure to the IPA might seem bewildering, most people eventually find the system easy to learn and apply in vocal study.

Introduction to Vowels

Vowels may be thought of as the different tonal colors or timbres that are produced with no vocal tract constrictions. Most scientists concur that effective vowel resonation is dependent upon tuning the vocal tract cavities, either separately or as a total unit. Because each vowel is recognized by the human ear as having specific acoustical properties—created by a unique configuration of the vocal tract—slight adjustments within this delicately balanced tonal system produce the entire spectrum of vowels used in all languages. Because most singing occurs on vowels, vocal study usually begins with the student practicing accurate vowel formation, which provides a firm foundation for producing efficient vocal tone.

Vowel formation is a complex activity involving shaping of the resonators by the articulators (jaw, tongue, lips, teeth, etc.), which, in turn, produces certain overtone structures characteristic of specific vowel sounds. Factors that determine the subtle differences in vowel formation are (1) individual vowel characteristics, (2) individual differences in articulating organs, (3) gender differences, (4) range of vocalization, (5) peculiar dialects or accents, (6) intended emotional effects, and (7) dynamic levels. Given all the preceding factors, singers must strive to produce the most efficient vowels possible.

Vowels can be better understood by looking at such characteristics as pitch, timbre, and action of the articulating mechanism (tongue, jaw, and larynx). The two exercises that follow illustrate how our perceptions of pitch and timbre (tone quality) are determined by the basic vowels used in speech and singing.

Exercise 9-1   PITCH PERCEPTION AND TIMBRE

Sing a sequence of vowels from "ee" [i] to "oo" [u] on a single, comfortable pitch, and notice that the higher frequencies of the [i] vowel's second formant seem a brighter timbre, and subsequent vowels gradually appear lower as one sings through "ay" [e], "ah" [ɑ], "oh" [o], and finally [u], which sounds the lowest because lower formants predominate. The vowel sequence can be reversed, beginning with [u], a darker, lower-pitched timbre, and ending with [i], a brighter, higher-pitched timbre.

Exercise 9-2   STAGE WHISPERING AND CHEEK THUMPING

To better understand the effects of formant frequencies in the absence of vocal-fold vibration, use a stage whisper to produce the vowel sequence [i-e-ɑ-o-u]. Next, whisper from [i] to [u] back and forth at various speeds to observe the changes in pitch. You can also experience this acoustical phenomenon by thumping on your cheeks with your index finger while shaping the articulators for each vowel, again using the [i-e-ɑ-o-u] sequence. Then try it from [i] to [u] back and forth, and notice the pitch change. What interval do you hear? Find the pitch on a keyboard instrument.

Tongue and Larynx Positioning

The tongue is the most important factor in varying the size of the vocal tract resonator for vowel formation, which occurs principally through high-low and front-back adjustments. For instance, the tongue moves through the vowel sequence from a high frontal position on [i] to a middle position on [ɑ], and lowers to an arched-back position on [u]. Other vowels are shaped by graduated tongue adjustments between the [i] to [u] positions.

Exercise 9-3 helps explain how tongue positioning affects vowel formation. This exercise is most effective when you use a mirror to closely observe your mouth and tongue action.

Exercise 9-3   VOWEL TONGUE POSITIONS ON [i-e-ɑ-o-u]

Place a clean finger on the central portion of the tongue and sing through the [i-e-ɑ-o-u] vowel sequence. As you experiment with singing this sequence of vowels on a sustained, comfortable pitch, you will notice that the tongue is frontally arched for [i] and gradually lowers and moves slightly backward as you sing toward [u]. You can also reverse the sequence, from [u] to [i]. Next, try other vowels, including those found in Figure A-1. Be careful not to exaggerate lip or jaw movements.

As you experiment with Exercise 9-3, place your finger on your larynx and notice that the larynx is in its highest position on [i], due to frontal tongue arching that causes a slight lift of the larynx, and gradually moves through the vowel sequence to its lowest position on [u]. Under ideal singing conditions, laryngeal movement should be very slight, with the larynx remaining comfortably situated throughout the vocal range.

Laryngeal positioning in vowel production is affected by activity of the articulators, namely the jaw, lips, and tongue. Sundberg (1977) reports several studies of singers showing that the larynx is lowered with rising phonation frequency, which coincides with increased jaw opening on ascending pitches. He also claims that lip rounding (oval mouth shape) tends to lower the larynx, whereas lip spreading (lateral mouth shape) tends to raise it. Furthermore, depressing or relaxing the tongue (and jaw), especially when singing the darker vowels [ɑ], [o], and [u] will effectively lower the larynx; raising the tongue, especially when singing the brighter vowels [i] and [e], will raise the larynx.

By experimenting with the cat's familiar "meow" (Ex. 9-4), you can experience all of the preceding vowel characteristics—subtle pitch and timbre changes and corresponding jaw, tongue, and laryngeal adjustments—as the vowel sequence migrates from the frontal vowel [i] to the back vowel [u].

Exercise 9-4   THE CAT'S "MEOW"

Simply mimic the sound of a cat by slowly voicing "meow" [m-i-ɪ-e-ɛ-æ-a-ɑ-ɔ-o-u-ʊ], first on a single sustained pitch level and then using inflected pitch levels. You will observe that almost all standard English vowel sounds appear to be incorporated in this exercise.

Categories and Classification of Vowels

Vowels can be categorized and classified in several ways, most of which are included in this section.

Tense/Closed and Lax/Open Vowels

Because the basic vowels [i], [e], [a], [o], and [u] require a more active involvement of the tongue for shaping them, these are often described as either "tense" or "closed" vowels. Their counterparts [ɪ], [ɛ], [ɑ], [ɔ], and [ʊ] are termed "lax" or "open" because their formations require less tongue elevation. Figure A-2 presents a comparison of the primary tense/closed and lax/open vowels.

Nasal and "Nasty" Vowels

The four French *nasal vowels*—[ɛ̃], [ɑ̃], [ɔ̃] and [œ̃]—are vocalized by allowing the velum (soft palate) to relax and the nasal port to remain slightly open, thereby allowing the tone to resonate more in the nasal cavity. Refer to Figure A-3.

The less nasal vowel [æ], often referred to as the unpleasant "nasty" vowel (as in the word "n*a*sty"), is used rather frequently in the English language, but more so in American English. North American speech uses a more nasal version than British pronunciation, which in many words tends toward more of an [ɑ] than [æ], as heard in such words as "path" or "bath." Some linguists contend that the North American [æ] is a close cousin to the French nasal [ɛ̃], For vocal development, both phonemes can be used in vocalises to encourage more vocal twang or ring, an especially helpful objective for singers with such vocal deficiencies as breathiness, weakness, darkness, or throatiness. Because it is sometimes difficult for students to initially vocalize the [æ] correctly, a competent teacher's guidance is needed. Some singers have a tendency to press or tighten pharyngeal and laryngeal muscles in an effort to create the [æ] sound, when sensations should be experienced more in the upper pharyngeal and eye/forehead areas. Singers can gain strength, brilliance, and projection by vocalizing both [æ] or [ɛ̃], followed by [a] or [ɑ], and returning to [æ] or [ɛ̃], as illustrated in Exercise 9-5.

Exercise 9-5

IPA: [ɲæ _ ɑ __ ɲæ _ ɑ __ ɲæ]
[ɲɛ̃ _ ɑ __ ɲɛ̃ _ ɑ __ ɲɛ̃]

Umlaut (Mixed) Vowels

The **umlaut** vowels may be thought of as a mixture of two vowels. For example: [y] is a combination of [u] and [i]; [ʏ] combines [ʊ] and [ɪ]; [Ø] combines [o] and [e]; and [œ] combines [o] and [ɛ]. If this is confusing, be patient. It is normal for beginning singers to experience some difficulty in producing these mixed vowels (see Fig. A-3). However, by listening carefully to native speech and singing and by practicing (with feedback from a teacher or tape recorder), foreign phonemes will eventually sound more authentic.

Neutral Vowels

The vowels that occur at the ends of words, plus many monosyllabic single words, are often thought of as neutral sounds, basically because they do not require prolonged vocalization. Such vowels present problems in singing, sometimes requiring a more Italianate [ɑ] vowel in lieu of the neutral vowels, especially on higher, sustained pitches. The [ə] vowel, sometimes referred to as "schwa vowel"—a

Hebraic/German derivative—is frequently found in German (lieb*e*), and French (j*e*), while the "dull" neutral vowel [ʌ] is primarily found in English (e.g., "the").

Semivowels (Glides)

Semivowels, or **glides,** are a combination of at least two vowels that effectively merge to become one sound, as found in such English words as "which,"[hwɪtʃ] "you" [ju], and "word" [wɜˑd]. Six examples are illustrated in Figure A-4, including the three listed here with IPA transcriptions.

Diphthongs and Triphthongs

Diphthongs are double vowels, sounded together as a single unit with a primary emphasis on the first of the two vowels, which is especially emphasized when singing. Similarly, **triphthongs** are triple vowels sounded together as a single unit. Because French does not use either diphthongs or triphthongs, it is conspicuously absent from the chart listed in Figure A-5. Although there are approximately 29 possible diphthongs and eight triphthongs, only some of the more commonly used ones are illustrated.

One problem common to untrained singers is the tendency to give premature attention to the second vowel in a diphthong. In almost all instances, the first vowel in a diphthong should be lengthened and the second vowel minimized, as illustrated in Exercise 9-6.

Exercise 9-6

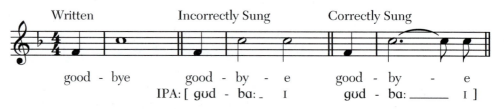

One diphthong syllable combination that American singers have problems with is the [uɚ], as found in the words *your* or *sure.* The tendency in some regions of the United States is to pronounce these words as "yore" or "shore." The English and general American accents require a [u] in lieu of [o] and only a hint of an [r], if any at all. Ideally, the words are pronounced [juɚ] and [ʃuɚ]. Refer to Figures A-6, A-7, and A-8 for a list of major consonant phonemes.

Vowel Modification and Efficiency

The laws of acoustics require that vowels be modified by slight physical adjustments, particularly when one is singing from low-to-high range. Although there is some controversy within the voice profession regarding the concept of **vowel modification,** there is sufficient scientific and empirical evidence to support it. Vowel modification partly explains what happens when the voice is dynamically balanced throughout the vocal range—creating a tone characterized by both bright and dark qualities. Vowel modification can be helpful in remedying vocal productions that are strident, spread, or piercing in timbre.

Because singers spend most of their time singing vowels, it is desirable to produce all vowels as efficiently as possible. As discussed briefly in chapter 8, singers try to align their vocal tract formants with the overtones of the fundamental frequency of the vibrating vocal folds. This is accomplished by manipulating their vocal tract to a certain degree, in an effort to match the formants of the vocal tract with the overtones, a process known as *formant tracking* or *formant tuning*.

However, singers must also pay heed to the creative intentions of composers, who dictate which vowels of a text are to be sung on given pitches, so singers' vocal tracts must produce sounds recognizable as specific vowels. Tongue and jaw adjustments are limited to those that will produce the desired vowels, or degree of vowel modification a singer is willing to produce, which is especially problematic in the case of female singers singing at very high pitches. For acoustical reasons too complex to explain at this time, sopranos have difficulty singing recognizable vowels in their upper range, where most vowels gravitate toward [ɑ].

Vowel modification occurs primarily when negotiating the transition zones between registers (for example, between chest and head for male voices), reaching a crucial peak at the pivotal register transition point. The typical lyric tenor, for instance, will experience a major register event around F♯4, at which time the vowel must be adjusted acoustically in order for G4 to sound secure and balanced in resonance. The important point to bear in mind is that vowel modification will occur naturally when the singer maintains (1) a properly aligned body and vocal tract, (2) sensations of head placement, (3) a natural speechlike involvement of the articulating organs requiring more jaw drop in the high vocal range, and (4) sufficient breath flow. When approaching the higher register transition zones, most singers, especially females, might find it more helpful to modify vowels toward more open, relaxed mouth/throat space in conjunction with increased jaw dropping. On the other hand, male singers might benefit from mentally closing or narrowing vowels when singing through their upper passage zone in an effort to avoid overloading the voice. In other words, it may help to image a vertical inner mouth/throat space, an egg-like shape that becomes proportionately more tall and deep as ever-higher notes are sung. In all cases, singers should be cautioned against using manipulative tactics to superficially "cover" or darken the tone in negotiating register transitions.

This narrowing approach is also related to the *pure vowel* concept some teachers use to indicate vowels that are speechlike, lean, and undistorted. Moreover, another related Italian concept, known as *closed vocal timbre*, is the opposite of open or spread timbre. One effective approach to achieving a closed voice timbre is to *think* of singing vowels in their most efficient formations—formations nearer to tense/closed vowel positions than lax/open ones (see Fig. A-6). Some singers tend to pronounce vowels with a spread, "mouthy" position, which is contrary to the desirable high-placed head position advocated throughout this text. It becomes more possible for the closed vowel to be experienced by concentrating on closed vowels throughout the singing range, all the while maintaining a sensation of head resonance at a level of the hard palate, eyes, nose bridge, and forehead. Successful ventriloquists, by way of illustration, are masters at employing the minimal vowel to project a variety of voice types.

A good example of vowel clarity is the often problematic [e] vowel, which is usually pronounced as a diphthong in English in such a words as "day," which can be voiced either [deɪ] or [dɛɪ]. For singers who sing too open or wide, it may help to vocalize "day" using the closed [e] that's common in German and French, which is experienced in a higher mouth position, closer to [i]. The same holds true for other vowels. This does not imply that the so-called open or relaxed vowels should be avoided, for one should have no problem making distinctions in subtle vowel coloring—after establishing a correct concept of the "vowel-placement tract."

Exercise 9-7 will help you experience the principle of vowel modification when singing from low to high and back to low range. Please note that this exercise is primarily descriptive of what appears to happen naturally; it is not necessarily pre-scriptive of what a singer should do to achieve a balanced vocal tone with accurate vowel formation.

Exercise 9-7

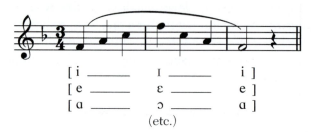

[i _____ ɪ _____ i]
[e _____ ɛ _____ e]
[ɑ _____ ɔ _____ ɑ]
(etc.)

Vowels are also used to develop a legato vocal style. **Legato** literally means "bound," and in singing it means singing in a smooth, connected manner. Legato singing technique is based on the practice of sustaining pure vowel sounds by avoiding the prolongation of consonants (keeping them crisply energized) and postponing the final vowel of a diphthong by giving primary attention to the first vowel. Although it may take time to develop these skills, one way to achieve this "vocal line" is to practice singing all vocal literature on the textual vowel sounds minus the consonants. A phrase excerpted from "Amazing Grace" demonstrates how a singer can apply this technique to any song (Ex. 9-8).

Exercise 9-8

A - maz - ing _ Grace, how sweet the sound,
IPA: [ʌ   e   i __   e   ɑʊ   i   ʌ   ɑːʊ]

Introduction to Consonants

Consonants are phonemes—other than vowels—that are produced by closing, diverting, or constricting the air passing from the lungs through the larynx, by means of the speech articulating organs: lips, teeth, alveolar ridge, hard and soft palates, tongue, cheeks, and jaw. Some examples of each type are: (1) *closing*—[p, b, t, d, k, g]; (2) *diverting*—[m, n]; and (3) *constricting*—[f, v, s, z]. Figure A-6 explains these categories in greater detail, with descriptions of which articulating organs are involved in producing each consonant.

Consonants carry more "information" than do vowels because they clarify and reveal the meaning and expressive power of languages. Consonants also aid in voice projection by generating positive noise in the acoustic spectrum. The power of consonants to add meaning can be quickly demonstrated by speaking a sentence or singing a phrase of a song text using only the vowels of the text (see Ex. 9-8), followed by singing it again, this time with consonants added.

By voicing consonants in a greatly exaggerated stage whisper, followed by louder dynamic levels of speaking and singing, one can experience the expressive power of consonant articulation (see Exs. 9-9 through 9-12). Beginning students are very much encouraged to strongly energize and exaggerate consonant articu-lation, to the extent that listeners report distinctly hearing every consonant and word. This exercise often seems very strange to novice singers, who are under-standably shy and unaccustomed to exaggerated speech. The results, however, are

90

Adventures in Singing

almost always an improvement in both overall vocal tone and expression of text, and are well worth taking the risk. Caution: Excessive whispering is not recommended, as it can be an unhealthy vocal practice, drying the vocal folds and promoting breathy voice production.

Although consonants can be classified in several ways, the most logical way is according to "place" of articulation; that is, positions of articulating organs (lips, tongue, soft palate, cheeks, and jaw) in relationship to the stationary mouth organs (teeth, dental ridges, and hard palate). The other two major ways of classifying consonants are based on "manner" of articulation and **voiced** and **unvoiced** characteristics. Some examples of unvoiced/voiced pairings are (1) unvoiced consonants—[p, t, f, k, t, tʃ, θ], and their corresponding (2) voiced consonants—[b, d, v, g, dʒ, ð]. The three categories are summarized in Appendix A (Fig. A-6), followed by a chart of consonants (Fig. A-8). A key to the chart (Fig. A-7) is supplied to familiarize you with the examples and symbols used in each of the six columns.

Sounding Consonants

All consonants can be problematic for certain individuals, especially in cases of speech impediments caused by missing teeth, malocclusion ("buck teeth" or "overbite"), cleft palates, TMD (*temporomandibular disorder*, also known as TMJ), and neurological ailments. However, a few consonants seem to be especially difficult for many people to articulate correctly, notably "r," "l," and most consonants that end words. IPA symbols and word examples of all problematic consonants are found in Figure A-8.

Typical Problematic Consonants

The "r" is classified as a semivowel and can be used in several ways depending on language peculiarities. For example, the rolled or trilled [r̃] is accomplished by air flowing over the top of the tongue as it touches the alveolar ridge, causing the tongue to flutter. It is used extensively in Italian, less so in German, French, and British English, and very infrequently in American English, except for dramatic effects. An example in British English would be the word "break" which sounds "br-r-r-eak" [br̃ek].

The flipped [ɾ] is a single flutter that sounds somewhat like the substitution of a [d] for an "r" as in "veddy" for "very." Though rarely used in American English, the flipped [ɾ] is frequently used in most languages, especially when occurring between two vowels, as it occurs in the Italian word "amo*r*e" (love).

The uvular "r" sound, in which the velum is fluttered against the back of the tongue, is typically used in spoken French and by French cabaret singers and is almost never used in singing classical song repertoire or in refined dramatic speech. This throaty consonant is related to the uvular "ch" [x] that occurs at the end of the German word "ach" [ɑx].

Finally, the retroflex [ɝ] or [ɚ] sound is the typical American "r," but when exaggerated it becomes the type of twangy, nasalized sound heard in some parts of the Midwest and South. For example, when the word "are" sounds "ar——," the rather unpleasant effect is referred to in linguistic parlance as *rhotacizing*. This type of "r" is the culprit of an overactive tongue, one that curls back and up, in its extreme position touching the soft palate, in effect shutting off the nasal port and causing nasality. One can improve the quality of a retroflex "r" by relaxing the tongue, and perhaps even thinking more toward a neutral vowel, such as [ə], the "schwa" vowel used in German and French, which is similar to the American "uh" [ʌ], but higher placed. It should be noted, however, that although this sound might sound unpleasant when used in standard diction, it has its merits as a tone-building device, especially for singers who tend to sing with a dark tone and throat orientation. When the articulators are relaxed and ample resonating space is provided, the retroflex "r" can help develop the desirable high-placed, frontal head sensations discussed earlier.

The "l" is a particularly obvious problem for certain regional Americans who tend to "swallow and wallow" in it. The late movie actor Jimmy Stewart typified this problematic consonant in a rather endearing way. In contrast, the European version is produced with the tongue tip placed forward on the upper dental (**alveolar**) ridge rather than on the front of the hard palate. The tongue and jaw exercises (Exs. 7-2a,b) use the "lah-lah-lah" technique to help achieve a high, forward-placed tongue in articulating a proper [l]. Even when singing English, the singer is encouraged to lean more toward the European pronunciation rather than the American version.

Most singers exhibit some minor difficulties articulating all consonants clearly, regardless of when or where they occur. Typically, however, there seems to be a preponderance of slip-ups when sounding final consonants. For example, [d] is often weakly voiced or eliminated altogether, and when voiced, is often voiced as [t]. This practice changes the word God [gɔd] into [gɔt] which is correctly pronounced only if one is singing in German. (The American pronunciation of *God* is usually more toward an [ɑ] vowel instead of the more acceptable [ɔ] vowel.) Another final-consonant problem can occur when ending strongly by adding an extra syllable. For example, "soun*d*" becomes "soun-duh" [sɔʊndʌ] and "mine" becomes "mine-uh" [mɑːɪnʌ]. It takes practice to articulate precisely without adding a pronounced extra syllable.

Some singers, particularly in the U.S. Midwest, tend to omit the final "ng" [ŋ] in such words as "sing*ing*" by substituting "een" [in] for the final syllable. Like many other diction problems, these habits take awareness of the specific problem and lots of practice to rectify.

Voice-Building Consonants

The value of consonants in assisting and enhancing correct voice functioning has been discussed previously in this book, particularly the use of the nasal consonants [m], [n], [ɲ] and [ŋ] (chapter 8) for inducing nasal resonance or head placement; [j], [l], and [r̄] for developing a flexible tongue and jaw (chapter 4); and [h] for achieving a healthy, relaxed, nonpressed vocal onset (chapter 6). Other consonants helpful in freeing the articulators and causing the natural voice to emerge are [bl] as in "blah" and [fl] as in "flah." The voiced consonants [ð] "th," [z], and [v] are useful in inducing both sufficient airflow and mask sensations, and [g] and [k] are particularly good for exercising soft palate and tongue coordination. In addition, there is a difference in the acoustic energy of consonants. For example, the relative acoustic power of the consonant [r̄] is 200 times as intense as [θ], which is the weakest.

All of the preceding consonants can be coupled with the primary vowels in vocalises based on the musical scales and arpeggios listed earlier throughout this book—for instance: 5–4–3–2–1; 1–5–4–3–2–1; 1–2–3–4–5–4–3–2–1; 1–3–5–3–1; 1–3–5–8–5–3–1; 1–2–3–4–5–6–7–8–9–8–7–6–5–4–3–2–1. All exercises can be sung in various tempi (slow, moderate, and fast), dynamics (soft, moderately loud, and loud), and styles (legato, staccato, and marcato).

Though the possible combinations of vocalises are extensive, it is best to limit most vocalizing to a few simple scales and arpeggios for warming up the voice. Then, to continue giving attention to specific technical objectives, one can treat suitable song repertoire as vocalises by singing the vocal line with various vowel and consonant combinations. For example, if your major problem is related to jaw and tongue tension, it might help to sing the entire song on "blah" [blɑ] in conjunction with the primary vowels [i], [e], [ɑ], [o], and [u]. If tonal placement is too dark and in the throat, it might help to sing the song using various combinations of nasal consonants in conjunction with vowels; for example, "nyahm" [njɑm] or "ming" [miŋ]. Although most singers will benefit from using traditional generic vocalises, others should be invented or tailored to suit specific problems.

Suggestions for Improving Diction

How does one set about developing good singing diction? In general, overall diction will improve as you learn to release unnecessary tensions in the articulating organs. This muscular freedom is only a starting point, however, for you must make a concerted effort to master all the elements of dynamic expression discussed thus far.

First, you must imprint an "aural image" of crisp, expressive diction. This can be accomplished by listening to vocal artists who exemplify the best singing diction in all languages being studied. Then, in a large space, use an exaggerated diction level while repeatedly practicing and perfecting all vowels and consonants until every phoneme is easily intelligible. But diction is effective only when you master the subtle points of expression, including dynamics, word stress, and meaning. The following exercises should help you become a more dynamic communicator.

Exercise 9-9   STAGE WHISPERING

With intense emotion—like a crazy person—use a stage whisper to voice the consonants of a song text in an exaggerated manner, slowing down the tempo and prolonging the consonants. If you don't have a song with an appropriate English text, experiment by reading Emily Dickinson's poem, "It's All I Bring Today" (page 206).

Exercise 9-10   DRAMATIC READING

Read a selected song text aloud in a dramatic, oratorical manner with a fully supported voice, perhaps the same one you used in Exercise 9-9. Concentrate on exaggerated articulation of consonants, accurate pronunciation, strong word emphasis, and expressive interpretation. Next, chant the text on a single pitch and in the rhythm of the song. Even better, try to contour your speech to closely coincide with the melodic voice line, in effect approaching speech-singing.

Exercise 9-11   TEXTS WITH ALLITERATION

Practice speaking complex texts that employ alliteration to emphasize specific consonants. For example, use the familiar "Peter Piper picked a peck of pickled peppers" and "Sister Sue sells sea shells down by the seashore." Some excellent examples can be found in David Blair McCloskey's book, *Your Voice at Its Best* (1972).

Exercise 9-12   "PATTER" SONGS

Study a song with a text that requires rapid articulation, such as certain selections from Gilbert and Sullivan operettas. Prior to singing, recite the text aloud using suggestions in Exercise 9-10.

Exercise 9-13   MINIMIZING "JAWING"

To avoid overusing the jaw when working toward effective diction skills, try to minimize jaw movement by adjusting the jaw drop to suit the demands of dynamics and range. You can work on this by placing the top of one hand horizontally under your jaw to sense the amount of jaw movement; even better, observe your jaw movements in a mirror. The important objective is to keep the jaw loose and floppy, never tensed or overworked. Pretending you are a ventriloquist might also help, as long as articulation remains loose and crisp.

Diction Assessment

Vowels.   Do you understand vowel characteristics as based on pitch perception, timbre, and tongue position? Are you aware of the subtleties of tongue and jaw positions on all vowel sounds as you speak or sing them? Do you allow the vowel sounds to be natural, without undue shaping of the mouth and lips? Do you understand the differences between open and closed vowels? Have you experimented with the cat's "meow"? Are you aware of singing diphthongs correctly when they occur on sustained pitches, for example, "n*igh*t" or "b*y*"? Are you aware of vowels being modified as you sing from low to high pitch range? Are you able to sing a song comfortably using *only* the vowel sounds of the words and not the consonants?

Consonants.   Are you aware of all the articulating parts of the vocal mechanism? Do you understand voiced and unvoiced consonants? Do you have any problems articulating specific consonants? Can you demonstrate how to use all the forms of "r," particularly the rolled and flipped versions? Are you able to recite a song text without leaving out any consonants, especially the final "d's" and "t's"? Can you articulate an "l" with your tongue tip on the upper dental ridge?

General Diction.   Do you have facility in languages other than English? If so, are you aware of both the differences and the similarities with English, notably how vowels and consonants are sounded? Which language do you most enjoy singing? Why? Do you understand the differences among the uses of articulation, pronunciation, and diction? Do you understand the difference between jawing and floppy jaw? When learning a song, do you make it a practice to read the text aloud in a dramatic, expressive manner?

Go to www.mhhe.com/ais4 to learn about additional Web-based resources that supplement the content of this chapter.

10

Coordinating The Vocal Process

Singers listen to themselves too much. I think we sing infinitely more by radar than sonar . . . . Ultimately, all that stuff *[voice studies]* ought to inform what you do as a singer, but it ought not to dominate. We are up there to use our voices as expressive tools to touch people.

—Thomas Hampson, baritone

Coordination in singing refers to the effective interrelationship and unity of all components of the vocal process—volition, respiration, phonation, resonation, and articulation—for the sake of expressive communication. Because each component is influenced by the functioning of the others, all must be considered and understood as parts of a whole, united in a single act or response. The miracle of this complex coordinated activity is that it occurs instantaneously, usually within seconds. The coordinated processes and their characteristic actions are summarized next.

- **Volition.** The brain (thought or will) and body interactively transmit instructions throughout the body, resulting in an instantaneous chain reaction of neuromuscular responses.

- **Respiration.** Air is inhaled and momentarily suspended in the lungs.

- **Phonation.** Airflow, released by passive forces of exhalation in combination with action of the abdominal wall muscles, meets resistance by the vocal folds.

- **Resonation.** The vibrating vocal folds excite the air column in the vocal tract (laryngopharynx, oropharynx, and nasopharynx).

- **Articulation.** Finely tuned movements of the articulating organs produce vocal sounds that take shape as words.

- **Communication.** Ideas, moods, and actions are expressed.

Elements of Dynamic Vocalism

Only when the voice is well coordinated is a singer capable of dynamic performance in a wide range of musical styles suitable for his or her specific voice type. Hence, a balanced, flexible coordination, or complete "hook-up," is the ultimate goal of all aspiring singers. An efficiently produced and well-coordinated voice demonstrates some principal characteristics associated with accomplished singers, such as accurate intonation, a normal vibrato pattern, agility, sustaining power, and dynamic flexibility, each of which we will now consider.

Intonation

The topic of tuning in music performance is a complicated one, requiring more explanation than is necessary for our purposes. Suffice it to mention that there are two major systems—*just intonation* and *mean-tone intonation*—which you may want to explore independently. For vocal reasons, we refer to **intonation** as the ability to sing "in tune," that is, to reproduce accurate pitches of music scales and modes (major, minor, etc.) with a relative degree of accuracy. A singer who is "out of tune" is said to have poor intonation, whereas an in-tune singer is said to have a good "musical ear."

It has been established that intonation is highly affected by the ability of singers to tune their resonators with their fundamental frequencies, which helps explain why singers with good musical ears but poor technique can sing "off key." As far as the so-called tone-deaf person is concerned, there is mounting evidence that it may be possible for anyone to achieve a respectable level of in-tune singing, with patient, nurturing training, regular practice, and physical maturation.

Although out-of-tune singing is frequently attributed to faulty hearing, the reality is that singing either flat or sharp in pitch is usually the result of one or more malfunctioning components of the vocal process (respiration, phonation, registration, resonation, and articulation) and is often difficult to diagnose. For example, "flat singing" is commonly caused by a lack of breath energy or proper vocal-fold adjustment, but it can also be the result of "over-singing," or tense articulators, as when using a heavy, dark vocal production. On the other hand, "sharp singing" can result from forcing too much air through the folds, another form of stressful vocalism. Such singing might also seem strident and "spread-toned." When the tone is properly coordinated, intonation is accurately perceived as being "on pitch," or "in tune."

Vibrato

Vibrato may be defined as the audible, regular pulsation, oscillation, or fluctuation of a single pitch that varies no more than a semitone or a third of a whole tone. Such a variation in pitch is normally perceived by the ear as a quality characteristic of the tone rather than a pitch deviation.

Vibrato occurs when the nerves supply impulses to the laryngeal muscles as an alternating current, creating movements alternating between muscles, one relaxing (agonist) and the other contracting (antagonist). This action is combined with the activity of the breathing muscles and diaphragm, resonating cavities, and laryngeal cricothyroid muscles. As a result, vibrato is integrally related to pitch, timbre, airflow, and intensity (nerve energy).

Normally, the frequency of vibrato pulsations is between 5.5 to 7.5 times per second. Any frequency pattern faster than 7.5 pulsations per second is considered a **tremolo** or **bleat,** which is usually caused by a hyperactive manipulation of laryngeal muscles. A vibratory pattern slower than 5.5 is known as a **wobble** and is usually caused by overloading the voice or creating a "false vibrato" (or "flutter") by pulsing the abdominal muscles. Irregularity in the vibrato pattern usually indicates some form of malfunctioning in the vocal process, such as hyperfunctional or hypofunctional muscular activity, emotional imbalance, physical and vocal fatigue, nervous system disorders, or vocal-fold injury.

Voices lacking a vibrato are usually described as breathy, dull, straight, spread, or yell-like. One explanation of vibratoless (straight) tone is that intrinsic laryngeal muscular tension causes the mechanism to be rigid or static instead of the relaxed and flexible condition necessary for proper vibrato functioning. This might suggest a good reason to avoid excessive use of straight-tone singing techniques often associated with pop music styles and some choral music.

Finally, one must be cautioned against manipulating vibrato patterns to satisfy personal tastes. According to principles of efficient vocal production, the natural vibrato pattern occurs only when appropriate conditions result in a well-coordinated voice.

Agility

Agility in singing is based on the singer's ability to negotiate musical challenges nimbly and quickly, including wide pitch intervals, coloratura (fast-note) scales and passages, and dynamic variations. A sensation of elasticity and suppleness must ever be present in the singer's technique to safeguard against potentially negative muscular tensions and to counterbalance the technical requirements of sustained singing.

One characteristic of agility is illustrated by the singer's technical ability to produce a **trill** (which can be thought of as an exaggerated vibrato), produced by rapidly alternating between two notes, usually at an interval of a major (whole-step pitch) or minor (half-step pitch) second (see chapter 11). One way to understand a trill is to think of it as an exaggerated vibrato. Trilling is primarily an involuntary action, with the exception of the beginning and ending, which are controlled.

Trills should be practiced if for no other reason than to encourage agility in the vocal mechanism, at least at the intermediate to advanced levels of study. Typically, beginning singers have more fundamental concerns and therefore are not usually expected to produce an effective trill until the basics are firmly in place. As a matter of experimenting with learning how trills work, however, Exercises 10-1 and 10-2 may be helpful. Both may be sung on all vowels, beginning with [ɑ] on middle-range pitches, and moving to higher-range pitches based on level of ease and comfort.

Exercise 10-1

[ɑ] _____

Exercise 10-2

[ɑ _ ɑ _ ɑ _ ɑ _ ɑ _ ɑ _ ɑ _]

The ability to sing each note of a rapid scale passage (coloratura phrase) with agility and precise intonation requires total freedom of the singing mechanism. When sung at slower tempi, rapid scale work is normally felt as originating from the abdominal musculature. In contrast, fast-scale singing is associated with continuous steady breath pressure and a vocal articulation that seems to occur in the larynx as an almost involuntary flutter, somewhat similar to giggling. Ideally, one only has to think vowel and pitch when applying a steady breath pressure to the larynx to achieve an accurate execution of a fast-moving scale. Although the practice of articulating an [h] on every note of a fast scale may be a helpful technique for the beginning singer, the advanced student is cautioned against it, except perhaps in extremely fast passages where the **aspirato** (using "h's" to articulate fast notes) technique can be particularly helpful.

Vocal exercises for agility include scale work plus fast tempi musical phrases from the vocal literature of such composers as Purcell, Handel, and Bach. You might try using the giggling or "h" approach on the vowel [ɑ] while voicing the pitches of the "Woody Woodpecker Song" (1–4–6–8–6) two times as quickly as possible. The following vocal exercises (Exs. 10-3 and 10-4) illustrate types of scales useful in developing agility. Perform both exercises using [ɑ] at first, followed by random use of all primary vowels.

Exercise 10-3

Exercise 10-4

Sostenuto

Sostenuto refers to the sustaining capabilities of the voice and depends on coordination of respiration, phonation, resonance, and articulation. Primarily because of the pervasive "beat" commonly experienced in popular music forms, especially rock, most beginning voice students are extremely challenged by energetic sustained singing. The long, sustained phrases in certain vocal compositions of such composers as Handel, Mozart, Verdi, and Brahms, for instance, demand high energy and skillful execution. Two fine examples from the song anthology are "O Sleep, Why Dost Thou Leave Me" (p. 199), by Handel, and "Ridente la calma" (p. 226), by Mozart.

One of the main objectives of sostenuto singing is to find the delicate balance between using energy and remaining free of negative tensions. For example, when singing ascending vocal lines directed toward dramatic high notes, one is often tempted to over-sing. Conversely, when descending from high-note peaks, the opposite tendency of over-relaxing frequently occurs, resulting in a fizzling-out tone toward the end of phrases. Thus, the goal of every singer should be to sing or sustain the entire musical phrase with an eye toward the final note, never flagging in intent and physical energy.

Adventures in Singing

The following sostenuto exercise (Ex. 10-5) may be sung on either a single vowel such as [ɑ] or a combination of vowels. Begin with comfortable medium keys and work up and down in various keys to exercise and stretch the voice throughout the entire singing range. The tempi might begin moderately fast and gradually slow down as greater muscular and vocal control is gained.

Exercise 10-5

The basis of sostenuto is legato, the vocal result of binding or connecting one phoneme and note to the next throughout a musical phrase. When delivering a song text in legato style, for instance, singers are usually instructed to lengthen vowels and crisply articulate consonants in a smooth, flowing manner. However, vocal experts are not in complete agreement as to how legato singing style is best accomplished. While some experts suggest that singers focus on vocal sound to shape and move a phrase, others concentrate on diction or interpretive details. Both approaches are valid, but beginning singers are well advised to concentrate primarily on vocal technique in achieving sostenuto.

Dynamic Flexibility

Controlling dynamic levels is a prerequisite for artistic, expressive singing. Ultimately, the singer must be able to sing easily and effectively in all musical styles: legato (smooth and connected), marcato (strongly accented), staccato (crisp and detached), and aspirato (using h's to articulate fast notes). In addition to achieving dynamic flexibility by performing appropriate vocal literature, specific exercises can be designed to incorporate all dynamic levels and styles, including sustained, arpeggiated, and coloratura passages, as Exercise 10-6 illustrates.

Exercise 10-6

One of the traditional devices for mastering a wide range of dynamic variations is the messa di voce, which is soft-to-loud-to-soft singing on a sustained pitch while maintaining uniform timbre (see Ex. 7-5). The technique can be compared to what happens when a radio volume control knob is turned up and down, slowly and gradually, from soft to loud, then back to soft.

A singer's control over soft-to-loud-to-soft dynamics is determined principally by the ability to balance inspiratory and expiratory musculature. While maintaining the "sensation of inhalation," concentrate on release of articulator tensions, high-placed head sensations (above the hard palate and around the eyes), a coordinated, well-focused vocal onset, and increased airflow to sing louder. The trick is to start the tone with clarity and intensity at a low dynamic level, without pressing or forcing, and allow the tone to expand as it swells to the louder dynamic level. Diminishing a sustained tone requires even more concentration and coordination of inspiratory and expiratory muscles, with very little decrease in focused tone during the process. As adequate technique develops, you will discover that the mind will control vocal dynamics according to expressive considerations. For a messa di voce exercise, see Exercise 7-5, p. 70.

Young singers must be forewarned not to be overly zealous in practicing the messa di voce exercise on high pitches, especially in register transition zones at loud dynamic levels. Because the laryngeal cartilages are not secure until the singer is in his or her mid-twenties, loud singing should not be the primary objective. With time and coordination of the vocal process, the voice will continue to grow in strength and quality. As explained earlier, this exercise is very demanding, especially in higher ranges, so novice singers cannot be expected to master it until all other technical means are secure.

Range Extension

Although advanced-level singers may be able to vocalize a three-octave range, it does not necessarily follow that their effective singing range will encompass such wide parameters of pitch. In fact, most singers manage to sing most of the vocal repertoire for their voice types by performing within a range of one-and-a-half octaves, occasionally stretching to two octaves for more demanding repertoire, such as coloratura soprano arias and contemporary vocal music encompassing extended techniques. The truth is that most singers are evaluated in terms of their tonal quality, not their singing range. Nevertheless, as a precautionary safety net, it helps if a singer can vocalize beyond the normal singing range, both high and low.

In general, the voice will extend itself when inhibiting tensions are relieved and vocal efficiency is established. In practice, the use of the high mechanism (head voice) will aid in extending the upper range, and the low mechanism (chest) will help in extending the lower range. Below are some exercises for assisting range extension, all of which should be explained and monitored by a voice instructor. Singing the cardinal vowels [i, e, ɑ, o, u] using an octave arpeggio (1–3–5–8–5–3–1; see Ex. 10-5) in various vowel combinations and low-to-high keys is recommended for most of the following exercises.

Exercise 10-7 PITCH CONCEPTS

Because pitch is actually the frequency of vibrations per second, singers should be cautioned against thinking of pitches as high or low. Yet, the concept of high and low pitches might be put to good use in stabilizing the vocal range. Suggestions: When singing high, think low; when singing low, think high. Visualize pitch on a horizontal plane, with the lower pitches near you and higher pitches out and away from you. Use your hand to physically depict this imagery by singing an octave scale ascending and then descending. Move your hand and forearm smoothly in (low pitches) and out (high pitches) in synchronization to the rising and falling pitches.

Exercise 10-8 JAW POSITIONING

When singing an ascending scale, as in Exercise 10-5, the jaw should gradually drop, effectively enlarging the resonating cavity. This action is reversed on the descending scale until reaching the lower range, when, again, the jaw drop might be more necessary to allow the singing mechanism to function freely. The main thought should always be to let go of any tensions in the jaw by allowing it to drop and unhinge without force and tension.

Exercise 10-9 HIGH/LOW BODY CONNECTION

Concentrate on a combined high/low feeling when singing. This sensation of stretching incorporates the qualities described earlier in discussions of the bright-dark tone known as chiaroscuro. In terms of imagery, the "high sensation" is a tonal placement in the top of the head, as though there were an open dome for resonance, whereas the "low sensation" is an anchoring of tone to the supporting musculature of the middle/lower abdominal area, primarily below the waist. Using this imagery, you will become more aware that "the body sings the tone." The octave arpeggio can be used in progressively higher keys.

Exercise 10-10 TONAL FOCUS

The changing direction of tone focus as you sing up and down the scale has been discussed (see chapter 8). Tonal sensations should be experienced in the frontal head area, above the hard palate, and in the region surrounding the eyes. It might help to be aware that the tone focus for low notes is directed more toward the hard palate and gradually moves backward along the roof of the mouth (toward the soft palate) as you ascend into the top range. Rather than sticking or forcing the sound into any specific place, simply *allow* the tone to be sensed in the mask. Use the octave arpeggio in low-to-high keys while observing these tone-focus sensations.

Exercise 10-11 HEAD/CHEST REGISTRATION

When ascending a scale, concentrate on using more head-voice registration, which requires a thinner adjustment of the vocal folds. For singers who tend to employ too much of the lower mechanism when descending in pitch, it may help to lighten the voice and refrain from pressing.

Exercise 10-12 HIGH/LOUD PITCHES

When singing louder, particularly in the upper vocal range, increase breath flow, remain free of nonproductive tensions, and trust the vocal mechanism and ear to execute pitches accurately. Higher singing normally requires a relatively louder dynamic level, hence more breath energy.

Exercise 10-13 POSITION OF LARYNX

Although the larynx should remain relatively low and neutralized throughout the vocal range, there will be a slight lifting (caused by the upward pull of the cricoid cartilage in response to cricothyroid contraction) when ascending into higher-pitch range. The larynx should be allowed to float freely, and it should never be forced or depressed beyond its comfortable range of motion. Refer back to Figure 7-1 and the accompanying explanation and octave-leap exercise for a better understanding of laryngeal movement in singing higher pitches.

Classification of the Singing Voice

Do you know what type of voice you have? Because of potential difficulties associated with accurate voice classification, this delicate subject has been saved for inclusion at this time. According to all preceding information, accurate voice classifications can be made only when the singing voice is coordinated, which means efficient functioning. Physical maturation will also determine when to classify the voice and what type of voice you may have. In fact, most voices continue to change throughout the aging process, which means singers must be receptive to possible reclassification.

The four primary factors that help determine voice type are (1) timbre, the color or tone quality characteristics, (2) vocal range, the comfortable extent of the singing range, low and high, (3) tessitura, the comfortable pitch level a singer can sustain for a prolonged period without obvious strain, and (4) register changes, the points of transitions or passages (pitches in the scale) where the voice changes when in correct function.

As considered from the highest to lowest voice types, most young singers usually fit the solo classifications of **coloratura-soprano, soprano, mezzo-soprano, tenor, baritone,** and **bass.** Most young singers tend to have mid-ranged voices (at least at the outset of study). The rarest types are coloratura-soprano (highest) and bass (lowest). Of course there are several other voice classifications reserved for mature, professional opera singers, mostly large-voice types generally referred to as "dramatic," but they are beyond the scope of this text. Moreover, the majority of young, beginning-level singers benefit more from having lighter voice types as role models. As you continue your studies, you will become more familiar with an array of rare voice types, including large-voiced opera singers.

Reconciling Opposites

Italian singing technique has traditionally been concerned with establishing efficient, coordinated vocal function based on natural principles. The Italian masters coined the term **appoggio** (literally, "to lean") to describe the sensations one experiences when the vocal mechanism, with its many parts and processes, is in dynamic equilibrium. Although most written sources refer to the importance of breath management as a central coordinating function, scant information is available about the literal meaning, "to lean." The concept of leaning into the sound probably derives from (1) the psycho-physical acts of concentrating the sound "forward" in the vicinity of the upper head, lips, teeth, and hard palate, (2) lifting the chest and expanding the rib cage "outward," and (3) imagining the tone materializing "out there" beyond the singer's body. Appoggio represents the epitome of the reconciliation of opposites concept because precise mind/body functioning requires interdependence and synergy. In the words of G. B. Lamperti: "The singing voice in reality is born of the clash of opposing principles, the tension of conflicting forces, brought to an equilibrium" (Brown, 1973, p. 63).

Vocal Coordination Skills Assessment

Intonation.   Are you aware when singers are out of tune? Are you able to tell when and if you have pitch problems? Does it bother you to hear faulty intonation? What do you think causes it?

Vibrato and Trill.   Are you aware of your vibrato when you sing? When singing on a sustained pitch at various levels (low, medium, and high) and dynamic levels (soft, moderately loud, and loud), how many pulses do you count per second? Are you aware of vibrato when listening to others sing? Do you think it enhances the overall effect of the voice or does it detract? Can you tell the differences between a tremolo (bleat), a wobble, and a healthy vibrato? Using the two listed exercises

(Exs. 10-1 and 10-2), are you able to sing a trill? (If not, don't worry. Give it time to develop.)

Agility, Sostenuto, Flexibility, and Dynamics. Does your voice move easily when singing "runs" or fast-note passages, or do you find it difficult? What technique do you use when singing runs? How does it feel and how do you *think* you do it? Are you able to sustain a single pitch or musical phrase with a steady, flowing tone? Can you sing the messa di voce exercise on a single pitch with a change in dynamics and consistent tone? Are you able to change dynamic levels without changing your vocal production, or do you have to make obvious adjustments to do so? Can you sing Exercise 10-3 according to the suggested dynamic markings?

Vocal Classification. Do you have an idea of what type of voice you have? Has some vocal expert suggested a voice-type classification with which you either agree or disagree? What criteria should you use in determining voice classification? Do you understand the difference between choral and solo voice designations? What voice types have you heard, and which ones are unfamiliar?

Vocal Coordination. Do you understand the appoggio concept? What do you think of Lamperti's explanation of coordination? Based on what you experience when you sing, do these explanations make sense, or does the coordination process remain elusive?

Go to www.mhhe.com/ais4 to learn about additional Web-based resources that supplement the content of this chapter.

CHAPTER

11

Learning a Song

Basic Musicianship and Music Fundamentals

To develop full vocal potential, the singer needs a solid foundation in the fundamentals of music. Ideally speaking, one should have basic musical training *before* undertaking voice study; but if you happen to lack music skills, you can learn as you proceed, provided you have the interest, patience, and discipline to stick with it.

Practical musicianship includes a working knowledge of five fundamental areas of music: (1) rhythm, (2) pitch, (3) harmony, (4) form, and (5) dynamics, phrasing, and articulation. If you are already proficient in music reading skills, you might prefer to skip this section and go to the section titled "Song Study and Preparation."

> I came by music very honestly and easily . . . I had to take piano and voice and violin lessons, and dance lessons—I had a real stage mother. But it's paid off.
>
> —Renée Fleming, soprano

Music Notation

Notation is a system of symbols used for writing, reading, and performing (playing) music. Using Figure 11-1 as a reference, you can associate terms discussed next with their corresponding line and space letters.

Figure 11-1
Treble and Bass Staves with Pitch Letterings

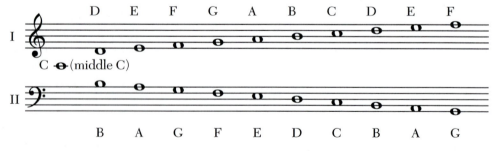

Music is written on a *staff* consisting of five lines and four spaces. Two staves (plural) appear in Figure 11-1, a *treble staff* (I) above and a *bass staff* (II) below. You will notice that the two staves use different letters for the same lines and spaces. Since mnemonic devices facilitate learning and memorization, the letter names (representing pitches) of lines and spaces on both staves are presented. The following words should be read upward from the bottom lines and spaces:

Treble clef lines:	**E**very **G**ood **B**oy **D**oes **F**ine.
Treble clef spaces:	**F**–**A**–**C**–**E**
Bass clef lines:	**G**ood **B**oys **D**o **F**ine **A**lways.
Bass clef spaces:	**A**ll **C**ows **E**at **G**rass.

Rhythm

Rhythm is the whole feeling of movement in music in relation to time. Time values are signified by symbols (notation) that indicate length of beats occurring within a given tempo (speed). Figure 11-2 lists the most common note values used to depict both sounded values and their corresponding silent value (rests).

Figure 11-2
Note Values: Sounded and Silent

Note Value Name	Sounded	Silent (rest)	No. of pulses (beats)
Whole Note	o		4
Half Note	♩ or ♩		2
Quarter Note	♩ or ♩		1
Eighth Note	♪ or ♪		1/2
Sixteenth Note	♬ or ♬		1/4

Bar lines are the regularly recurring vertical lines on a staff. They signify units of time measurement; hence, the spaces between these lines are known as *measures*.

Meters are used to indicate regular rhythmic **pulses** (beats) occurring within measures. The meter designation is usually placed only at the beginning of a song or at any measure when the meter changes. The top (first) number indicates the number of beats in each measure, and the bottom (second) number indicates the type of note that receives one beat. For example, in $\frac{4}{4}$ meter there are four beats to the measure, and the beat lasts a quarter note in duration (four quarter notes to the measure). The same procedure is used for $\frac{2}{4}$, $\frac{3}{4}$, and $\frac{6}{8}$, some of the standard meters found in music.

All of the previously mentioned terms (bar lines, measures, and meters) are illustrated in Figure 11-3.

Figure 11-3
Bar Lines, Measures, and Meters

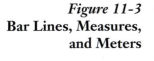

Tempo (singular), or tempi (plural), is an indication of speed, from slow to fast. Traditionally, Italian terms are frequently used to designate tempo, for example, **largo** (slow), **moderato** (moderate), **allegro** (fast), and **presto** (very fast). A tempo marking, placed above the time signature, is usually given at the beginning of a piece.

Pitch

Pitch refers to the location of a musical sound in the tonal scale. *Key signatures* are used to notate the tonal scale, or the arrangement of pitches upon which music is constructed. These signatures appear in the first measure of each staff and are notated by means of *sharps* (♯) and *flats* (♭). Sharps are used to raise pitches by a half step, and flats are used to lower pitches by a half step.

Thus, if one flat is indicated in the key signature, it will be located on the middle or third line of the treble clef, which is the pitch B. This indicates the key of F Major (Fig. 11-4), which contains only one flat in its scale (a stepwise organization of rising pitches) that begins on F at the bottom and continues through G, A, B♭, C, D, E, concluding with F on the top. This means that every B sounded within the key of F Major will be B♭ (the black key between A and B on the keyboard).

Figure 11-4
F Major Scale

Sometimes, particularly in the harmonic chord structure, sharp and flat pitches are altered by means of lowering sharp pitches or raising flat pitches by a half step. The notation used in such cases is a *natural sign* (♮). A natural sign appears before the note and cancels the sharp or flat, thus returning the note to its original pitch.

Major scales and keys are represented by a series of pitches that include half steps and whole steps. The scale of F Major, for example, is constructed on whole steps (F–G, G–A, B♭–C, and C–D) with the exception of pitches A–B♭ and E–F, which are half steps. This same configuration applies to all 12 major keys and scales; that is, all major scales have half steps between pitches 3 and 4 and pitches 7 and 8. In Figure 11-5, a keyboard segment illustrates all eight pitches that compose an **octave**, with the half steps indicated in brackets. Observe that the black-key notes may be labeled either sharp or flat, depending on the key of the scale used.

Figure 11-5
Octave Keyboard Indicating Whole and Half Steps

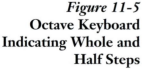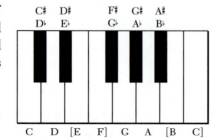

Some of the more frequently encountered major scales in the Song Anthology are C, G, D, F, and B♭ (Fig. 11-6).

Figure 11-6
Common Key Signatures

A minor key (scale) is often described as sounding somewhat sad. A good example is the Nicaraguan folk song "Niño precioso" (Song Anthology, p. 150). **Minor scales** are distinguished by an organization of pitches that includes a half step between pitches 2 and 3 (instead of 3 and 4, as in the major scale). The 6th and 7th pitches of the scale are flexible, capable of being raised or lowered, depending on the intent of the composer.

An **interval** indicates the distance between two pitches. Because two notes of the same pitch are not recognized as an interval, they are commonly referred to as **unison.** This term is often used to describe the practice of all instruments or voices sounding the same pitch simultaneously. For example, when a group of people sing the melody of a song together, they are singing in unison. Figure 11-7 depicts the major scale pitch intervals, beginning with the interval of a second and ending with an octave.

Figure 11-7
Pitch Intervals

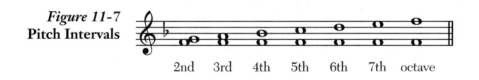

Harmony

Harmony is the vertical chord structure of music that plays a crucial role in creating the overall effect of any composition. Harmony is constructed upon **chords,** which result from the simultaneous sounding of three pitches (*triad*) or more. Though there are numerous chord configurations based on each note of a scale, the chord constructed on the first note of a scale is the most common. For example, Figure 11-8 illustrates a chord formed on the first note of the F Major scale.

Figure 11-8
Chord (Triad) Constructed on the First Note of an F Major Scale

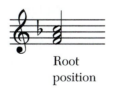

Harmonic progression is the rhythmic movement and chord changes (strong and weak) that occur throughout a music composition. The most common chord progression here is the I–IV–V–I pattern (Fig. 11-9), consisting of tonic (first scale-note chord construction), *subdominant* (fourth scale note), *dominant* (fifth scale note), and return to tonic. Variations of this progression are frequently heard, especially in performances of **folk songs** and **hymns.**

Figure 11-9
I–IV–V–I Harmonic (Chord) Progression

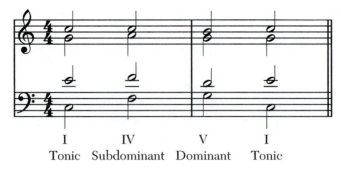

I   IV   V   I
Tonic Subdominant Dominant Tonic

Form

Form exists in nature and in art. It is especially observable in architecture, notably in classical style. For example, most of the state capitol buildings throughout the United States reflect the classical ABA form. The middle section, consisting of the columned entryway topped with a dome, represents the B section, and the flanking and usually identically matching (balanced) wings represent the A sections. A similar kind of ABA structure is found in songs; for example, "Simple Gifts" (in the Song Anthology, p. 154), which is discussed later in this chapter in the section related to song study.

There are several kinds of **song form,** the most common being the following:

Strophic.   All stanzas of a text are set to the same music, as found in folk songs and hymns.

Two part (binary or AB).   Two principal contrasting sections that are mutually dependent, form a complete musical idea, and may be repeated.

Three part (ternary or ABA).   Three principal sections, the first (A) and third (A prime) essentially the same musical idea but often modified. The **da capo aria** may also be considered a three-part form.

Through-composed.   New music is used for each stanza throughout the composition.

Dynamics, Phrasing, and Musical Articulation

When learning the basics of musicianship, you should give serious attention to some of the finer points of musical performance, including dynamics, phrasing, and musical articulation.

Dynamics refers to degrees of loudness; for example, soft = **piano** (*p*); moderately loud = **mezzo forte** (*mf*); and very loud = **fortissimo** (*ff*). One related aspect of volume is that of **accent,** the amount of emphasis or stress treatment placed on specific pitches. Two symbols connoting variations of emphasis are marcato (>), which is heavily stressed, and staccato (•), which is detached and crisp.

Phrasing refers to the separation of melody into its constituent parts (**phrases**). It also refers to performing music intelligently with meaning, somewhat comparable to an expressive poetic reading. Musical articulation (which is different from linguistic articulation) normally refers to the subdivision of a melodic phrase into smaller units. Figure 11-10 presents a three-measure phrase, with phrasing (a) indicated by an arching line over the entire three measures and the articulation (b) indicated by the shorter slur marks that connect the descending pairs of quarter notes in the second measure.

Figure 11-10
**Phrasing and Musical
Articulation**

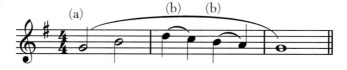

After the ABCs of music are learned, the whole world of vocal music (like the world of literature for the person who learns to read) opens up to everyone who has a desire to sing. If you lack musical skills and want to continue improving, you might consider enrolling in a music fundamentals course and/or a piano class. Should you immediately need additional materials and assistance, consult your teacher or the Society for Music Theory Fundamentals Web site (www.societymusictheory.org/), which contains a list of useful materials, including a link to computer programs that enable independent study.

Song Study and Preparation

Most professional singers approach song learning in a systematic way, with a definite strategy in mind. In this section we will look at a systematic method that should be very helpful for the novice interested in learning a song using a step-by-step approach.

First, any song you study should be both musically and textually worthy. It should also suit your particular vocal and musical abilities, which usually means that the song should not be too difficult nor too demanding to learn. On the other hand, you may occasionally be ready for repertoire that will challenge and stretch you. Consult with your teacher for recommendations of appropriate literature.

The most efficient way to learn a song is to study each component separately until it is mastered independently, in contrast to using rote repetition, a technique reserved for the final stages of memorization. A logical order of study might include the following steps.

Introduction and Overview

Begin by listening to the entire song, which may be accomplished by (1) attending a live performance, (2) listening to a recording, or (3) participating in a read-through session with a competent pianist. In group instruction, it is beneficial to hear the song sung in unison by the entire group. As noted previously, you will have a better understanding of the song if you learn as much as possible about the composer and the textual source. A little research will reveal information concerning creative and historical aspects of the song, a practice that will increase your appreciation, interest, and enthusiasm for any song.

Component Study

Component study involves detailed examination of (1) text, (2) rhythm, meter, and tempo, (3) melody, (4) form, (5) voice, (6) harmony, and (7) dynamics, phrasing, and musical articulation.

Text. Begin by reading the text through silently for pronunciation, inflection, articulation, phrasing, and meaning. When you're satisfied that you understand the text, read it aloud, first in a normal poetic reading and then in a dramatic manner with attention to word emphasis and expression.

Numerous repetitions will make you comfortable and secure with the text *before* voicing it to the rhythm of the song.

Rhythm, meter, and tempo. After checking the time signature ($\frac{6}{8}$, $\frac{4}{4}$, $\frac{3}{4}$, etc.), count aloud the number of pulses per measure ("*one*, two, three," etc.) with slight emphasis on the downbeat, or first beat of each measure. Now clap or tap the rhythm of each musical phrase until you have mastered the entire song. When starting out, clap in a slow tempo. As you feel more secure with the song's rhythm, clap it in the correct tempo. The important objective is accuracy, not speed.

Melody. After determining the key signature (treble and/or bass clefs), check the notated pitches either by playing them on a piano or by sight-reading them. Because you want to avoid unnecessary, careless singing, learn the melody by singing it mentally before vocalizing aloud.

Form. Examine the song for its underlying song structure: strophic, AB, ABA, or through-composed forms. Look for major musical sections, themes, and repetitions of musical material. Knowing the form of a song will help you to "frame" it mentally for learning purposes. For example, the arrangement of the folk song "Simple Gifts" reveals an ABA song structure. The A (first part) section begins with the piano introduction in measure 1 (m. 1) and ends with "love and delight" (m. 10). The B (second part) section commences with "When true simplicity" (m. 11) and ends with "comes 'round right" (m. 18). The return to the A section begins in measure 19 and continues to the end (**coda**).

Voice. Now you can focus on trying to achieve efficient vocal production with a fully resonated, physically supported vocal tone. First, sing through the song on a single vowel, a combination of vowels, or a single phoneme, such as "njam" [ɲɑm]. Next, sing on the vowels of the words. This procedure will help you gradually build up to full-voiced singing, including the use of dynamic levels. At this stage it is not necessary to use an accompanying musical instrument.

Harmony. If your keyboard skills are limited, engage an accomplished pianist to record the accompaniment for you so you can hear and imprint the harmonic sounds into your memory. This will greatly accelerate your overall learning pace. Be aware of changes in harmony and tonality and also of the nature and relationship of particular chords to the text.

Dynamics and musical articulation. Some dynamic levels will have been worked out throughout the process of studying the song, especially textual dynamics. Now is the time to give more thought to fine-tuning the dynamics and articulations as indicated by the composer's and/or editor's markings in the musical score.

Component Synthesis and Memorization

When all components have been mastered, you are probably ready to integrate them by singing the whole song with **accompaniment.** At this point you can use either a recorded accompaniment or, better yet, a competent accompanist ("artist collaborator").

Although rote repetition is an acceptable way to memorize a song, especially in the final stage, three techniques are particularly helpful for enhancing recall.

> I am a good pianist and this allows me to save a lot of time and energy. I work anywhere, when my colleagues are chasing their coaches [accompanists] with whom they have to sing every day . . . With my personal preparation at the piano, I can afford to hum at half voice.
>
> —Placido Domingo, tenor

One is to select and memorize key words in each phrase to help trigger memory. An even more effective technique involves dramatizing the song aloud in an exaggerated, melodramatic manner. Finally, you can stage the song, complete with props and all imagined trappings (scenery, locale, supporting cast, etc.), as though it were an opera aria or musical theater selection. These "acting-out" techniques will aid you in creating a matrix of visual, auditory, and kinesthetic sensations, greatly facilitating recall.

Musicianship and Learning Assessment

Basic Musicianship. Do you have a grounding in music fundamentals, or is music like a foreign language to you? Are you able to read music at sight? What general rating would you give your musicianship upon starting this course (excellent, good, fair, or poor)? After studying this chapter, do you have a better grasp of how music is notated and how to apply your newfound knowledge to reading and learning music? Do you appreciate the ability to read music in order to truly enjoy the substance of music and music making? What are your plans for continuing to improve your musical skills?

Song Study. Are you able to learn your songs after hearing the vocal lines several times, or do you have difficulty in learning them? Does the piano accompaniment confuse you when you try to sing with it, or do you adjust quickly with practice? What musical experiences (instrumental study, band, chorus, etc.) have you had that have helped you with song learning? Do you systematically study your songs according to the musical components of melody, rhythm, meter, harmony, form, and dynamics? Have you tried using key words and staging (acting out) techniques to facilitate memorization?

Go to www.mhhe.com/ais4 to learn about additional Web-based resources that supplement the content of this chapter.

CHAPTER 12

Performing a Song

Style in Vocal Performance

At the highest level of proficiency in any art form (poetry, dance, painting, or architecture) we speak in terms of *style*, a characteristic manner or mode of expression. In vocal music it is helpful to distinguish between two kinds of style: style in composition and style in performance. Generally, a singer's performance style must follow the composition style. An individual's imprint is always present, but in a proportion that allows the music and text to predominate. In other words, the singer's goal should be to portray the style of the song, rather than overshadow the song with his or her personal style. This dictum is more widely recognized in classical vocal performance than in the pop arena, as many highly personalized pop renditions of "The Star-Spangled Banner" demonstrate.

Vocal music has many styles, and in vocal literature each particular style bears characteristic manners and modes of expression. For example, some popular musical styles familiar to contemporary singers are soft rock, hard rock, rap, easy listening, jazz, country-western, gospel, and musical theater.

Most of the vocal music performed today in the Western world was written in the past 600 years. These six centuries are usually divided (approximate dates) into at least five historical periods: (1) **Renaissance** (1425–1600), (2) **Baroque** (1600–1750), (3) **Classical** (1750–1825), (4) **Romantic** (1825–1875), and (5) Modern/Contemporary (1875–present). Because each of these periods exhibits uniquely distinct, musical stylistic features, the period of origin of an unfamiliar song can often be identified on the basis of its general musical characteristics.

In the Appendix B notes (see the section "Information about the Art Songs and Arias"), some of the most prominent historic, national, and generic styles of vocal music in Western civilization are discussed briefly. Please consult the Bibliography for more thorough treatments and examples.

Expressive Use of Body and Voice

A performer is concerned not only with "what" is communicated but "how" it is communicated. How a singer communicates the inner feeling of a song brings us to a second vital skill in addition to musicianship: the ability to portray a song's poetic and dramatic content.

When performing, the singer is understandably preoccupied with producing beautiful vocal tones. But singing also involves language, and the primary literary genre of vocal literature is *poetry*—the language of imagination and intense perception. A thorough understanding of poetry (including denotation and connotation, imagery, figurative language, allusion, meter, tone, and pattern) can help the singer understand and express not only the sound, but also the meaning of songs.

Beyond poetic insight and feeling, singing calls on the ability to physically portray and communicate the inner drama of a song. It is not possible within the scope of this book to cover the field of acting as thoroughly as its importance to singing would justify. Therefore, three increasingly advanced-level books by H. Wesley Balk are recommended for further reading: *The Complete Singing Actor* (1977), *Performing Power* (1985), and *The Radiant Performer* (1989), all formerly published by the University of Minnesota Press.

Song Performance

Vocal performance can be divided into three stages: (1) preparation, (2) performance, and (3) postperformance.

Preparation

There is no substitute for thorough preparation of music to be performed in public. Whatever anxiety or stage fright you may feel prior to and occasionally during a performance, painstaking preparation is the best antidote. When dealing with stage fright, it is best to accept the normalcy of the affliction and to use the rush of adrenaline to your advantage. Peak performance preparation involves several factors associated with mind and body health. To review some information contained in chapter 1, the following suggestions will help you with "performance jitters."

> If the three most important things in real estate are location, location, location, then three most important things in singing are meaning, meaning, meaning! When you sing with very specific meanings, the technique on which you have worked so hard is allowed to fly. Try saying phrases several different ways and watch the technique respond. Do the vocal homework; just make sure you don't let it define your poetic choices.
>
> —Richard Leech, tenor

General health. Stay healthy by eating and sleeping well and by avoiding overstressing the mind and body in advance of the performance. You need energy to perform well. Avoid depressants (alcohol) and stimulants (caffeine) because they will only aggravate nervous symptoms. Remain sufficiently hydrated, particularly the day prior to a major performance.

Positive thinking. Avoid negative thoughts ("I can't," "I'm scared," "They won't like me") by focusing on your desire to perform, the value of the performing experience to you personally, the aesthetic and expressive content of the song or songs, and the needs of your audience. Program your thinking with positive affirmations and with repeated visualizations of yourself performing well. See your audience enjoying the performance and giving you an enthusiastic ovation.

Relaxation. Concentrate on your breathing by relaxing physically and taking slow, deep breaths while focusing on your body's "center," located slightly below the navel. By releasing physical tensions and slowing your breathing, your anxiety should dissipate gradually. Refer to Exercise 3-1 for a recommended relaxation/meditation routine.

Performance

In place offstage. Assuming all musical preparations have been made and physical conditions arranged (piano, piano bench, lights, and so forth), you are now offstage and standing ready to go on. Take a few moments at this point to concentrate on your entrance and to set the proper mood. Relax, take a slow, deep breath, straighten your posture, and tell yourself: "This is the moment I've prepared for with eager anticipation, and I'm really looking forward to it."

Stage entrance. As you enter the performance area slightly ahead of your accompanist, your bearing should be one of confidence and purpose. Walk enthusiastically and briskly to the "crook" area of a grand piano or to the side of an upright piano. Bow graciously as if to say "Thank you for your welcoming applause. I appreciate your coming to hear me." If there are no programs listing musical selections and performers' names, introduce yourself, your accompanist, and your selections in a firm, moderately paced, audible voice. Wait a few moments for the pianist to make preparations and the audience to become quiet. Concentrate on the mood of the first song and its message. Singer-pedagogue Carol Kirkpatrick offers an effective technique for setting a proper mood and preparing your accompanist and audience for your opening presentation.

Exercise 12-1   UNROLLING THE CARPET

When you're ready to begin, imagine that you are standing on a luxurious carpet (of your favorite color, size, etc.). Lower your eyes comfortably to view the carpet rolled up at your feet, and capable of extending to the back of the performing space when unrolled. Take your time, and when you feel focused and ready to sing, imagine kicking the carpet gently and watching it as it unrolls moderately slowly toward the back of the hall. Your head should rise gradually as your eyes follow the unrolling carpet, which, ideally, lies on a floor that's raked toward the back of the room, thereby allowing your gaze to be slightly up or at least on an horizontal level with the stage floor. All the while maintain a calm expression of anticipation toward communicating the song's mood and intent. Practice this exercise alone using a full-length mirror, as well as in class, where you can receive feedback from your instructor and classmates.

Presentation. The song actually begins just prior to the accompaniment, when you perform the carpet unrolling exercise, with the mood having been set by your psychophysical demeanor. Because it is very amateurish to treat piano introductions, interludes, and postludes as simply "marking time" when you're not singing, try to maintain the desired character throughout the entire song. During the performance you need only to honestly portray what you feel the song is about. You don't have to *do* something to "sell" it to the audience. It's enough to let the song flow through you, as though you are a mere vessel containing and then releasing the song's contents. It will help greatly if you are able to project your visualization and inner experience of the song, as it will provide something upon which to concentrate so that your eyes will not wander aimlessly. The idea is that what you see, the audience also will see, or at least the audience will be aware you are personally experiencing something, whether it is an idea, event, emotion, or mood. As the song ends, maintain your concentration to the very end, carefully pacing the amount of time you need to release the final mood. With a serious song, the release will be slower than with a fast, upbeat song. At the right moment, recognize the audience's applause by bowing graciously from the waist, saying under your breath, "Thank you very much." Recognize your accompanist and share a duet bow.

Stage exit. After the solo and duet bows, exit briskly ahead of the accompanist to offstage. Should the audience continue applauding, quickly enter again with your accompanist to take another duet bow at center stage. The number of bows is normally a matter of sensing the audience's response. Extra bows and encores are normally expected only when presenting an extended program.

Postperformance

Depending on the scope, nature, and outcome of your performance, you probably will breathe a sigh of relief for having survived the experience relatively unscathed. Your feelings at this point very likely will reflect your satisfaction or dissatisfaction with some aspects of your performance. You also will critique your performance based on the audience's general reaction and the comments made by individuals thoughtful enough to offer them. Although most people welcome constructive criticism in the right place and at the right time, the period immediately following a performance is normally reserved for well-wishers with their congratulations. The exception to this might be in educational situations where immediate critical feedback is expected.

It is important that you maintain a confident attitude regarding your performance, even though you may think it was not up to par. Though every minor mistake might have been painfully apparent to you, the chances are the audience didn't notice anything amiss. The point is to avoid volunteering unconstructive critical comments about your performance and to accept congratulations graciously. Keep reminding yourself that now is the time to celebrate your courage, determination, and success in performing publicly. Celebrate the occasion by going out with relatives or friends for fellowship and refreshments. Give yourself a well-deserved reward.

When you are ready to be objective about your performance (the time will vary with each person), take a few minutes to honestly evaluate what happened. Ideally, you will have access to an audio or video recording of your performance, which is an invaluable way to study your performance from the audience's perspective. If you have a knowledgeable friend or teacher, someone whose opinion you respect, consult with them regarding your performance. Try not to take any criticism personally. Instead, look at your performance objectively with the eyes and ears of an interested observer. Ask yourself what went well and what needs improvement. Break your evaluation down into the areas discussed in this text: (1) *musicianship*—accuracy in pitch, rhythm, tempo, dynamics, and phrasing; (2) *vocal technique*—breath management, tone quality, and coordination; (3) *diction*—pronunciation and articulation; (4) *stage presence*—posture, poise, and specific body language; and (5) *music/dramatic presentation*—interpretation, style, and expression.

Don't be too hard on yourself in your self-evaluation. Be realistic in considering your present level of development and in forgiving your shortcomings. It takes a lot of productive time and energy to learn all the skills used in vocal performance. In short, you need to be patient, yet persistent.

Continuing Your Vocal Study

Now that you've completed this course of study, you may be wondering, "What's the next step?" Depending upon your level of commitment, there are three levels of participation you can undertake as a singer: (1) amateur, (2) semiprofessional, and (3) professional. Each of these categories offers opportunities for you to continue pursuing your love of singing.

- **Amateur.** An amateur is simply someone who does or takes part in an activity for pleasure rather than remuneration, a category that includes the majority of singers who sing in community, religious, and educational musical/dramatic organizations on a volunteer basis. A "hobby singer" can be just as capable as any professional, provided he or she has the requisite talent and skills and is willing to devote the necessary time and effort. If this is your chosen level of participation, you will have lots of good company and loads of respect from all who enjoy listening to music.

- **Semiprofessional.** There are many well-trained, experienced singers who have found a compromise solution between the amateur and professional categories that suits them well. These singers normally manage part-time or even full-time nonmusic jobs that allow opportunities for evening and weekend professional singing engagements with choral and music/opera organizations, and the like. They may be highly trained professionals and, for whatever reasons, have intentionally chosen a semiprofessional status. Many freelance singers hold part- or full-time jobs in fields other than music, but it's fairly common for vocal music teachers, both private and those associated with educational institutions, to pursue part-time singing engagements. For example, many college/university voice professors manage part-time singing careers on the side.

- **Professional.** A professional singer is one who pursues a full-time singing career that provides remuneration to cover all living necessities. Because of such factors as marketplace supply and demand, heavy financial burden, lengthy study and apprenticeship periods, enormous competition, and lifestyle, the professional should enter into such a challenging career armed with an unwavering dedication and commitment to succeed.

If you are interested in investigating the possibility of pursuing a vocal music career—either on semiprofessional or professional levels—you might begin by seeking the evaluations and advice of several respected professionals. One appropriate resource is a book by this author titled *The Singer's Life: Goals and Roles* (Birch Grove Publishing, 2005), which discusses 20 professional and personal roles of singers. The chapter "The Singer as Amateur or Professional" addresses the three categories of singers—amateur, semiprofessional, and professional—in addition to the issues of vocal music potential, qualifications for a professional career, benefits, and drawbacks associated with a vocal music career. Another chapter, "The Singer as Business Manager," explains the need for singers to have business skills and succinctly outlines what it takes to build a successful career based on a business model in connection with selling products or services. Whether promoting a product or service, the major business concerns are (1) quality, (2) reliability, (3) packaging, (4) market niche, (5) financial support, (6) marketing, and (7) distribution. As human service products, career-oriented singers must address such concerns about their product—themselves, and the music they perform. In sum, any serious-minded singer interested in furthering his or her singing objectives, regardless of age or stage of development, must pay heed to such concerns, including any eager and talented high school or college student who wants to perform leading roles in music productions, compete in vocal contests, or obtain desirable vocal engagements.

Regardless of which of these three paths you decide to take, you will need someone to guide and counsel you. Begin by consulting your current teacher for suggestions, securing a list of voice teachers in your area who are members of the National Association of Teachers of Singing, or inquiring among respected area singers for recommendations. When you have narrowed your prospects down to two or three teachers, spend some time observing their students in action. Perhaps you can get permission from both the student and teacher to observe a lesson or two. What's important is your having confidence in the teacher's professional expertise, personal qualities, and concern for your personal growth.

> In my opinion, the quality of a person's singing is not only determined by beauty of timbre, natural talent or an accomplished technique, but also by what he or she carries inside: experiences, beliefs, as well as the cultural, social and emotional background . . . All these elements have an influence on the characteristics of a singer's artistry.
>
> —Ramón Vargas, tenor

As stated earlier in this book, anyone can learn to sing, and because singing is one of the best disciplines for overall self-improvement, everyone can benefit from vocal study. If *Adventures in Singing* has aided you in the exploration, discovery, and development of your vocal talent, then the original goal of the book has been fulfilled. There is no greater satisfaction for a teacher than to guide others on paths that lead to greater self-understanding and self-expression.

In the words of an anonymous sage: "Develop the wisdom to know yourself, and the courage to be yourself." Such advice certainly applies to the study of voice. May your unique voice adventure continue to be one of opening up to new possibilities in personal growth and fulfillment through a love of singing.

Performance Skills Assessment

Stylistic Skills. Do you have a clear understanding of what style is and how it applies to performance? Do you have a unique, personal performing style? Do you try to present each song's style in performance? Can you differentiate among the various styles associated with musical periods and nationalities and between popular and classical vocal music styles?

Dramatic Skills. Are you an outgoing, expressive person, one who uses gestures and vocal dynamics when communicating, or are you reserved and quiet-spoken? Are you adept at pretending or mimicking the actions and voices of others, or do you find it difficult to "be someone else"? What stage experiences have you had with public performance? Are you willing to make a fool of yourself in the process of becoming a more expressive person? What kind of persona do you portray to the public, to your friends and relatives, and to yourself when alone? Do you study your songs with the objective of "acting out" the song's textual content in a staged practice presentation?

Performance Skills. When performing, are you able to concentrate on technical objectives and the communication of the song's meaning, or do you find yourself thinking about unrelated, distracting matters? Are you able to suspend self-judgment and self-criticism during performance situations, or do you constantly chastise and berate yourself for real and even imagined mistakes? Do you really *enjoy* the act of performing or is it just something you *have* to do? Do you maintain your concentration from the very beginning of each song to its ultimate conclusion, or does your focus tend to wander? Do you always remember to acknowledge your accompanist at the appropriate moment? Following the performance, do you accept compliments graciously, or do you offer excuses and apologies for your performance?

Future Study and Performance. Are you enthusiastic or disheartened about your vocal studies to date? Have you been encouraged or discouraged in any way during your studies? Based on what you have learned about yourself, what are your assets and liabilities as a singer? Do you have plans to continue your vocal studies? If so, at which level will you be content to function: avocational, semiprofessional, or professional? Have you sought professional guidance regarding your singing interests and talents? Do you have a plan of action for exploring your future as a singer?

> Does luck play a part? You bet! What is luck? That's when "opportunity and preparation collide!"
>
> —Jennifer Larmore, mezzo-soprano

Song Anthology

Musical Theater Songs

Dona Nobis Pacem
(Traditional)

We Are Singing
(American/C. Ware)

Let Us Sing Together
(Adapted from Czech Folk Tune)

Let Us Sing Together lyrics:

1. Let us sing to-geth - er, Let us sing to-geth - er, One and all a joy - ous song.

2. Let us sing to-geth - er, One and all a joy - ous song.

3. Let us sing a - gain and a - gain, Let us sing a - gain and a - gain,

4. Let us sing a - gain and a - gain, One and all a joy - ous song.

Make New Friends
(American)

Make New Friends lyrics:

Make new friends but keep _____ the _____ old; _____

One is sil - ver and the oth - er gold.

Music Alone Shall Live
(Die Musici—German)

(3 parts)

All things shall per - ish from un - der the sky;
Him - mel und Er - de müs - sen ver - gehn;

Mu - sic a - lone shall live, mu - sic a - lone shall live,
a - ber die Mus - i - ci, a - ber die Mus - i - ci,

Mu - sic a - lone shall live, nev - er to die.
a - ber die Mus - i - ci, blei - ben be - stehn.

O How Lovely Is the Evening
(Traditional)

(3 parts)

O how love - ly is the eve - ning, is the eve - ning,

When the bells are sweet - ly ring - ing, sweet - ly ring - ing,

Ding! Dong! Ding! Ding! Dong! Ding!

Hail to Music

(American/C. Ware)

Hail to mus - ic and to sing - ing, with warm hearts and voi - ces ring - ing.

Beau - ty truth and ar - tis - try, all our lives are bless - ed by thee,

As we join in migh - ty chor - us. Lift our spir - its and re - store us!

Note: Musical score plus orchestrated accompaniment available on Web site (www.mhhe.com/ais4)

Row, Row, Row Your Boat

(Traditional)

(4 parts)

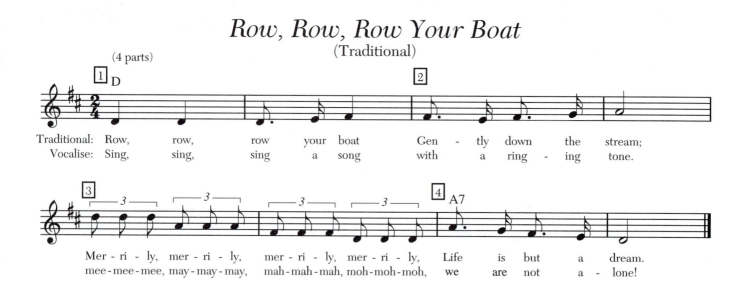

Traditional: Row, row, row your boat Gen - tly down the stream;
Vocalise: Sing, sing, sing a song with a ring - ing tone.

Mer - ri - ly, mer - ri - ly, mer - ri - ly, mer - ri - ly, Life is but a dream.
mee - mee - mee, may - may - may, mah - mah - mah, moh - moh - moh, we are not a - lone!

Adventures in Singing

Shalom, Chaverim!
(Farewell, My Friends–Israeli)

*IPA pronunciation: Figure C-1, p. 325

Vive L'Amour
(Long Live Love–College Song)

Enthusiastically
Soloist

Let ev - 'ry good fel - low now join in a song.
A friend on your left and a friend on your right,
Now wi - der and wi - der our cir - cle ex - pands,

*Vi - ve la com - pag - nie!

Soloist

Suc - cess to each o - ther and pass it a - long,
In love and good fel - low-ship let us u - nite,
We sing to our com-rades in far - a - way lands,

Vi - ve la com - pag - nie!

Faster

Vi - ve la, vi - ve la, vi - ve l'a - mour,
Vi - ve la, vi - ve la, vi - ve l'a - mour,

vi - ve l'a - mour, vi - ve l'a - mour, vi - ve la com - pag - nie! _____

*IPA pronunciation: Figure C-2, p. 325

The Star-Spangled Banner

Text by Francis Scott Key

Music by John Stafford Smith

*Refer to the Web site for an orchestral accompaniment

We Sing of America

C. Ware & B. Ware

*Refer to the Web site for an orchestral accompaniment

Adventures in Singing

*Vocalizing Fun

C. & B. Ware

* May be sung in progressively higher keys

All through the Night

Text Traditional

Welsh
Arr. by Bettye Ware

Balm in Gilead

Text Traditional

African-American Folk Hymn
Arr. by Bettye Ware

Amazing Grace

Text by John Newton

English/American Folk Hymn
Arr. by Bettye Ware

Adventures in Singing

Through man - y __ dan - gers, toils, and snares I have al -

read - y __ come; _____ 'Tis grace _____ that _ brought me safe _____ thus _

far, And grace will __ lead me home. _____

Con qué la lavaré
(Oh, What Can Wash Away)

Spanish Text Unknown
English Text by Clifton Ware
and Bettye Ware

Spanish Folk Song
Arr. by Bettye Ware

vo - me yo cui - ta - da, con pe - nas y do - lo - res.
wash my griev - ing sor - row, with pain and end - less suf - fring.

con pe - nas y___ do - lo - res.
with pain and end - less___ suf - fring.

Down in the Valley

Text Traditional

American Folksong
Arr. by Bettye Ware

Drink to Me Only with Thine Eyes

Text by Ben Jonson

Old English Air
Arr. by Bettye Ware

Farmers' Song

English Text C. Ware

Chinese-Taiwanese Folksong
Arr. by B. Ware

Moderately (♩ = 69-72)

1. Spring comes a - gain; we sow our
3. Hum - ming this tune, as we go

seeds; work in the fields, and help plants grow. Farm - ing pro -
home, wear - y from work - ing all day long. Dark - ness des -

vides for all our needs; this year we pray that
cends, no more we roam; led by the North Star,

full crops show.
we hum our song.

1st time, steady tempo
2nd time, broader to the end

Fine

Adventures in Singing

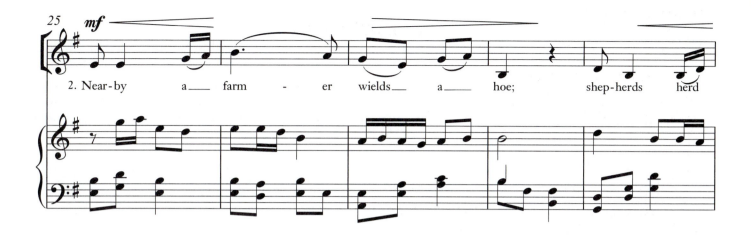

2. Near-by a farm - er wields a hoe; shep-herds herd

cat - tle to far pond. Men plough the fields and

wo - men sow; backs wet with sweat, all share one bond.

D.S. al Fine

Greensleeves
(What Child Is This)

Text Traditional

English Folksong
Arr. by Bettye Ware

*Christmas Carol verses

Green - sleeves was _ all my joy, _____ Green - sleeves was _
This, this is _ Christ the King, whom_ Shep - herds guard and _

my de - light, Green - sleeves was my heart of gold, And, _
an - gels sing; Haste, haste to _ bring Him laud, The _

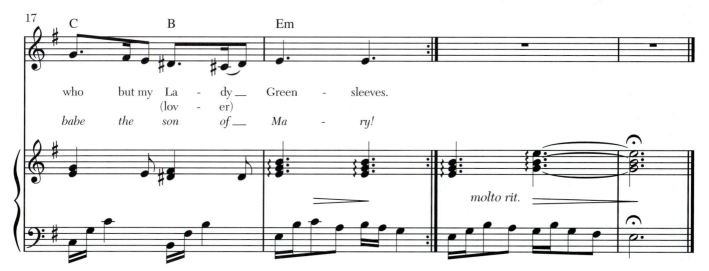

who but my La - dy _ Green - sleeves.
(lov - er)
babe the son of _ Ma - ry!

Long Time Ago

American Folksong
Arr. by Bettye Ware

Text Traditional

1. On the lake where droop'd the wil-low
2. Rock and tree and flow - ing wa-ter

long time a - go
long time a - go

Where the rock threw back the bil - low
Bird and bee and blos - som taught her

bright - er than snow.
love's ____ spell to know.

Dwelt a maid be -
While to my fond

lov'd and cher-ish'd __ by high and __ low
words she lis-ten'd __ mur - mur-ing __ low

But with au-tumn leaf she per-ish'd __ long _____ time a - go.
Ten - der-ly her blue eyes glis-ten'd __ long _____ time a - go.

poco rit.

Niño precioso
(Precious Child)

Text Traditional

Nicaraguan Folksong
Arr. by Bettye Ware

O Shenandoah

Text Traditional

Traditional American Folksong
Arr. by Bettye Ware

Adventures in Singing

Simple Gifts

American Shaker Tune
Arr. by Lawrence Henry

Text Traditional

'Tis the gift to be sim - ple, 'tis the gift to be free, 'Tis the gift to come down where we ought to be, And when we find our - selves in the place just right, 'Twill be in the val - ley of

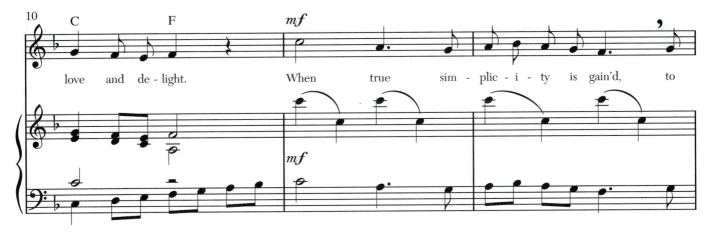

love and de-light. When true sim-plic-i-ty is gain'd, to

bow and to bend we ___ shan't be a-sham'd, to turn, turn will

be our de-light, 'Till by turn-ing, turn - ing we come 'round right.

mp 'Tis the love and de-light.

D.S. al Coda Coda

Sometimes I Feel Like a Motherless Child

Text Traditional

African-American Spiritual
Arr. by Bettye Ware

The Happy Singer

Text by C. Ware

Music by B. & C. Ware

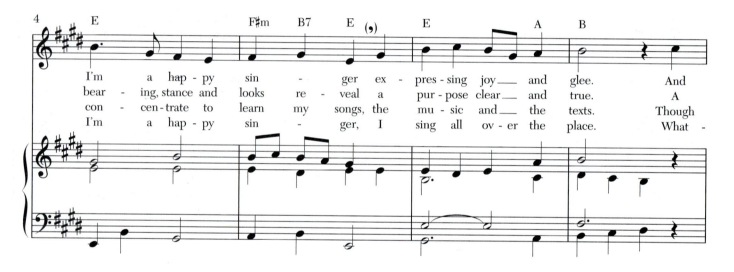

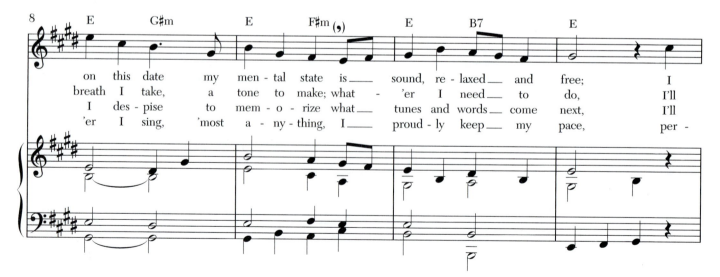

The Water Is Wide

(O Waly, Waly)

Text Traditional

British Folksong
Arr. by Bettye Ware

row, _____ my love and _____ I
way _____ like morn-ing _____

2. I leaned my back _____ up a-gainst an oak. I thought it was _____ a trus-ty ___ tree, but first it bent _____ and then it ___ broke _____ as did my love _____ prove false to ___ me.

dew.

Over the Meadows

Original Textual Source Unknown
Text by Clifton Ware and Bettye Ware

Czechoslovakian Folksong
Arr. by Bettye Ware

Energetically (♩ = 104–112)

O - ver the mea - dows green and wide,
O - ver the fields we stroll a - long,

Spring grass is grow - ing, spring grass is grow - ing high,
Sing - ing to - geth - er, Sing - ing a song of joy,

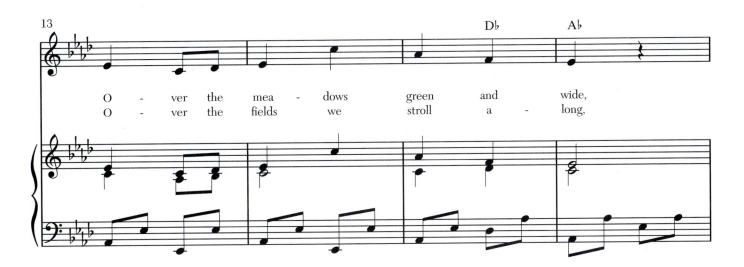

O - ver the mea - dows green and wide,
O - ver the fields we stroll a - long,

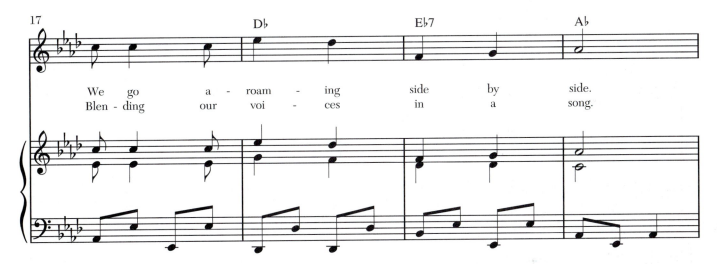

We go a - roam - ing side by side.
Blen - ding our voi - ces in a song.

Melt - ing from win - ter's snow, stream - lets from moun - tains flow,

Join - ing   as   on they go,   Sing - ing   their   songs so   mer - ry.

Melt - ing   from win - ter's snow,   Stream - lets   from   moun - tains flow.

Join - ing   as   on they go,   cal - ling   to   me.   Hi!

optional
2nd verse

An die Musik
(To Music)

Franz Schubert (1797–1828)
Op. 88, No. 4
Ed. by C.W.

German Text by F. von Schober
English Text by Clifton Ware

war - mer Lieb' ent - zun - den, hast mich in ei - ne__ bess' - re Welt ent-
heart with love__ and__ glad - ness, and shown to me a__ bet - ter world and

rückt __ in ei - ne bess' __ re Welt __ ent - rückt!
life __ a bet-ter world, __ a bet - ter life!

Oft hat ein Seuf - zer
Strains from your harp come

dei - ner Harf ent - flos - sen, ein süss - er, hei - li - ger Ak-
sigh - ing of - ten__ 'round me; a sweet - er, ho - lier sound I've

kord_ von _ dir
ne - ver _ heard.

den Him - mel bess' - rer _
The hea - vens o - pen _

Zei - ten mir er - schlos-sen, du hol - de Kunst ich _ dan - ke dir da-
wide to show _ such _ beau - ty; O won - drous Art my _ thanks to you I

für, _ du hol - de Kunst, _ ich dan - ke dir!
sing _ O won-drous Art, _ my thanks _ I sing!

A Memory

Text by Minnie K. Breid

Rudolph Ganz (1877–1972)

Bist du bei mir
(If You Are Near)

Anonymous
(Attributed to Johann Sebastian Bach)
(1685–1750)
Ed. by C.W.

German Text Anonymous
English Text by Clifton Ware

Bist du bei mir, geh' ich mit Freu - den zum Ster - ben __
If you are near I go with glad - ness to death __ and __

und zu mei - ner __ Ruh', zum _____ Ster - ben und zu mei - ner Ruh'.
to e - ter - nal __ rest, to _____ death and to e - ter - nal rest.

29

dei - ne schö - nen __ Hän - de mir __ die ge-treu - en Au - gen zu.
with your lov - ing __ hands __ my __ faith - ful eyes to gent - ly close.

33

Ach, wie ver - gnügt wär so mein End - de: Es drück - ten __
Ah, plea - sant thought would be my end - ing: by touch - ing __

38

D.S. al Fine

dei - ne schö - nen __ Hän - de mir __ die ge-treu - en Au - gen zu.
with your lov - ing __ hands __ my __ faith - ful eyes to gent - ly close.

D.S. al Fine

Caro mio ben

(My Dearest Love)

English Text by C. Ware

Music by Tommaso Giordani
Edited by C. & B. Ware

Verse 1 (under staff, lines 5–8):

Ca - ro mio ben,   cre - di - mi al - men,   sen - za di te   lan - gui-sce il
My dear - est love,   *in Hea'vn a - bove,*   *now with-out you*   *pain____ fills my*

cor____   ca - ro mio ben,   sen - za di te lan - gui - sce il
heart.__   *My___ dear - est love,*   *now with-out you__ pain_ fills___ my*

cor.
heart.

Il tuo fe-
Your faith-ful

del   so - spi-ra o - gnor.___   Ces - sa, cru - del,___ tan - to ri -
one   pines   far a - part,___   Gone   is   the   sun,___ now___ we   de -

gor!   Ces - sa, cru - del,   tan - to ri - gor,___   tan - to ri -
part.   Gone   is   the   sun,   now   we   de - part,___   now   we   de -

gor!_____ Ca - ro mio ben, cre - di - mi al - men, sen - za di te lan - gui - sce il
part!_____ My dear - est love, in Hea'vn a - bove, now with-out you___ pain___ fills___ my

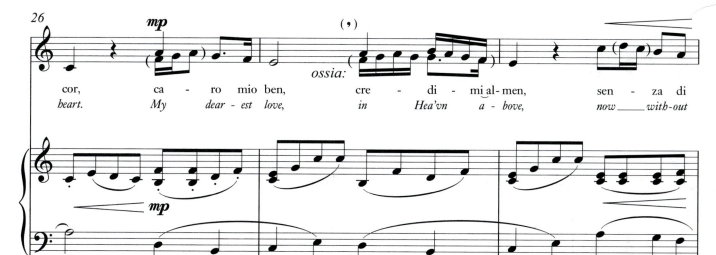

cor, ca - ro mio ben, cre - di - mi al - men, sen - za di
heart. My dear - est love, in Hea'vn a - bove, now ___ with-out

te_____ lan - gui - sce il cor.
you, _____ pain___ fills___ my heart.

Cara, Cara e Dolce
(Dearest Liberty)

English text C. Ware

low voice

Music by Alessandro Scarlatti
edited by C. & B. Ware

Come Again, Sweet Love

John Dowland (1563–1626)
Arr. by Lawrence Henry

Text Anonymous

Andante (♩ = 96–100)

1. Come a - gain, Sweet love doth now in - vite Thy
2. Come a - gain, that I may cease to mourn Thro'

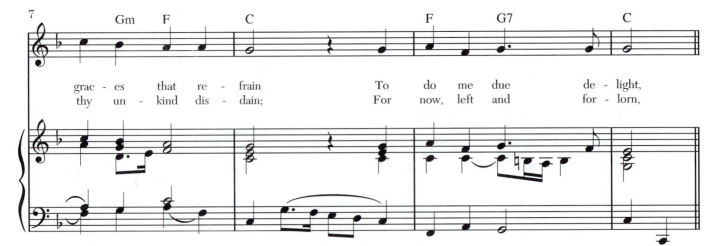

grac - es that re - frain To do me due de - light,
thy un - kind dis - dain; For now, left and for - lorn,

To see, to hear, to touch, to kiss, to die _____
I sit, I sigh, I weep, I faint, I die _____

With thee a - gain in sweet - est sym - pa - thy,
In dead - ly pain and end - less mis - er - y.

poco rit. (2nd Time)   D.S. 2nd verse

Dream Valley

Text by William Blake

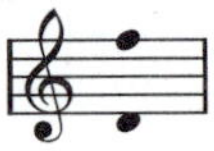

High Voice

Roger Quilter (1877–1953)

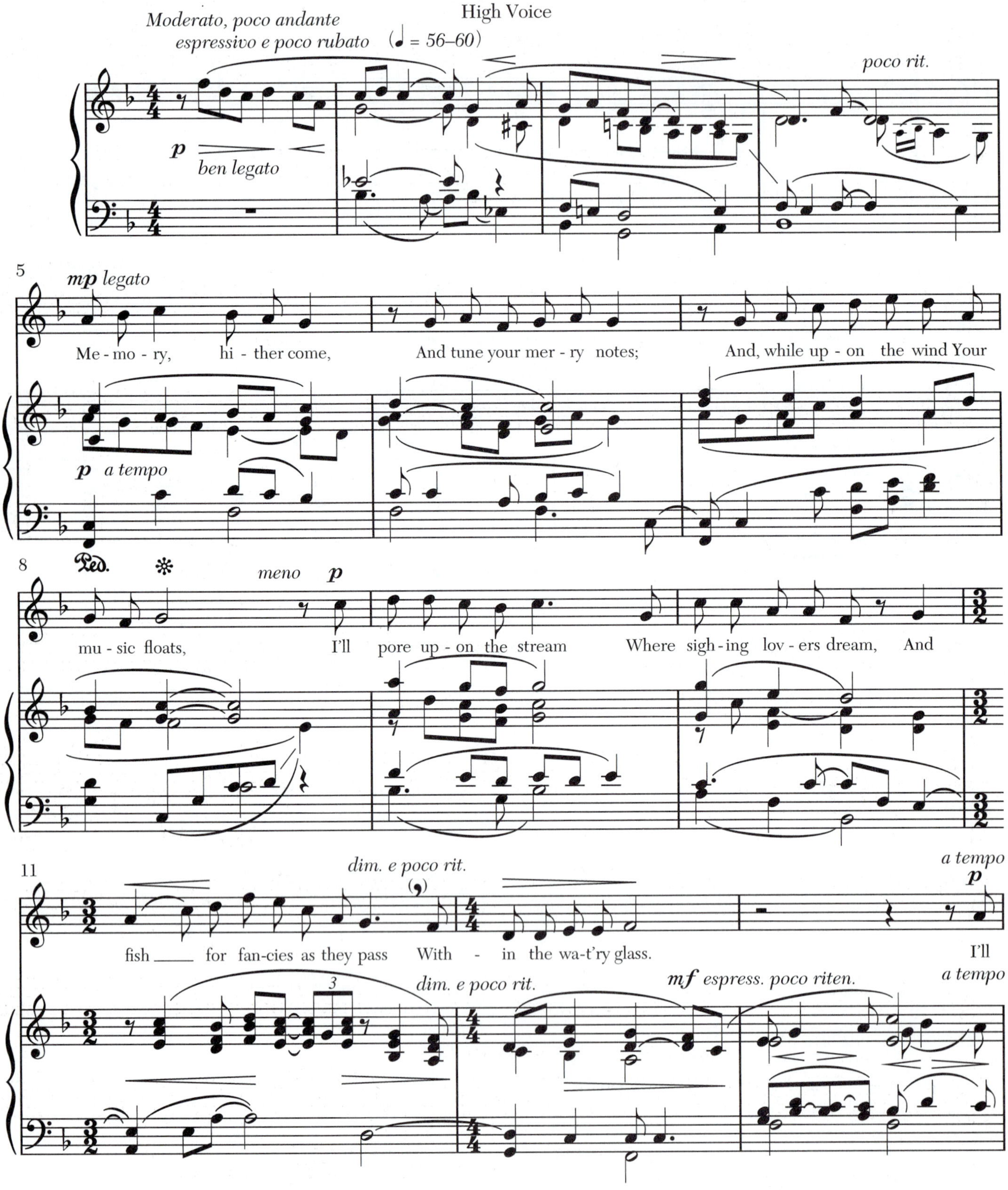

Moderato, poco andante
espressivo e poco rubato (♩ = 56–60)

poco rit.

p
ben legato

mp legato

Me - mo - ry, hi - ther come, And tune your mer - ry notes; And, while up - on the wind Your

p a tempo

Ped. ✳

meno *p*

mu - sic floats, I'll pore up - on the stream Where sigh - ing lov - ers dream, And

dim. e poco rit.

a tempo
p

fish ___ for fan - cies as they pass With - in the wa - t'ry glass. I'll

dim. e poco rit.

mf espress. poco riten.

a tempo

Dream Valley

Text by William Blake

Low Voice

Roger Quilter (1877–1953)

Moderato, poco andante
espressivo e poco rubato   (♩ = 56–60)

poco rit.

p
ben legato

mp *legato*

Me - mo - ry,   hi - ther come,   And tune your mer - ry notes;   And, while up - on the wind Your

p *a tempo*

meno **p**

mu - sic floats,   I'll   pore up - on the stream   Where sigh-ing lov - ers dream,   And

dim. e poco rit.

a tempo
p

fish _____ for fan-cies as they pass   With - in the wa-t'ry glass.   I'll

dim. e poco rit.

mf *espress. poco riten.*

a tempo

Adventures in Singing

Du bist wie eine Blume

(You Are So Like a Flower)

German Text by Heinrich Heine
English Text by Clifton Ware

Robert Schumann (1810–1856)
"Myrthen," Op. 25, No. 24

Flocks Are Sporting

(Christ Is Risen)

Text by Henry Carey
Sacred Text by Clifton Ware

Henry Carey (1689–1743)
Ed. by C.W. & B.W.

Joyfully (♩ = 138–152)

1. Flocks   are   sport - ing,   doves are   court - ing,   Warb-ling   lin   -   nets
2. Flocks   are   bleat - ing,   rocks re -   peat   - ing,   Val - leys   e - cho
1. *Christ is   ri - sen,   from death's   pri - son,   In His   vic - t'ry*
2. *From Christ's   teach - ing,   and His   preach - ing,   All who   know Him*

sweet-ly   sing,   Ah! _____
back the   sound,
now re -   born,   A -   le - lu - jah!
shall be   free,   A -   le - lu - jah!

Program notes page 317
CD 1, track 34

E l'uccellino

(And the Little Bird)

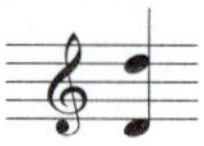

Italian Text by Renato Fucini
English text C. Ware

Music by Giacomo Puccini
(1858–1924)
edited by C. Ware

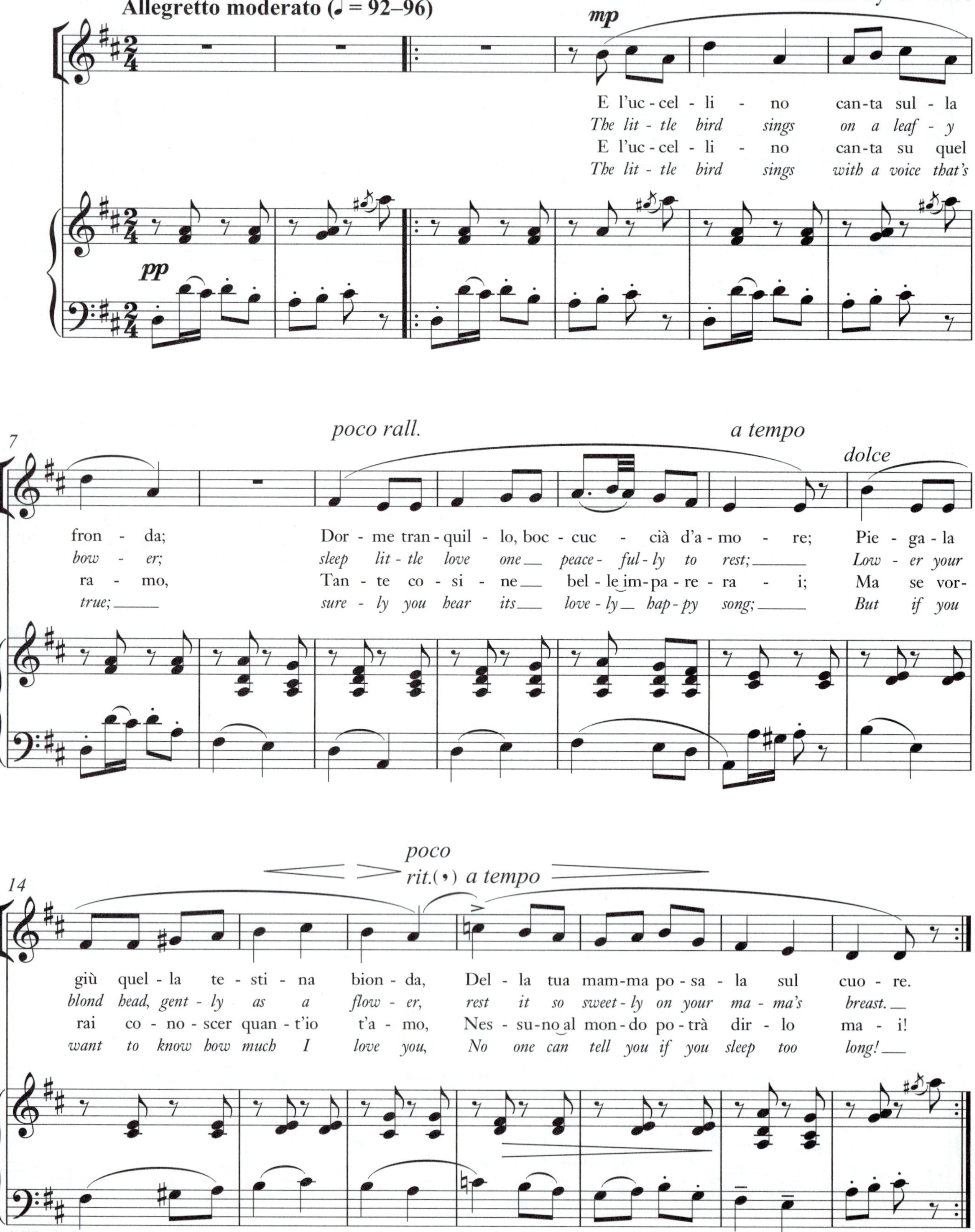

Allegretto moderato (♩ = 92–96)
mp
pp
E l'uc-cel-li-no can-ta sul-la fron-da; Dor-me tran-quil-lo, boc-cuc-cià d'a-mo-re; Pie-ga-la giù quel-la te-sti-na bion-da, Del-la tua mam-ma po-sa-la sul cuo-re.
The lit-tle bird sings on a leaf-y bow-er; sleep lit-tle love one peace-ful-ly to rest; Low-er your blond head, gent-ly as a flow-er, rest it so sweet-ly on your ma-ma's breast.
E l'uc-cel-li-no can-ta su quel ra-mo, Tan-te co-si-ne bel-le im-pa-re-ra-i; Ma se vor-rai co-no-scer quan-t'io t'a-mo, Nes-su-no al mon-do po-trà dir-lo ma-i!
The lit-tle bird sings with a voice that's true; sure-ly you hear its love-ly hap-py song; But if you want to know how much I love you, No one can tell you if you sleep too long!
7
poco rall.
a tempo
dolce
14
poco rit. (,)
a tempo

E l'uc-cel-li - no can-ta al ciel se - re - no;
The lit - tle bird sings high up in the sky, ___

Dor - mi te-
Sleep now my

so - ro mio qui sul mio se - no.
trea - sure, here u - pon my breast lie.

Heavenly Grass

Text by Tennessee Williams

Paul Bowles (b. 1910)

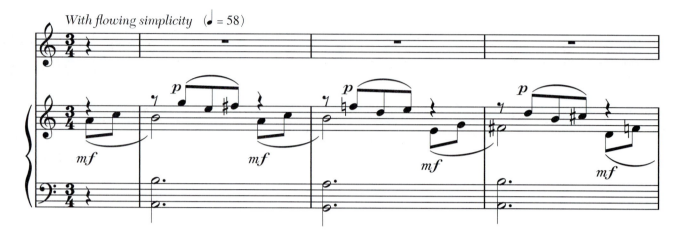

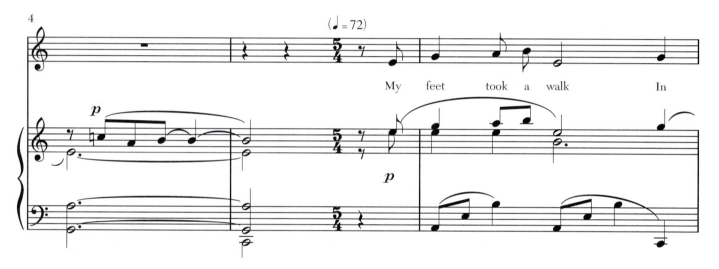

feet took a walk In heav-en-ly grass.

All __ night while the lone - some __

stars rolled past, Then my feet come down to walk on earth And my

moth - er cried When she give me birth.

I Attempt from Love's Sickness to Fly

Henry Purcell (1659–1695)
Arr. by Lawrence Henry

Text by John Dryden

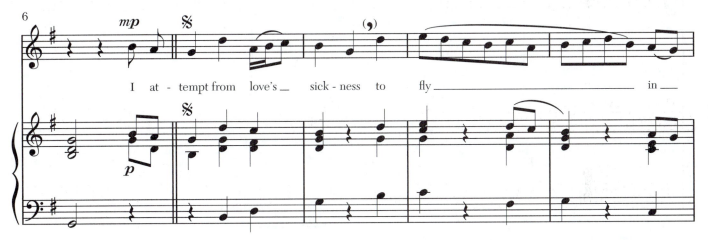

I at - tempt from love's sick - ness to fly in

vain, Since I am, my - self, my own fe - ver, Since I am, my -

self,   my   own   fe - ver ___ and ___ pain.   No   pain.

more now,   no   more now,   fond ___ heart,   with   pride   no more   swell,   Thou

canst not ___ raise ___ for - ces,   thou   canst not ___ raise ___ for - ces   e - nough   to re -

bel;   I   at - tempt from   love's ___ sick - ness   to   fly _____   in ___

Ich liebe dich
(I Love You Dear)

German Text by Karl Friedrich Herrosee
English Text by Clifton Ware

Ludwig van Beethoven
(1770–1827)

14

tra - gen; du trö - ste - test im Kum - mer mich, ich _ weint' in dei - ne
glad - ness; you com - fort me when I am low, my _ tears _ as - suage your

18

Kla - gen, in dei - ne Kla - gen. D'rum _ Got - tes Se - gen
sad - ness, as - suage your sad - ness. May _ God's kind bles - sings

22

ü - ber dir, du mei - nes Le - bens Freu - de, Gott _ schü - tze dich, er - halt' dich mir, schütz'
be on you, my love, my life, my treas - ure; may _ God pro - tect and hold you near, and

Adventures in Singing

Oh, Sleep, Why Dost Thou Leave Me?

from *Semele*

(*O Lord, Hear My Prayer*)

Original Text by W. Congreve
Sacred Text by Clifton Ware

George Frederic Handel (1685–1759)
Ed. by C.W.

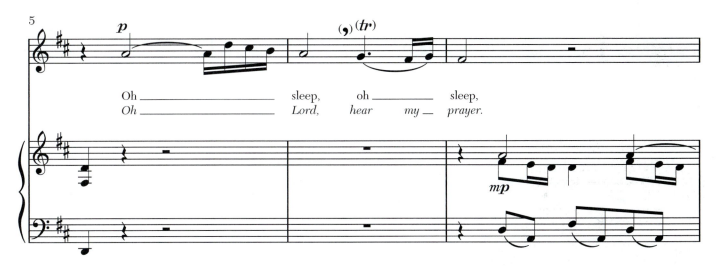

Oh _____ sleep, oh _____ sleep,
Oh _____ Lord, hear my _ prayer.

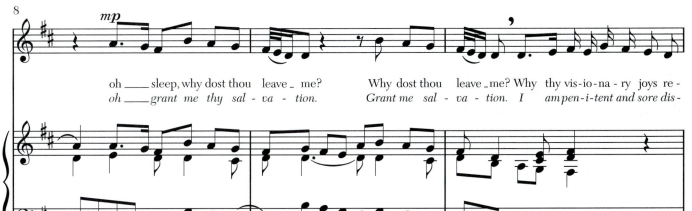

oh _____ sleep, why dost thou leave _ me? Why dost thou leave _ me? Why thy vis-io-na-ry joys re-
oh _____ grant me thy sal - va - tion. Grant me sal - va - tion. I am pen-i-tent and sore dis-

move?
tressed!

Oh ————————— sleep, oh ———— sleep, oh
Oh ————————— Lord, hear my — cry, and

poco cresc.

sleep, a-gain de-ceive me, oh sleep, a-gain de-ceive me, to my arms re-store my wan-d'ring
hear the sup - pli-ca-tion, oh hear the sup - pli-ca-tion of my heart, Re-store my wan-d'ring

mp

poco cresc.

cresc.

love, my wan - d'ring love, my — wan -
soul, my wan - d'ring soul, my — wan -

cresc.

If Music Be the Food of Love

Text Attributed to H. Heveningham

Henry Purcell (1659–1695)
Arr. by Lawrence Henry

It Was a Lover and His Lass

Text Attributed to
William Shakespeare

Thomas Morley (1557–1603)
Ed. by C. W.

It's All I Bring Today

Text by Emily Dickinson

Ernst Bacon (1898–1990)

Andante (♩ = 60–66)

It's all I have to bring — to - day,

mp smoothly and with quiet warmth

This, and my heart be - side, This, and my heart, and

all the fields, And all — the mead - ows — wide. _____ Be

Adventures in Singing

sure you count, _____ should I for - get, Some - one the

richly

sun could tell, This, and my heart, and all _____ the

bees _____ Which in the clo - ver dwell. _____

Lascia ch'io pianga
(Let Me in Weeping)
[O Lord, I Pray Thee]

Italian Text by Giacomo Rossi
English Texts by Clifton Ware

George Frederic Handel (1685–1759)
Ed. by C.W.

Le Charme
(The Charm)

French Text by Armand Silvestre
from "Chanson des heures"
English Text by Clifton Ware

Ernest Chausson (1855–1899)
Op. 2, No. 2

Adventures in Singing

My Lovely Celia
(O, My Beloved)

Textual Source Unknown

George Monro (1680–1731)
Ed. by C.W.

°Alternate words

love _ ease my trou - bled mind.

O, let _____ me _ gaze _____ on your _____ bright _ eyes, Where melt - ing _

beams so oft _____ a - rise; My heart's _ en - chant-ed with _____ thy _

charms, O, take _____ me, _ dy - ing, to _____ your arms. _____

Nel cor più non mi sento
(My Heart Has Lost Its Feeling)

Italian Text by Giuseppe Paloma
English Text by Clifton Ware

Giovanni Paisiello (1740–1816)
Ed. by C.W.

Adventures in Singing

piz - zi - chi, mi stuz - zi - chi, mi pun - gi - chi, mi
pinch   me, you ex - cite _ me,   you prick _ me and you

mas - ti - chi; che co - sa è que - sta ohi - mè? pie - tà, _ pie - tà, _ pie -
bite _ me; what spite - ful things _ you do! Have mer - cy, have pi - ty, be

tà! _ A - mo - re è un cer - to che, _ che di - spe - rar _ mi
fair! _ Oh Love it's sure - ly you! (ʼ) Oh why _ do you drive me to _ de -

fa.
spair.

Non lo dirò col labbro
(At Evening)

Italian Text by Nicola Haym
English Text by Clifton & Bettye Ware

George Frederic Handel (1685–1759)
Arr. by Lawrence Henry

218

Preach Not Me Your Musty Rules

Text by John Dalton
From: *Comus* by John Milton

Thomas A. Arne (1710–1778)
Arr. by Lawrence Henry

sen - ses al - ways rea - son well.

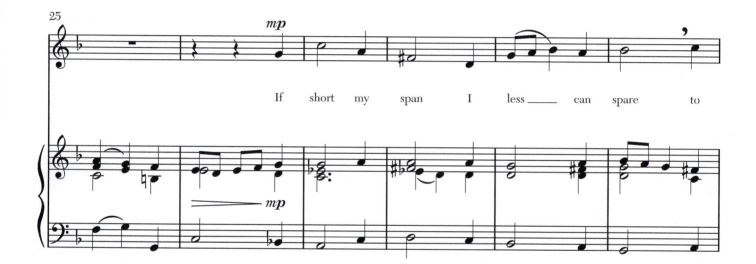

If short my span I less——— can spare to

pass a sin - gle plea - sure by:

Adventures in Singing

An hour — is long — if lost — in care;

They on - ly live, they on - ly live, They on - ly live who

life — en - joy.

Program notes page 312
CD 2, track 11

Now Is the Month of Maying

Text Anonymous

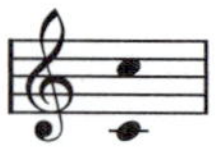

Thomas Morley (1557–1603)
Ed. by C.W.

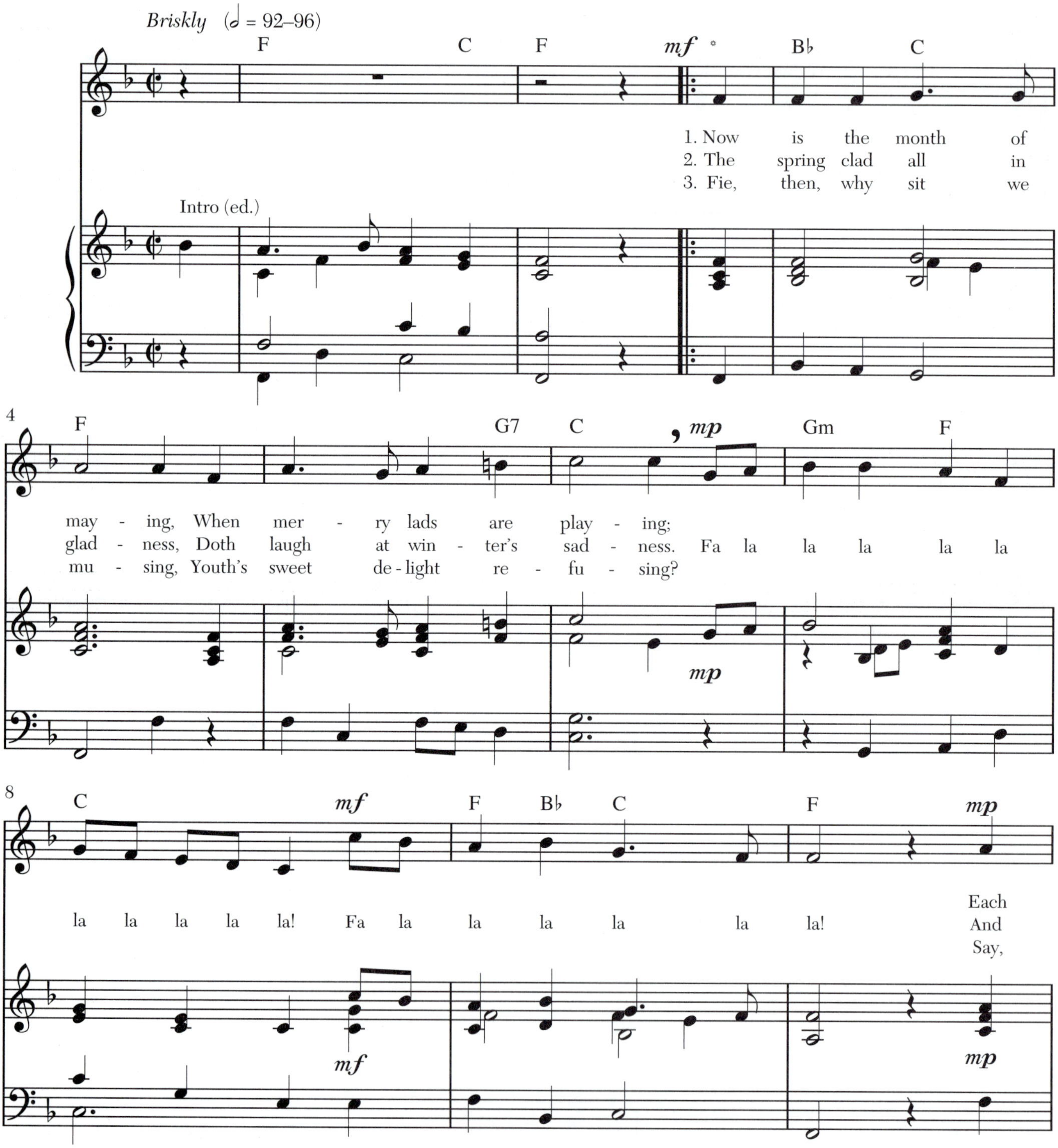
Briskly (𝅗𝅥 = 92–96)
F
C
F
mf *
B♭
C
1. Now is the month of may - ing, When mer - ry lads are play - ing;
2. The spring clad all in glad - ness, Doth laugh at win - ter's sad - ness.
3. Fie, then, why sit we mu - sing, Youth's sweet de - light re - fu - sing?
Intro (ed.)
4
F
G7
C
mp
Gm
F
Fa la la la la la
mp
8
C
mf
F
B♭
C
F
mp
la la la la la! Fa la la la la la la!
Each
And
Say,
mf
mp

*Each verse may be sung by a different singer, and the fa-la-la chorus sung by all

with his bon - ny lass,   A - danc - ing on the grass,   Fa la
to the bag - pipes' sound,   The nymphs tread out their round
dain - ty nymphs, and speak,   Shall we play bar - ley - break?

la   la   la!   Fa la la la la la la   la   la la la   la!

Ridente la calma

(May Calm Joy Awaken)

Italian Text Unknown
English Text by Clifton Ware

Joseph Mysliveček (1737–1781)
W.A. Mozart (1756–1791)
Ed. by C.W.

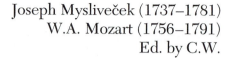

Adventures in Singing

cal - ma nell' al - ma si de - sti, ne re - sti più se - gno di
wa - ken my quiet peace - ful spi - rit, nor let there re - main here no

sde - gno e ti - mor,_ ne re - sti più se - gno di sde - gno e ti -
an - ger or fear._ Nor let there re - main here no an - ger or

mor, di sde - gno e_ ti - mor.
fear, no an - ger or fear.

Romance
(Romance)

French Text by Paul Bourget
English Text by Clifton Ware

Claude Debussy (1862–1918)
Ed. by C.W.

lis?
flow'r?

N'est — il plus un par-fum qui res — — te.
Is there no per-fume yet re-main — ing,

De la su-a-vi-té cé-
Of pure ce-les-tial fra-grance

les — — te, Des jours où tu m'en-ve-lop-pais D'u-ne va-
reign — ing, Of days when you en-vel-oped me In va-p'rous

peur sur-na-tu-rel — le
su — per-na — t'ral won — der,

Fai — te d'es-poir,
Fash — ioned of hope,

d'a-mour fi-dè — le,
and faith-ful lov — ing,

De bé-a-ti — tude _____ et de paix?
Blessed with ho-ly joy, _____ peace pro — found?

Seligkeit
(Bliss)

German Text by Ludwig Heinrich
Christoph Hölty
English Text by Clifton Ware

High Voice

Franz Schubert (1797–1828)
Ed. by C.W.

Adventures in Singing

21

En - geln und __ Ver - klär - - ten, wie __ die Vä __ ter
Harf' __ und Psal - ter klin - get, und __ man tanzt __ und
ei - nen Blick __ der sa - get, daß __ ich aus - ge -
An - gels sing __ the glo - ry, of __ God' an - cient
Harp __ and psal - ter cling - ing, all __ are danc - ing,
When your eyes __ in - form me, I'll __ no more __ for -

27 *mf*

lehr - ten. O, da möcht ich sein _____ und mich
sin - get. O, da möcht ich sein _____ und mich
kla - get. Se - lig dann mit ihr _____ bleib' ich
sto - ry. O, there would I be _____ for e -
sing - ing. O, there would I be _____ for e -
lorn be. Bliss - ful it will be _____ for e -

mp

34 *f*

e - wig freun, _____ und __ mich e - wig freun!
e - wig freun, _____ und __ mich e - wig freun!
e - wig hier, _____ bleib' ich e - wig hier!
ter - ni - ty, _____ for __ e - ter - ni - ty!
ter - ni - ty, _____ for __ e - ter - ni - ty!
ter - ni - ty, _____ for __ e - ter - ni - ty!

mf   *f*

Seligkeit
(Bliss)

German Text by Ludwig Heinrich
Christoph Hölty
English Text by Clifton Ware

Low Voice

Franz Schubert (1797–1828)
Ed. by C.W.

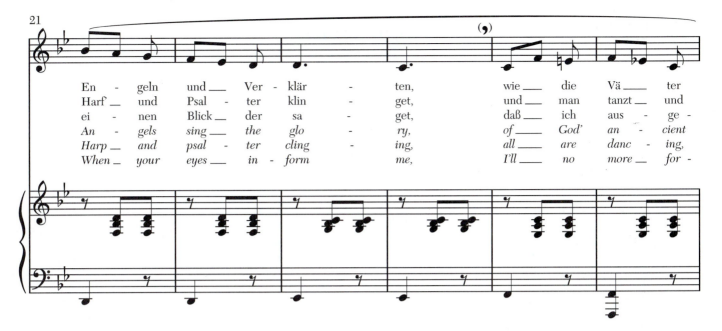

21

En - geln und __ Ver - klär - ten, wie __ die Vä __ ter
Harf' __ und Psal - ter klin - get, und __ man tanzt __ und
ei - nen Blick der sa - get, daß __ ich aus - ge -
An - gels sing __ the glo - ry, of __ God' an - cient
Harp __ and psal - ter cling - ing, all __ are danc - ing,
When __ your eyes __ in - form me, I'll __ no more __ for -

27

lehr - ten. O, da möcht ich sein _____ und mich
sin - get. O, da möcht ich sein _____ und mich
kla - get. Se - lig dann mit ihr _____ bleib' ich
sto - ry. O, there would I be _____ for e -
sing - ing. O, there would I be _____ for e -
lorn be. Bliss - ful it will be _____ for e -

mf
mp

34

e - wig freun, _____ und __ mich e - wig freun!
e - wig freun, _____ und __ mich e - wig freun!
e - wig hier, _____ bleib' __ ich e - wig hier!
ter - ni - ty, _____ for __ e - ter - ni - ty!
ter - ni - ty, _____ for __ e - ter - ni - ty!
ter - ni - ty, _____ for __ e - ter - ni - ty!

f
mf
f

Star vicino
(To Be Close)

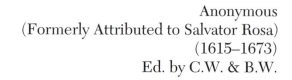

Anonymous
(Formerly Attributed to Salvator Rosa)
(1615–1673)
Ed. by C.W. & B.W.

Italian Text Anonymous
English Text by Clifton Ware

1. Star vi - ci - no al bel i - dol che s'a - ma,
   To be close to one's am' - rous be - lov - ed,
2. Star lon - tan - na co - lei che si bra - ma,
   To be far from one's am' - rous de - sir - ing,

è il più va - go di - let - to ___ d'a - mor, ___
Is the most char - ming as - pect ___ of ___ love. ___
é d'a - mo - re il più mes - to, ___ do - lor, ___
Is for love the most dole - ful ___ af - flic - tion.

The Call

Text by George Herbert

Ralph Vaughan Williams (1872–1958)

Feast, as mends in length: Such a Strength, as makes _____ his

guest. ___ Come, my Joy, __ my Love, __ my Heart: Such a

Joy, __ as none ___ can move: Such a Love, as none __ can

part: ___ Such a Heart, as joys _____ in love.

The Daisies

Text by James Stephens

High Voice

Samuel Barber (1910–1981)
Op. 2, No. 1

In the scent-ed bud of the morn-ing O, When the wind-y grass went rip-pling far! I saw my dear one walk-ing slow In the field where the dais-ies are. We did not laugh, and we did not speak, As we

Adventures in Singing

Program notes page 318
CD 2, track 23

The Daisies

Text by James Stephens

Samuel Barber (1910–1981)
Op. 2, No. 1

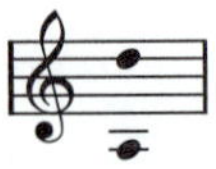
Low Voice

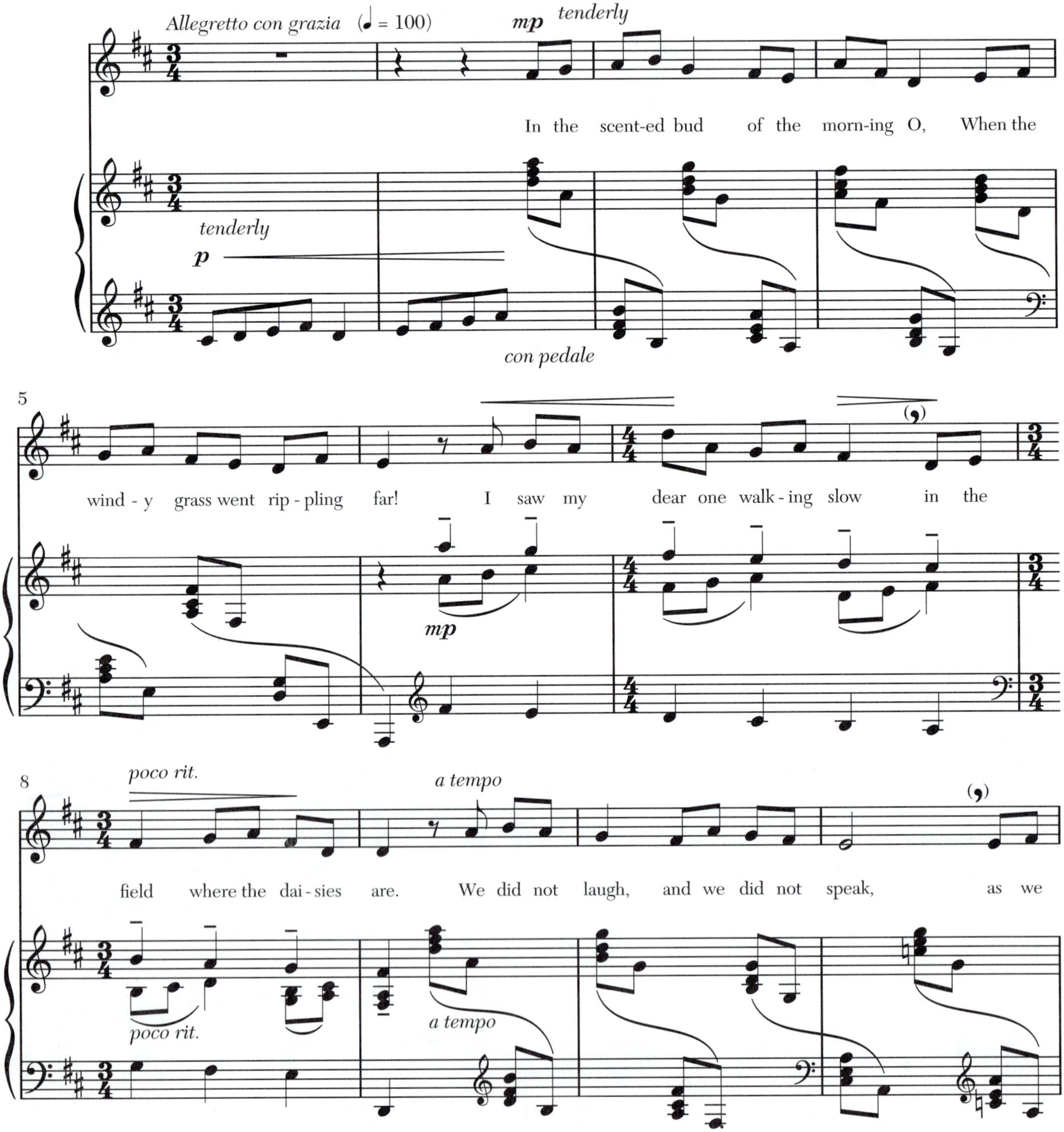
Allegretto con grazia (♩ = 100)
mp tenderly
In the scent-ed bud of the morn-ing O, When the
tenderly
p
con pedale
5
wind - y grass went rip - pling far! I saw my dear one walk - ing slow in the
mp
8
poco rit.
a tempo
field where the dai - sies are. We did not laugh, and we did not speak, as we
poco rit.
a tempo

wan-dered hap - p'ly, to and fro, I kissed my dear on ei - ther cheek, in the bud of the morn - ing O! A lark sang up, from the breez - y land; A lark sang down, from a cloud a - far; As she and (he) I went, hand in hand, In the field where the dais - ies are.

The Pasture

Text by Robert Frost

Charles Naginski (1909–1940)

wait   to watch the   wa - ter   clear, _____ I   may):

I   sha'n't be gone   long.—   You   come too.

I'm go - ing out   to   fetch   the lit - tle   calf   That's   stand - ing   by   the

moth - er. It's so young, It tot-ters when she

licks it with her tongue.

I sha'n't be gone long. You come too.

Adventures in Singing

The Side Show

Text and Music by
Charles Ives (1874–1954)

In a moderate waltz time (♩ = 144)

"Is___ that Mis-ter Ri-ley, who keeps the ho-tel?" is the
tune that ac-comp-nies the trot-ting track bell; An old horse un-sound,_ turns the
mer-ry-go-round, mak-ing poor Mis-ter Ri-ley look a bit like a
Rus-sian dance,___ Some speak of so high-ly, as_ they do of Ri-ley!___

This Little Rose

High Voice

Text by Emily Dickinson

Music by William Roy
Edited by C. Ware

Moderate, and in a free, gentle manner (♩ = 92–96)

slightly accelerate

a tempo

No-bod-y knows this lit-tle rose, It might a pil - grim be.

Did I not take it from the ways And lift it up to thee.

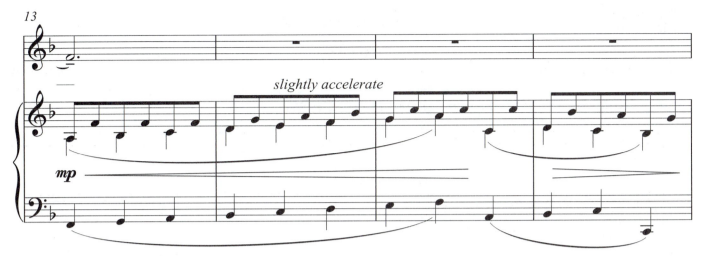

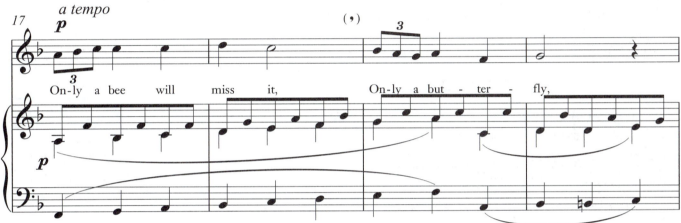

On-ly a bee will miss it, On-ly a but - ter - fly,

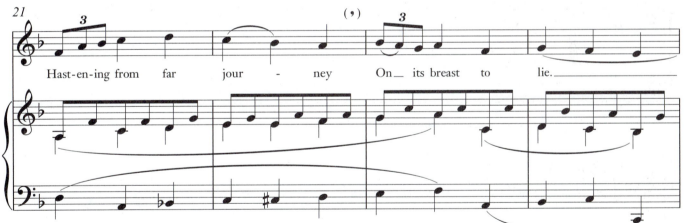

Hast-en-ing from far jour - ney On__ its breast to lie.___

Song Anthology

This Little Rose

Low Voice

Text by Emily Dickinson

Music by William Roy
Edited by C. Ware

Song Anthology

Adventures in Singing

Toglietemi la vita ancor
(Oh, Take Away My Breath, My Life)

Italian Text Unknown
English Text by Clifton Ware

High Key

Alessandro Scarlatti (1660–1725)
Ed. by B.W. & C.W.

Toglietemi la vita ancor

(Oh, Take Away My Breath, My Life)

Italian Text Unknown
English Text by Clifton Ware

Alessandro Scarlatti (1660–1725)
Ed. by B.W. & C.W.

Low Key

Vaga luna
(Lovely Moon)

Text Anonymous
English Text by Clifton Ware

Vincenzo Bellini (1801–1835)
Based on version by Pauline Viardot-Garcia

Andante cantabile (♩ = 66–69)

1. Va - ga lu - na __ che i - nar - gen - ti Que - ste ri - ve e que - sti
   Love-ly moon that __ co - vers with sil - ver all these banks and __ flow'rs re -
2. Dil - le pur, che lon - tan - nan - za, Il mio duol non - può le -
   Tell my love who __ longs __ so __ far a-way that my grief I __ can - not

fio - ri. Ed in spi - ri, ed in-spi - ri a-glie - le - men - ti, Il lin -
splen - dent, brea-thing life in - to all of na-ture's won - ders, the pure
nir __ Che se nu - tro, se nu-tro u-na spe - ran - za, El - la è
share, __ that I nour - ish and nur-ture ev - er - last - ing hope, that u -

guag-gio, il lin-guag-gio dell'a - mor,
lang-uage, the pure lang-uage of my love.
sol, si el - la è sol nell' av - ve - nir,
ni - ted, yet u - ni - ted we shall be.

Te - sti - mo - nio_or se - i tu
As my wit - ness you____ are all-
Dil - le pur che gior - no e
Say that ev - 'ry day____ and

so - la Del mio fer - vi - do de - sir____
know - ing of my fer - vor and de - sire____
se - ra Con - to l'o - re del do - lor; ____
ev - 'ning I count ev - 'ry hour a - part;____

Ed a lei, ed a lei che m'in-na-
Tell my love, tell my loved one of my
Che u - na spe - me, una spe - me lu - sin-
That a hope, that a bur - ning hope en-

mo - ra Con - ta_i pal - pi - ti, i pal - pi - ti_e_i so - spir,
pas - sion, Tell of trem - bling, of my trem-bling and my sighs,
ghie - ra mi con - for - ta, mi con - for - ta nell' a - mor,
ti - cing com - forts me, yes com-forts me in thoughts of love.

Ed a lei che m'in - na-
Tell my loved one of my
che u - na spe - me lu - sin-
That a hope, a hope en-

Weep You No More, Sad Fountains

Text Anonymous

Roger Quilter (1877–1953)

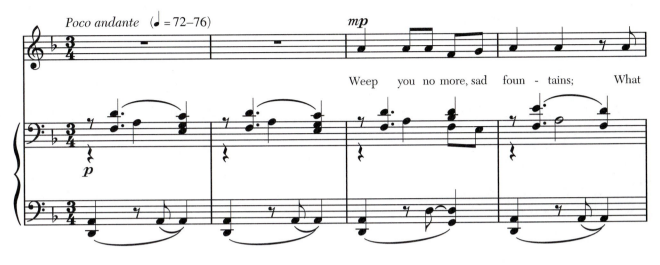

Poco andante (= 72–76)

mp

Weep you no more, sad foun - tains; What

need you flow so fast? Look how the snow-y moun - tains Heav'n's

sun doth gent - ly waste! But my Sun's heav'n-ly eyes view not your

sets? _____ Rest you, then, rest, sad eyes! Melt not in weep - ing,

While she lies sleep - ing, Soft - ly now

soft - ly lies sleep - ing, sleep - ing.

Almost Like Being in Love
(from *Brigadoon*)

Text by Alan Jay Lerner

Music by Frederick Loewe

Any Dream Will Do
(from *Joseph and the Amazing Technicolor Dreamcoat*)

Text by Tim Rice

Music by Andrew Lloyd Webber (b. 1948)

Adventures in Singing

But the world was sleep - ing. An - y dream will do.

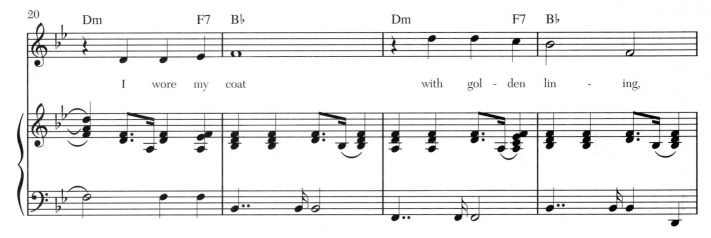

I wore my coat with gol - den lin - ing,

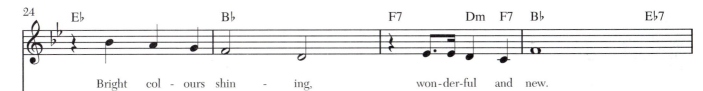

Bright col - ours shin - ing, won - der - ful and new.

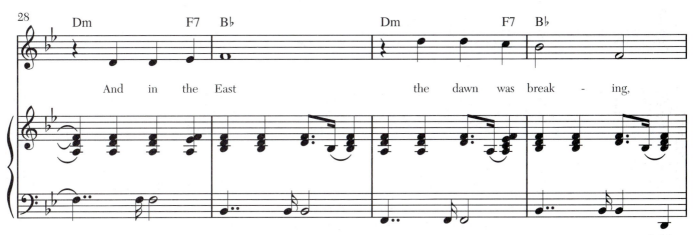

And in the East the dawn was break - ing,

to the be - gin - ning, The light is dim - ming

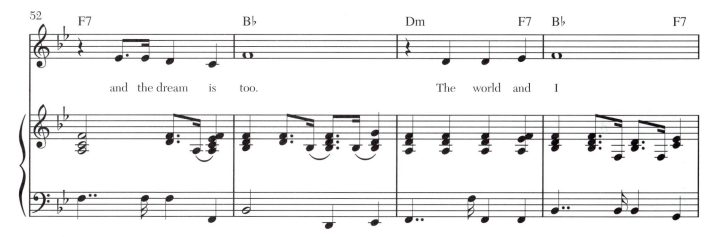

and the dream is too. The world and I

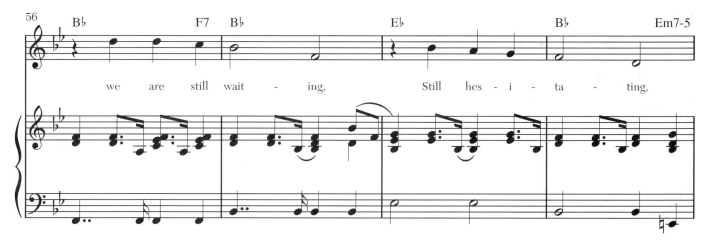

we are still wait - ing, Still hes - i - ta - ting,

a - ny dream will do, a - ny dream will do.

On a Clear Day (You Can See Forever)
(from *On a Clear Day You Can See Forever*)

Text by Alan Jay Lerner

Music by Burton Lane

Program notes page 320
CD 2, track 37

Oh, What a Beautiful Mornin'

(from *Oklahoma!*)

Text by Oscar Hammerstein II

Music by Richard Rodgers

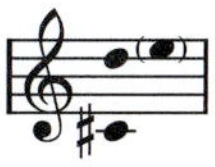

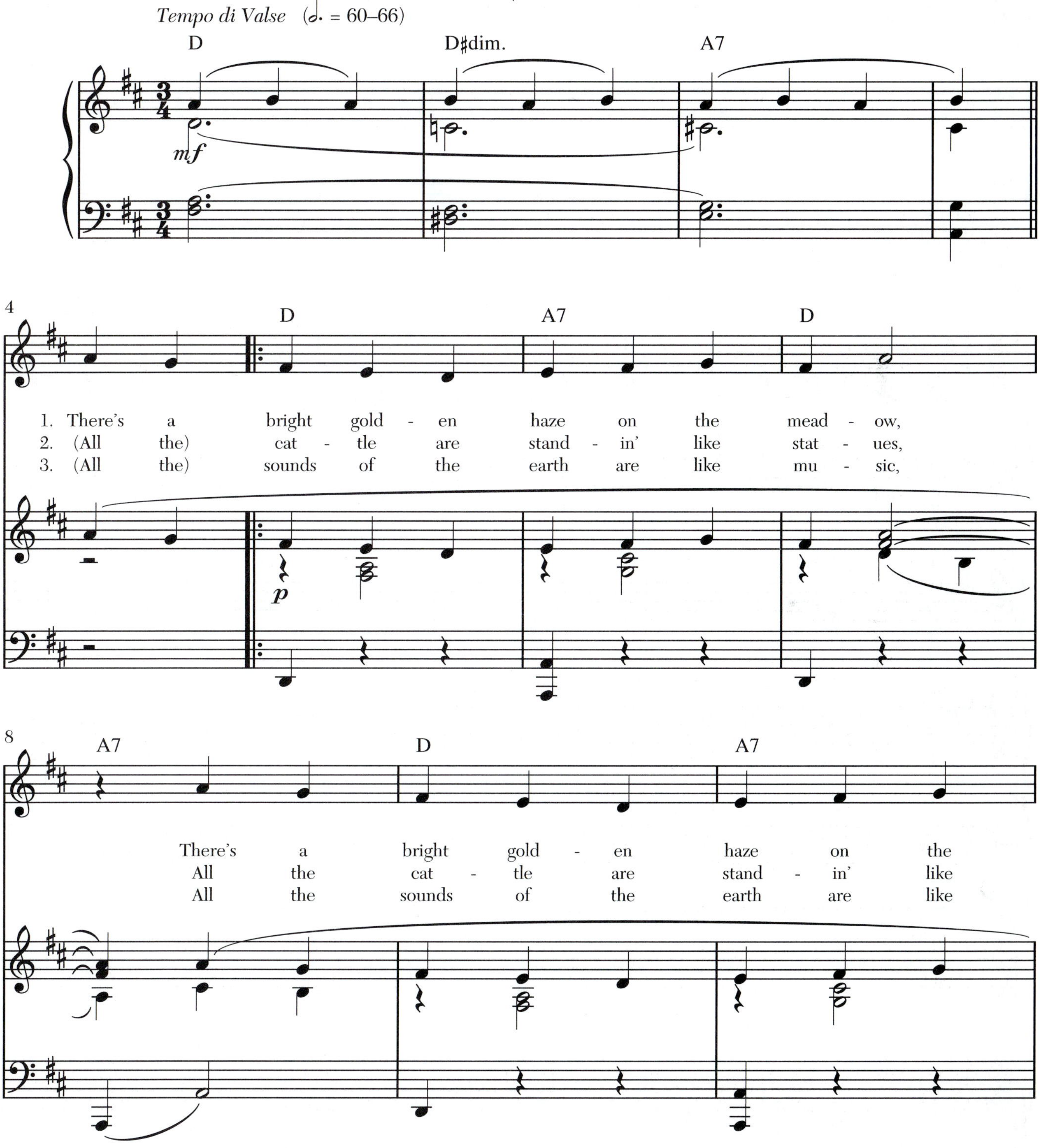

Tempo di Valse (♩. = 60–66)
D
D♯dim.
A7
mf
4
D
A7
D
1. There's a bright gold - en haze on the mead - ow,
2. (All the) cat - tle are stand - in' like stat - ues,
3. (All the) sounds of the earth are like mu - sic,
p
8
A7
D
A7
There's a bright gold - en haze on the
All the cat - tle are stand - in' like
All the sounds of the earth are like

Put On a Happy Face
(from *Bye Bye Birdie*)

Text by Lee Adams

Music by Charles Strouse

Time After Time

(from the Metro-Goldwyn-Mayer Picture
It Happened in Brooklyn)

Text by Sammy Cahn

Music by Jule Styne

Song Anthology

281

Chorus
a tempo

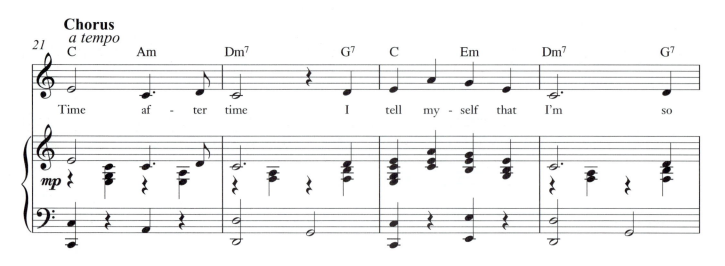

Time af- ter time I tell my- self that I'm so

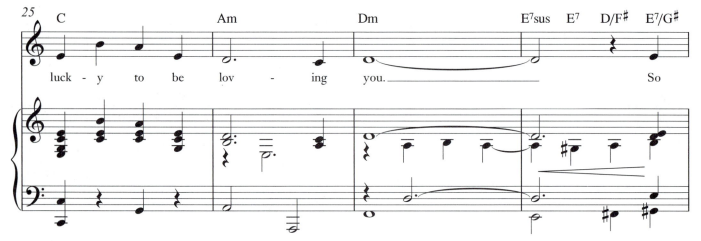

luck - y to be lov - ing you. _____ So

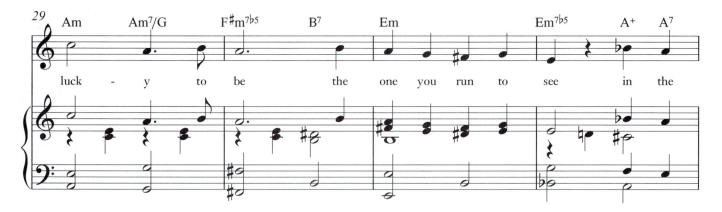

luck - y to be the one you run to see in the

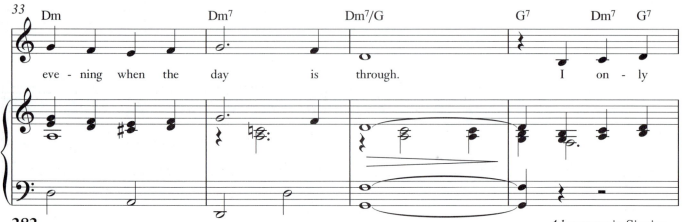

eve - ning when the day is through. I on - ly

Adventures in Singing

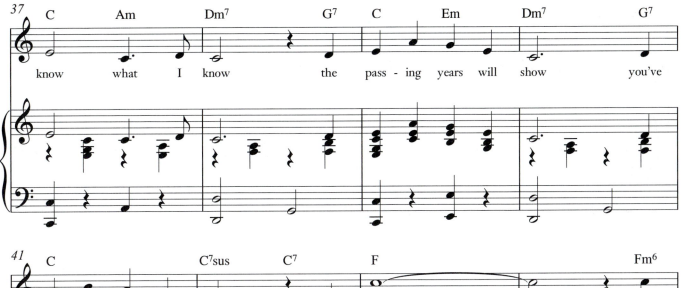

know what I know the pass-ing years will show you've

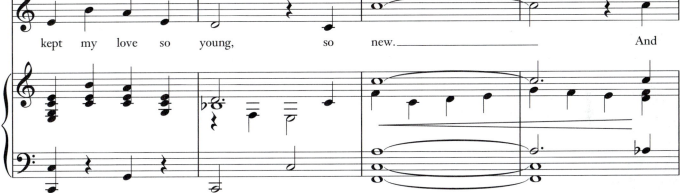

kept my love so young, so new. And

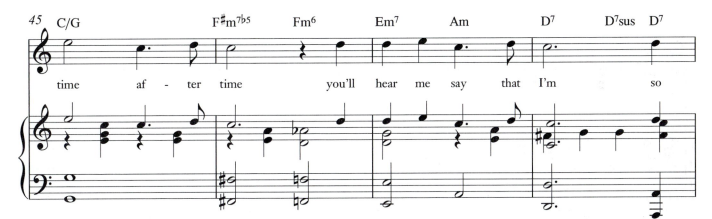

time af-ter time you'll hear me say that I'm so

Slightly broader

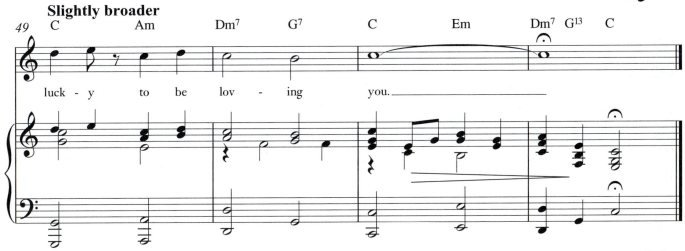

luck-y to be lov-ing you.

'S Wonderful

Text by Ira Gershwin

Music by George Gershwin

Note: If both verses are sung, observe the repeat sign.
If one verse is sung, use the second ending only.

Adventures in Singing

Till There Was You

(from Meredith Willson's *The Music Man*)

Text and Music by Meredith Willson

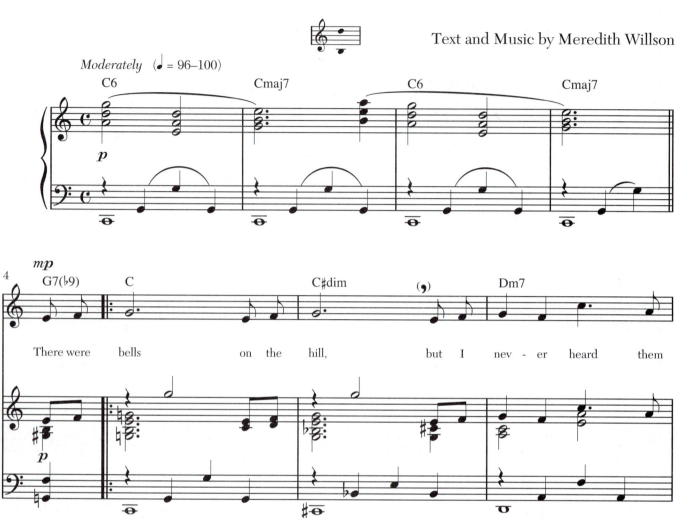

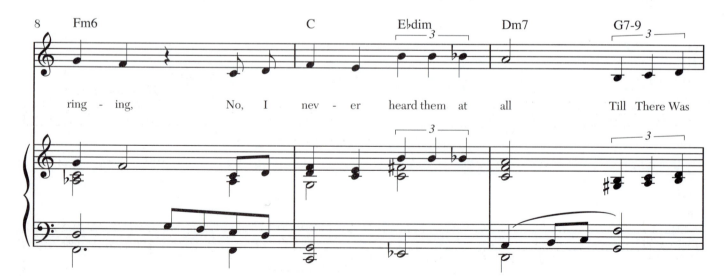

Adventures in Singing

Tipsy Song
(from *La Périchole*)

French Text by Ludovic Halévy
English Text by Clifton Ware

Jacques Offenbach (1819–1880)
Ed. by C.W.

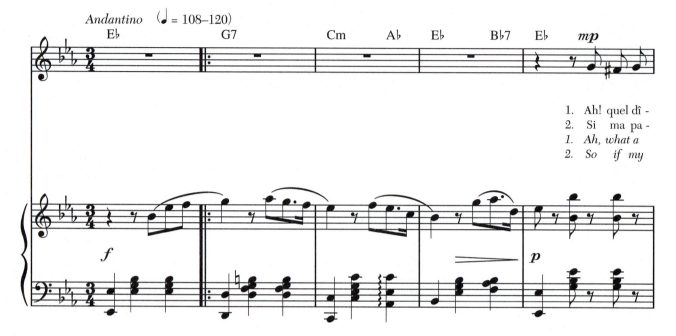

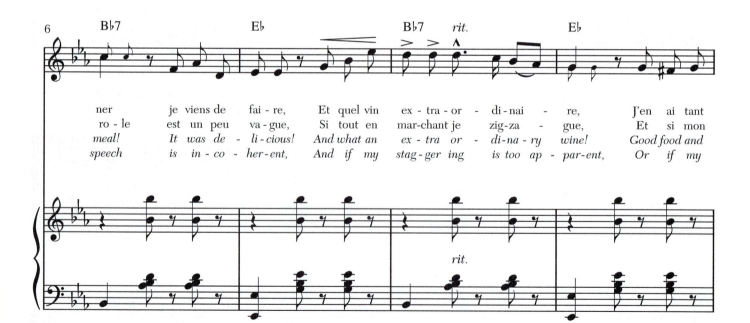

Try to Remember
(From *The Fantasticks*)

Text by Tom Jones

High Voice

Music by Harvey Schmidt

294

Adventures in Singing

Try to Remember
(From *The Fantasticks*)

Text by Tom Jones

Low Voice

Music by Harvey Schmidt

1. Try To Re - mem - ber the kind of Sep - tem - ber when life was slow and
2. Try To Re - mem - ber when life was so ten - der that no one wept ex -
3. Deep in De - cem - ber it's nice to re - mem - ber al - tho' you know the

oh, so mel - low. _ Try To Re - mem - ber the kind of Sep - tem - ber when
cept the wil - low. _ Try To Re - mem - ber when life was so ten - der that
snow will fol - low. _ Deep in De - cem - ber it's nice to re - mem - ber with -

Why Should I Wake Up?
(from the musical *Cabaret*)

Text by Fred Ebb

Music by John Kander

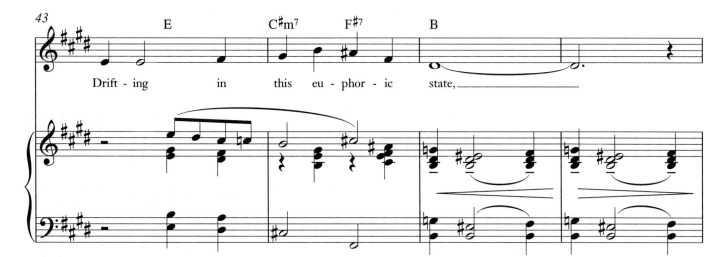

Drift - ing in this eu - phor - ic state,

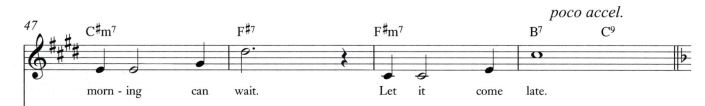

poco accel.

morn - ing can wait. Let it come late.

With motion

Why should I wake up? Why waste a drop of the wine?

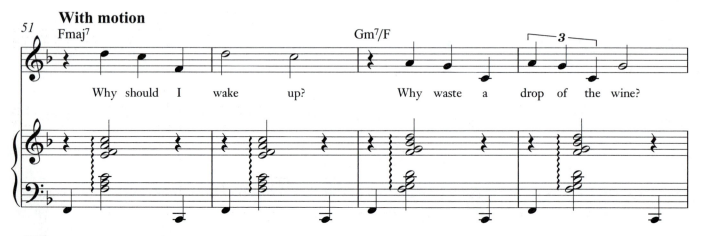

Adventures in Singing

Appendix A

INTERNATIONAL PHONETIC ALPHABET

Figure A-1   Basic English and Foreign Language Vowels

Basic phonemes	IPA Symbol	English	Italian	German	French
ee	[i]	s*ea*t	s*i*	s*ie*	h*i*ver
ih	[ɪ]	s*i*t		*i*mmer	
ay	[e]	d*ay*	v*e*ro	l*e*ben	*é*té
eh	[ɛ]	g*e*t	b*e*lle	d*e*nn	cl*ai*r
ae	[æ]	b*a*ck			
ah	[a]				p*a*rle
ah	[ɑ]	f*a*ther	c*a*sa	M*a*nn	r*a*s
aw	[ɔ]	cr*aw*l	gl*o*ria	k*o*mmt	f*o*lie
uh	[ʌ]	sh*u*t			
oh	[o]	t*o*ne	d*o*ve	s*o*	h*ô*tel
	[ʊ]	l*oo*k	*u*nd		
oo	[u]	s*oo*the	s*u*a	z*u*	b*ou*le

Figure A-2   Tense/Closed and Lax/Open Vowels

Tense/Closed			Lax/Open		
[i]		s*ea*t	[ɪ]		s*i*t
[e]		g*a*te	[ɛ]		g*e*t
[æ]		n*a*sty			
[a]		cr*o*p	[ɑ]		f*a*ther
[o]		m*o*le	[ɔ]		m*aw*l
[u]		sh*oo*t	[ʊ]		sh*oo*k
[y]	(G,F)	H*ü*te (G)	[ʏ]	(G,F)	H*ü*tte (G)
[ø]	(G,F)	G*oe*the (G)	[œ]	(G,F)	G*ö*tter (G)
[ə]	(G,F)	lieb*e*, j*e*	[ʌ]		th*e*, *u*p

Figure A-3 Vowels Peculiar to German and French

IPA Symbol	Type	German Word	French Word
[ə]	schwa (neutral)	Erd*e*	*je*
[ɛ̃]	nasal		sa*in*te
[ɑ̃]	nasal		bl*anc*
[ɔ̃]	nasal		b*on*
[œ̃]	nasal		*un*
[y]	umlaut /mixed (F)	*ü*ber	s*u*r
[ʏ]	umlaut	H*ü*tte	
[ø]	umlaut/mixed	sch*ö*n	d*eu*x
[œ]	umlaut/mixed	G*ö*tter	fl*eu*r

Figure A-4 Semi-Vowels (Glides)

IPA		English	Italian	German	French
[hw]		*wh*ich			
[w]		s*u*ave	q*u*ando		o*u*i
[j]		*y*ou	*i*eri	*j*ahr	h*i*er
[ɥ]					p*ui*s
[ɜ]	(silent r)	w*or*d			
[ɚ]	(silent r)	p*er*			

Figure A-5 Diphthongs and Triphthongs

	IPA	English Word	Italian	German
Diphthongs	[ɪɚ]	*ear*		
	[ɛɪ]	d*ay*		
	[ɛi]		s*ei*	
	[ɛɚ]	*air*		
	[ɑɪ]	s*igh*		M*ai*
	[ɑu]	n*ow*	*au*ra	
	[ɑʊ]			H*au*s
	[oɚ]	*ore, oar*		
	[ɔɪ]	b*oy*		
	[ɔi]		v*uoi*	
	[ɔʏ]			H*äu*ser
	[ou]	n*o*		
	[uɚ]	*sure*		
Triphthongs	[ɑɪɚ]	*fire*		
	[ɑʊɚ]	*our*		

A. *Place of Articulation*

1. *Bilabials.* Both lips working in coordination produce the consonants [p], [b], and [w].
2. *Labiodentals.* The lower lip working in contact with the upper teeth produces [f] and [v]. Loosely closed lips are used for [m].
3. *Lingua-dentals.* The tongue tip in contact with the upper teeth produces the voiceless "th" [θ] and voiced "th" [ð].
4. *Lingua-alveolars.* The tongue tip in contact with the upper dental ridge produces [d], [t], [l], and [n]; also, the flipped [ɾ] as in "ve*r*y" ("ve*dd*y").
5. *Lingua-velars.* The tongue body in contact with the velum produces "ng" [ŋ].
6. *Lingua-palato/alveolar.* The tongue blade in contact with the back of the alveolar ridge and hard palate produces "sh" [ʃ]; also the glide [j] as in "you."
7. *Lingua-palatals.* The tongue blade in contact with the hard palate produces [k] and [g].

B. *Manner of Articulation*

1. *Stops and Plosives.* Consonants halted abruptly include [d], [k], [p], and [t]. Stops are at ends, **plosives** at beginnings, and stop-plosives in middles of words.
2. *Continuants.* Consonants with prolonged sound (voiced and unvoiced) include [f], [l], [m], [n], [s], [v], and [z].

C. *Voiced and Unvoiced*

1. *Voiced.* Examples of consonants produced by vocal-fold vibration are [b], [d], [l], [m], [n], [z], [v], and [g].
2. *Unvoiced.* Examples of consonants produced without vocal-fold vibration are [h], [f], [p], [s], [t], and [k].
3. *Cognates.* **Cognates** are consonants produced with the same place and manner of articulation, differing only by unvoiced or voiced characteristics. Some examples:

Unvoiced	*Voiced*
[p]	[b]
[t]	[d]
[f]	[v]
[k]	[g]
[tʃ]	[dʒ]
[θ]	[ð]

Figure A-7 **Key to the IPA Chart of Consonants**

Column	*Key to Chart of Consonants*		
1. Consonants	IPA: International Phonetic Alphabet Symbol		
2. Word Example	**I** = Italian	**G** = German	**F** = French
3. Place	**l** = lip	**l (2)** = both lips	
	tt = tongue tip	**tb** = tongue body	
	ar = alveolar ridge	**hp** = hard palate	
	sp = soft palate	**te** = teeth	
	ute = upper teeth	**lte** = lower teeth	
4. Voiced/Unvoiced	**+v** = voiced	**−v** = unvoiced	
5. Manner	**s** = stop	**c** = continuant	
6. Other	**glides** (semivowels) = brief sound moving to another		

Figure A-8 **IPA Chart of Consonants**

1. IPA Consonant	2. Word Example	3. Position	4. Voiced/ Unvoiced	5. Duration	6. Other
[b]	*b*e	1 (2)	+v	s	
[ç]	*h*ue, i*ch* (G)	tb, hp	−v	c	glide
[tʃ]	*ch*urch	tb, hp	−v	s	
[ts]	i*ts*	tt, ar, te (closed)	−v	s	
[d]	*d*o	tt, ar	+v	s	
[dʒ]	*g*ym	ar, te, tb, hp,	+v	s, c	
[f]	*f*ast	l (lower), ue	−v	c	
[g]	*g*o	tb, hp	+v	s	
[h]	*h*ot	glottal	−v	c	
[hw]	*wh*en	glottal, l (2)	−v	c	glide
[j]	*y*es, *ia*to (I)	tb, hp	+v	c	glide
[k]	*k*itten, *c*at	tb, hp	−v	s	
[kw]	*qu*ick, *qu*ando (I)	tb, hp	−v	s	glide
[l]	*l*ove	tt, ar	+v	c	
[m]	*m*e	1 (2)	+v	c	
[n]	*n*ow	tt, ar	+v	c	
[ɲ]	o*ni*on, og*ni* (I) li*gn*e (F)	tb, ar, hp	+v	c	
[ŋ]	si*ng*, a*ng*ola (I)	tb, hp/sp	+v	c	
[p]	*p*et	1(2)	+v	c	
[r]	*r*are	tb, hp (retroflex)	+v	c	
[ɾ]	ca*r*o (I)	tt, ar (flipped)	+v	c	
[r̃]	*r*apido (I)	tt , ar (rolled)	+v	c	
[s]	*s*ee	tt, ar, (te)	−v	c	
[st]	hu*sh*ed, Mozart	tt, ar, (te)	−v	s	
[ʃ]	*sh*e	tb, hp, te	−v	c	
[t]	*t*o	tt, ar	−v	s	
[θ]	*th*in	tt, te	−v	c	
[ð]	*th*is	tt, te	+v	c	
[v]	*v*ine	l (lower), te	+v	c	
[w]	*w*e, o*ui* (F)	1 (2)	+v	c	glide
[x]	Ba*ch* (G)	tb, sp	−v	c	
[z]	*z*eal	tb, hp (te)	+v	c	
[zd]	ple*dg*ed	tb, ar, hp	+v	s	
[ʒ]	a*z*ure	tb, hp, te	+v	c	

Appendix B

SONG ANTHOLOGY GENERAL INFORMATION

This Song Anthology has been compiled according to several specific guidelines that have been adhered to as closely as possible. These guidelines are discussed below, providing information that explains how this anthology can be used most effectively

Texts

In most instances, song texts have been selected that are suitable for either female or male singers. In a few cases where song texts indicate either male or female—for example, "Greensleeves"—adjustments in wording will allow for a broader gender reference, in this particular song simply by substituting the word "lover" for "lady." Overall, the literary content of song selections is of high quality and varied in subject matter. Representative authors include Shakespeare, Goethe, Heine, William Blake, George Herbert, Ben Jonson, Tennessee Williams, and Emily Dickinson. In songs that feature English versions of foreign texts, an attempt has been made to be as faithful as possible to the original languages in producing a singable English text, an altogether very challenging undertaking. Because learning accurate pronunciations and translations of foreign texts is a fundamental aspect of voice study, Appendix C provides both International Phonetic Alphabet (IPA) transcriptions and word-by-word translations of all foreign language texts.

Song Sources

The preponderance of songs by English, American, German, French, and Italian composers is in response to professional expectations for training classical singers in the European vocal tradition, which has greatly influenced the vocal music curriculum in the United States, in addition to many other countries. The songs in this volume represent typical standard song repertoire, having proven over time their pedagogical, musical, and lit-

erary value. An attempt has been made to strike a judicious balance of musical styles, from folksongs and art songs to musical theater, with a wide representation of composers and arrangers.

Vocal Objectives

Perhaps the most important guideline has been to select songs that will assist with vocal music educational objectives, particularly regarding the development of technical skills. Careful attention has been given to selecting songs that allow for an easy to moderate level of vocal difficulty, with moderate keys and vocal ranges. The range of most songs is limited to approximately an octave or slightly more, and tessitura levels are comfortably challenging. Though keys of most songs are suitable for the majority of mid-ranged singers, there are a few songs in keys suitable for lower and higher voices. In addition, a few songs are presented in both high and low keys, and on the Web site are included higher and lower keys for some songs not included in the song anthology. As it is impossible to provide the ideal key for every song and voice, a sufficient number of songs have been included in the anthology to provide some options for all students. Although an attempt has been made to select songs with a variety of tempi, dynamics, and melodic line configurations (scales, arpeggios), there is an intentional preponderance of songs with moderate demands. In most cases, phrases are of short to moderate length with breathing places indicated as either an optional breath [(,)] or required breath [,].

Musical Objectives

The major guideline in selecting repertoire for this anthology was to include a variety of solo vocal musical styles representative of outstanding composers of the sixteenth through the twentieth centuries. Because individual instructional time is limited in voice class, most songs are brief and packed with musical substance. The piano accompaniment is usually supportive of the voice line, often duplicating it, and the harmonies are generally uncomplicated. An attempt has been made to keep the piano part simple enough for the average accompanist to master, yet musically challenging enough to maintain artistic interest. The basic elements of music—song form, dynamics, tempi, meter, harmony—are provided in a variety of combinations to enhance both learning and performing experience.

Support Materials

To aid the student in becoming a more knowledgeable vocal artist, the following information has been provided about each song: (1) background data on textual and musical sources, (2) performance suggestions, (3) word-by-word translations, and (4) figures simplifying IPA transcriptions for all foreign texts. Two CDs containing keyboard accompaniments and pronunciations of foreign language texts are provided for study and practice, and some synthesized, orchestrated accompaniments are available on the Web site (www.mhhe.com/ais4), allowing students an opportunity to sing with a full orchestral accompaniment.

INFORMATION ABOUT THE GROUP SONGS

As people have been increasingly lured into passive spectator participation in such fields as sports and music, group singing has declined as a social activity. Although at one time family members occasionally gathered around the parlor piano to sing as a group, one rarely hears of such activities today. Moreover, school music programs are being reduced or eliminated for economic reasons, resulting in less exposure to traditional group singing.

The question may well be asked, "What are the advantages of using group songs in a voice class situation?" First of all, group songs—especially **rounds**—are very easy to learn, enabling students to begin singing sooner, possibly during the first class. In addition to building group spirit, sharing the singing experience takes the pressure off individuals to perform solo in unfamiliar circumstances. The ease of learning and singing a very simple song gives the individual a sense of immediate accomplishment. It also allows the teacher and others in the class the opportunity to hear all class members as soon as possible, without undue pressure caused by musical and vocal concerns.

After warming up with vocal and physical exercises and prior to singing individual solo songs, students can sing group songs as an intermediate-level warm-up exercise. And, because of the short duration of a group song, it can provide an opportunity for everyone to sing during every class session. One useful approach is for individuals to sing group songs as solos. For example, three to four singers might perform a simple round such as "Row, Row, Row Your Boat" (also listed herein

as "Sing, Sing, Sing a Song"), each one singing the melody three or four times. As skill and confidence grow, more vocal independence can be developed by using more advanced songs, such as "Hail to Music" and "Vive L'Amour" (especially the latter, which has some simple four-part harmony). An approach that works well with this selection is to have individuals solo on the verses and the rest of the class join in on the **chorus**. It's a great rouser and spirit builder, too. "Hail to Music" may be performed several ways: in unison, a cappella, as a round, with guitar, or with the piano and orchestrated accompaniments located on the Web site.

The Star-Spangled Banner, page 127. Patriotic songs are of special interest at this particular juncture in the United States' post-9/11 era, and this great song tops the list. Francis Scott Key, a district attorney for Washington, D.C, wrote the poem in 1814 aboard a ship in Baltimore harbor following the overnight bombardment of Fort McHenry by British forces. At dawn's light, upon learning that the fort had survived, he proudly penned this poem, which was later set to an English drinking song, "To Anacreon in Heaven." In 1931 it was adopted as the official U.S. anthem. Though powerfully stirring to sing, its wide vocal range presents a challenge to most untrained singers, especially in certain keys. Garrison Keillor, creator of the NPR *Prairie Home Companion* radio show, wrote in the magazine *Atlantic Monthly* (May 2006, p. 28): "Francis Scott Key's magnificent poem isn't about national power and triumph; it's about survival, and that is its brilliance as a national anthem—so much is left unsaid. The song has been abused by aging divas and faded pop stars and every soloist who ever sang it, but when it's put in the people's key and sung by a crowd, it's thrilling." Well stated! Thus, singers are strongly encouraged to avoid self-indulgent interpretations, such as extreme ornamentation of the vocal line or irregular tempi. The orchestrated accompaniment (on the Web site) presents a version for solo or group performance that represents a more traditional standard format.

Vocalizing Fun, page 129. was written in 2003 as a vocal warm-up exercise for voice classes, with each verse addressing a specific area of vocal technique—breathing and breath hook-up, relaxation of articulating organs, clean vocal-fold phonation and resonance, and appropriate body alignment. It also provides a vehicle for all class members to sing (one verse each) in a relatively short time, and even have fun doing it.

We Sing of America, page 128. This song was written in 2004 for a national song competition that offered the prospect of presenting the winning song on a goodwill tour of China. Unfortunately, the contest was canceled when the Chinese government backed out of co-sponsoring the event. In writing the song I kept two basic guidelines in mind: I wanted a simple but engaging and stately melody and a text that focused on what I consider this nation's most positive qualities—its love of freedom and peace, its spaciousness and physical beauty, its opportunities for individual expression and prosperity, and its commitment to assist other nations in achieving freedom and a better way of life. It can be sung either as a solo or in unison as a group, preferably using the orchestrated accompaniment to lend full support.

In addition to the songs contained in this limited collection, there are innumerable high-quality group songs from all over the world, including two in foreign languages that are translated and provided with pronunciation guides in Appendix C: "Shalom Chaverim" (IPA: Fig. C-1, p. 325) and "Vive L'Amour" (IPA: Fig. C-2, p. 325). Class members with ethnic backgrounds other than European origins are encouraged to share their traditional songs with the class, perhaps as the first solo vocal performance assignment. This is an opportunity to become familiar with each person's unique socio-cultural background while broadening the musical horizons of all class members. Especially in situations where the class composition of ethnic backgrounds is widely mixed, this procedure is highly recommended.

INFORMATION ABOUT THE FOLK SONGS AND SPIRITUALS

Traditional songs form an historical musical continuity in all world cultures and civilizations. Many of the world's great composers have acknowledged the folk music of their respective countries or geographical regions as the inspirational source of their musical creativity, either directly or indirectly. There's ample evidence that the popular music traditions of the United States are outgrowths of folk music origins, such as country, blues, gospel, and folk ballads.

As part of the oral tradition of a people, the origins of folk song are hard to pinpoint. In most cases, folk songs are notated only after many years of evolving through essentially primitive forms, gradually becoming more and more refined. Some classical music composers have produced modern arrangements of some popular folk songs, with mixed results, as some become hybrid forms of folk and art song, while others retain much of the original folklike qualities. The folk songs and spirituals in this collection have been treated simply, but with an awareness of modern performance standards. Based on the premise that there is no "right" or "perfect" version, the arrangers and editors of this edition have taken minor liberties to enhance and adapt these folk songs for current performance practice.

All through the Night, page 130. The authorship of both the words and music are unknown. The first known printing of the melody was in 1784 with Welsh words and English translation, in Edward Jones's *Musical and Poetical Relicks for the Welsh Bards* (London, 1784). The song appears under the title "Ar Hyd Y Nos" and the English translation by Jones does not mention the phrase "all through the night." The first verse begins with words typical of a lullaby. However, the second verse reveals that it is actually a love song—for it is not a child, but one's beloved who is being watched over while asleep. The attitude should be one of tenderness and sincere attention to the task of keeping a nightly vigil. Be careful to pronounce the word "hover" to rhyme with "lover," not "over." A feeling of two beats to the measure will help smooth out the phrasing and make it flow more easily.

Amazing Grace, page 134. Although this well-known hymn is commonly thought of as American in origin, it is actually the composition of the Englishman, John Newton (1725–1807). As a youthful, godless sailor in the Royal Navy, he deserted, was recaptured, severely punished, and degraded. He spent several years of service in the slave trade and for some time as a captain of a slave ship. Some near misses with death at sea and his subsequent religious studies in Liverpool led to his conversion and eventual ordination as a priest in the Church of England. He became known as a great evangelical preacher and writer of several well-known hymns. The tune is of unknown origin, and appears for the first time in the "Virginia Harmony" (1831), compiled by J. P. Carrell and D. S. Clayton. In performing this particular version of the hymn, one should refrain from tendencies to embellish the basic melody, thereby maintaining the simple traditional nature of the hymn. The spirit of performance must be that of deep religious conviction, sung with quiet fervor. The meaning of the word *grace* in theological terms can be thought of as the freely given and unmerited love of God, the spirit of God working in persons, and the favor of God. The hymn begins with quiet wonder and amazement at God's love for one so unworthy, focuses on the conversion experience in the second verse, and ends triumphantly and victoriously with the final verse.

Balm in Gilead, page 132. The actual derivation of this hymn is unknown, but it is widely accepted as having origins as an African-American spiritual. Versions of it are included in such sources as *Folksingers Wordbook* (Irwin and Fred Silver) and *American Negro Songs and Spirituals* (John Work). The text is based on Jeremiah 8:22 and 46:11 with references such as: "Is there no medicine in Gilead? Is there no physician there: Why doesn't God do something? Why doesn't he help?"; and "Go up to Gilead for medicine, O virgin daughter of Egypt! Yet there is no cure for your wounds. Though you have used many medicines, there is no healing for you." Gilead is the ancient name of a country now designated as the area east of the river Jordan, extending from the Dead Sea to the Sea of Galilee. The term *balm* refers to healing medicine, which means that the singer should aim for a soothingly smooth vocal line in the first (A) section (mm. 2–11). The second (B) section (mm. 12–20) can be sung with more energy to suit the textual intent. *Gilead* should be pronounced without an abrasive sounding last syllable ("ad"), preferably with a more relaxed rounding of the vowel, but not an "ahd." A slight, graceful **portamento** (delayed slide) from the lower to upper pitch on the word *whole* is encouraged—but not a slow scoop.

Con qué la lavaré (Oh, What Can Wash Away), page 137. The origins of this plaintive Spanish song are loosely associated with the term *villancicos*, a reference to a poetical and music form that has undergone many modifications over the past few centuries. At least two arrangements are available in folk-song collections of sixteenth-century composers: Eduardo M. Toner's *Marváez* and Juan Vazques's *Coleccion de Vihuelistas Españoles del Siglio XVI*. Joaquin Rodrigo, a twentieth-century Spanish composer, also includes the song in his four-song set for voice and chamber orchestra titled, *Cuatro Madrigales Amatorious*. The mood set by the song's languid melodic and harmonic treatment reflects the quasi-religious nature of the text, an expression of anguish and penitence, possibly for committing some transgression which requires a self-imposed ritual of cleansing. The song should be sung legato, with deep feeling. (IPA: Fig. C-3, p. 325.)

Down in the Valley, page 140. Commonly thought to be an authentic "hillbilly tune," this popular American folk song stems from the Kentucky mountain region. The work first appeared in 1917 in G. L. Kittredge's "Ballads and Songs" in the *Journal of American Folklore*, Lancaster, Pennsylvania. It has subsequently been published in many versions and under various titles, such as "Bird in a Cage," "Birmingham Jail," and "Down on the Levee." Kurt Weill and Arnold Sundgaard based a one-act folk opera on the song in 1948. This song should be sung nostalgically and with great longing, as though writing a love letter filled with one's deepest feelings. In addition to the three verses included in this version, the verses that were omitted would give a more complete picture. For example, "write me a letter, send it by mail, send it in care of Birmingham jail," gives the impression the writer might not have long to live. Because of the strophic construction and repetitiveness, try to sing each verse with a different point of view, using varying dynamics to suit the meaning of the words.

Drink to Me Only with Thine Eyes, page 142. This well-known poem by Ben Jonson (1573–1637) was first published in a collection of poems titled "The For-

est" (1616), included in *The Works of Benjamin Jonson*. The original tune was titled "Song to Celia." Beginning around 1750, the poem was used in several other musical settings, but all of these have been forgotten. The present version of the tune was published in 1780 in a number of editions, several of which were set as *glees*, eighteenth-century genres of unaccompanied English choral music for three or more parts of solo men's voices. Although the composer is unknown, some speculation has been offered that a possible contender is J. W. Callcott, who included the song in a publication of his in which he claimed authorship. Because of the sophistication of the poem, this love song requires a delicate, sophisticated interpretation. The vocal line must be very smooth and the words well-articulated, especially the numerous voiced and voiceless "th's." To maintain a sustained, legato flow, feel main pulses as two to the measure instead of six.

Farmers' Song, page 144. For the past few years, an Asian folksong has been sought to include in the song anthology, and finally one has been found that suits all guidelines. A female graduate student from Singapore recommended it, along with a few other songs, but this one, which is most likely associated with Taiwanese folk traditions, proved to be the most appropriate. Because few Westerners have any experience with Asian languages, an English text that approximates as closely as possible the original meaning has been created. The arrangement of the accompaniment maintains the sparse harmonic treatment common to Asian folksong, with parallel movement of open intervals. The second verse—expressing how hard the farmers work—is arranged to provide a stronger contrast with the first and third verses, both of which are supported by the same harmonic accompaniment. In performing this hauntingly lovely song, you can imagine singing this song in various ways—while working in the fields, or plodding home from the fields at the end of a long day, weary and tired, or gathering wirh neighbors at the end of the day to celebrate the fruits of hard work.

Greensleeves, page 146. One of the most cherished English folk tunes, "Greensleeves" is equally well known as the Christmas carol/hymn "What Child Is This?" One of the earliest references to this tune is found in Shakespeare, with Falstaff's cry, "Let the sky . . . thunder to the tune of 'Greensleeves'." This accounting supports the evidence that the tune was originally a lively dance tune. The text was first published in 1580 as a separate ballad by Richard Jones, titled "Lady Greensleeves," and the melody's first printing was its inclusion (without words) in 1652 in *A Booke of New Lessons for the Cithern and Gittern*, under the title "Greensleeves." Because of its probable dance derivation, this version connects the last two pitches at the end of most measures. Consequently, the pickup word is sung on two pitches instead of only the last one, resulting in a snappy lilting effect. One should still try to sing the song in legato style, reflecting the tender emotional content of the text. The word *adieu* is pronounced "adyou" [adju] to rhyme with "true."

Long Time Ago, page 148. This lyrical ballad was first mentioned in 1837 as an anonymous, original tune adapted by George Pope Morris (words) and Charles Edward Horn (music). It is also included in the *Harris Collection*. The song has become more known by its inclusion in Aaron Copland's collection of *Old American Songs*. The singer can sing this nostalgic song from either a personal or narrative point of view. The descriptively quaint text paints a clear picture of the almost primitive natural surroundings in which the lovers knew one another. A suggested image: a small log cabin situated by a lake with a stream flowing into it, in a valley surrounded by mountains. A *billow* is a wave of water, caused by a rock being tossed into the lake, resulting in a sunlit white cap "brighter than snow."

Niño precioso (Precious Child), page 150. Although its origins are difficult to ascertain, this Nicaraguan folk song is a product of traditions related to both Spanish Catholic religious rites and Native Central-American Indian customs. The original two-part musical form and melodic characteristics substantiate its kinship with songs from the western European tradition. According to the text, the "God of love" is possibly a reference to the Christ child, indicating it could also be sung as a Christmas carol. The reference of the child being compared to precious ermine acknowledges the particularly luxurious fur common in Central America. The person singing must assume the role of one keeping peaceful, loving watch over a sleeping child. Artistic license has been exercised with the decision to have the song end with the return to the A section of the first verse, which effectively changes the form to ABA. (IPA: Fig. C-4 p. 326.)

O Shenandoah, page 152. Perhaps one of the most memorable of all sea chanteys in English, "Shenandoah" has been presented in many versions and in many forms over the years, several of which exist as choral arrangements. Discrepancies over its origins create a bit of mystery surrounding the song. According to one theory (James F. Leisy, *The Folk Song Abecedary*), the name *Shenandoah* is an adaptation of the name used by the Iroquois Indians for the mountains surrounding the Shenandoah valley in Virginia, meaning "land of big mountains." It was a popular tune among the voyageurs on the rivers west of the Mississippi, probably accounting for one version titled "Across the Wide Missouri." It became a capstan chantey known as "Shanandore" on American ships following the Civil War and later a favorite song of the U.S. Calvary during the Indian wars

in the West. In keeping with some of the free rhythmic traditions associated with the song, this version alternates between duple and triple meter to follow the textual inflections. Setting it to a consistent rhythmic pulse can restrain the natural suppleness of the melodic line, so a certain amount of freedom, or *rubato*, is acceptable. The loneliness of one who has been away from home for an extended period (seven years) is felt throughout the song. One can easily imagine singing casually with companions prior to retiring after a full day of travel and experiencing the homesickness this song conveys.

Over the Meadows, page 162. This cheerful up-tempo song is listed in several community song books as a Czechoslovakian folk song, but its exact origins are somewhat obscured by the scarcity of Czech editions. The musical and textual characteristics are similar to songs sung throughout the mountain areas of central and southern Europe where there are plenteous blooming meadows in springtime, nourished by the melting of winter snows. Based on available English edition translations, the song was originally sung by field workers as they hiked to and from mountainside fields at the beginning and close of spring days. It is also likely that, over the years, enthusiastic hikers have adopted this song. Employing a vigorous, marchlike tempo, the song stimulates a great-to-be-alive, "can-do" attitude. It may be sung in various ways using piano accompaniment: (1) as a solo, (2) with alternate soloists, (3) with soloist(s) and group, or (4) group only, in unison or in improvised two-part harmony. As with other folk songs, it may also be sung *a cappella* or with guitar accompaniment.

Simple Gifts, page 154. From the period 1837–1847, this song was a favorite of the Shakers, a celibate, communitarian religious sect located primarily in New York and New England at the end of the seventeenth century, who later established settlements in Ohio, Kentucky, and Indiana. The Shakers were known for neat, well-planned, peaceful villages, pure architecture and fine craftsmanship, progressive agricultural practices, concern for social betterment, and distinctive songs, dances, and rituals. Because of these peculiar Shaker characteristics, it is easy to understand the simplicity of this lovely song, popularized through several contemporary musical versions, including Aaron Copland's version in his *Old American Songs* for voice and orchestra (also piano). The basic message is that striving for true humility is "to come down where we ought to be," resulting in freedom from worldly cares and concerns, and eventually reaching "the valley of love and delight." The use of *turning* might mean to keep trying for human perfection until "you come round right," or it might simply be a literal dance movement response reflecting the music and text.

Sometimes I Feel Like a Motherless Child, page 156. The first account of this African American spiritual was in William E. Barton's *Old Plantation Hymns* (1899). Like all folk songs, the song has had many modifications over the centuries, yet its basic characteristics have remained intact. Several versions by contemporary composers have been arranged, including John Carter's unique rendition in his song cycle *Cantata*, based on four spirituals with a very challenging piano accompaniment. The simple text of mournful longing depicts the extreme feeling of separation from one's roots, interpreted as family, homeland, or even heaven. To be a "motherless child" is to say "I feel as though I don't exist . . . I'm completely useless . . . a nobody." Because so many slave children were sold off and separated from their families, it is easy to imagine their feelings of desolation and dejection as they strove to adjust to a harsh, strange, and often degrading existence. Hence, there is no single interpretation; the final choice is up to the singer. Because of the difficulty of simulating the appropriate authentic dialect, use your natural singing diction but with a slight relaxation of the diphthong vowels, such as [AI], on such words as "t*i*mes" and "l*i*ke." Also, there must be no hint of an "r" in the word "mothe*r*less."

The Happy Singer, page 158.   Though this song is not an authentic folk song, its simple components—melody, harmonic structure, and text—illustrate a basic nature and style common to American/British folk song. Typically, traditional folk songs were originally created by individuals and gradually became modified over many years of widespread use into present-day forms. John Jacob Niles (1892–1980), a well-known composer of folklike songs, composed "The Roving Gambler," which became the inspirational model for Clifton Ware's song "The Aging Singer" (1996). Finally, for this song anthology, it was converted into "The Happy Singer." The upbeat song is partially intended as a pedagogical tool, with each verse describing some positive aspect of singing—psycho-emotionally, physically, technically, musically, and expressively. The song should stimulate a very outgoing, confident, and happy attitude for the singer and a receptive response from listeners. So let go and have fun while performing it.

The Water Is Wide, page 160.   Known also as "O Waly, Waly," this plaintive love song originated in the southwest section of England known as Somerset. The eighteenth-century Austrian composer Josef Haydn produced one charming arrangement of this lovely anonymous folk song. *Waly* (also *wally* or *walie*) is an obscure word that has a cognate with *woe*, meaning an exclamation of sorrow. Although various verses have been used, the general theme of this beautiful song is essentially a story of young love and its sad dissolution. The first verse is hopeful. Although a gulf separates them, perhaps they could make things work if only they could find the means. The second verse reveals that one lover turned out to be unfaithful, and the third verse summarizes, philosophically, that even though love is sweet when new, nothing lasts forever. Communicating the changing moods of each verse is the major challenge. Sing the second verse more impassioned when expressing the trusty tree's bending and breaking.

INFORMATION ABOUT THE ART SONGS AND ARIAS

An **art song** is a composition of high artistic intent, the entirety of which is written by a musically sophisticated composer. With the exception of the textual source, all musical invention is the composer's responsibility. This is in contrast to a folk song arrangement where only the accompaniment part is invented. However, many folk songs (tunes and texts) have been arranged or incorporated into art songs at the hands of skillful composers. An art song in German is called a **"lied,"** and in French *"mélodie."* One of the distinguishing characteristics of an art song is the integration of harmony (accompaniment), melody (voice), and text into a cohesive art form. The characteristic art song as we know it today came into existence in the early nineteenth century through such composers as Beethoven and Schubert. This means that some earlier songs—such as the *lute songs* composed by Dowland and Morley—are not generally classified as art songs.

An **aria** is a solo vocal composition, usually from a major work (such as opera, cantata, or oratorio), with instrumental accompaniment. It is generally distinguished from the art song by greater length, expanded song form, and more emphasis on musical design and expression, often at the expense of the text. Five of the selections in this anthology may be classified as arias, including all Handel selections, "Nel cor più non mi sento," (Paisiello) and "Ridente la calma" (Mozart), which is similar to an aria in form and substance. It is standard practice to perform such works with piano accompaniment in lieu of orchestra, especially sixteenth- and seventeenth-century Italian songs and arias, which are widely used by beginning voice students. Some of these selections would sound traditionally appropriate with harpsichord and continuo instrument (cello on the bass line) playing the accompaniment.

The Renaissance Era

Most solo songs of the late fifteenth century, and throughout the sixteenth century, were created for courtly entertainment. With the growing popularity of the lute (a precursor to the modern guitar), composers began writing songs for voice with lute and bass viol accompaniment. Because accomplished lute and viol players are so rare, these songs are commonly performed with either piano or guitar (and sometimes cello) accompaniments in modern-day performances.

It Was a Lover and His Lass, page 204. As one of the outstanding composers in Renaissance England, Thomas Morley established a strong reputation as organist, first at St. Giles, Cripplegate, and subsequently at St. Paul's Cathedral in London. In 1598, he joined the Chapel Royal and obtained the monopoly of music printing. His secular works are more important than his church compositions, and his *Plaine and Easie Introduction to Practicall Musick* (1597) is valuable to the music historian. Composed by Morley for the play *As You Like It* by William Shakespeare (1564–1616), this song is unique as one of the surviving original songs created specifically for the great bard's plays. The song was first published by Morley in *First Book of Ayres* (1600). It occurs near the end of the play and is performed by two page boys as entertainment for a clown and his intended bride. Keeping this comic scene in mind should help maintain a lively, brisk tempo and mood. Some words needing clarification are *corn-field* meaning "wheat field"; *ring-time* meaning "wedding season"; *fools* meaning "folks"; and *prime* meaning "springtime." This song may be sung by several solo singers as an opportunity for more students to learn it, each taking a verse.

Now Is the Month of Maying, page 224. Set by Thomas Morley to an anonymous text and published originally as a five-part madrigal in the composer's *First Book of Ballets to Five Voices* (1595), this song has also been adapted in several versions for solo voice. In the same category as "It Was a Lover and His Lass," this selection is also very spirited and is about lovers frolicking in the springtime. It, too, may be effectively used as a group-singing activity, perhaps as a vocal warm-up. Individuals may be assigned a solo verse with the group joining on the "fa la la" refrains. Some words requiring clarification are *nymphs*, a reference to beautiful, graceful young women, and *barley-break*, which refers to a group game of "catch" played by both sexes in a corn-field (wheat field). The *break* is a reference to when everyone separates to get away from the "catcher."

Come Again, Sweet Love, page 178. Recognized as one of England's outstanding composers and lutenists, John Dowland (1563–1626) spent much of his career outside of England (Paris, Florence, and Denmark) before accepting patronage by Charles I. His primary contributions to music literature are his songs for voice and lute. His "Come Again, Sweet Love" is perhaps the most well-known song of this genre. On the surface this song appears, quite innocuously, as a typical tender love song. However, as is often the case with lyrics of this period (and also with some of the rock music today) there is an underlying meaning that reveals a more passionate subtext. Understanding both levels should provide a reason to sing this song with more than the customary straightforward approach. Almost any reasonable interpretation is acceptable when sung with substantiated conviction.

The Baroque Era

Around the turn of the seventeenth century, some major changes and developments in every field of human endeavor paralleled the creation of a new musical language. When opera began in Italy with Jacopo Peri's *Euridice* (1600), singing moved from an intimate art form to one of larger proportions. At first the aesthetic vocal ideal was to support and express the text with musical means, but as the century progressed, the equation between text and music evolved, eventually swinging more toward elaborate vocal display. Throughout the seventeenth century, and up to the middle of the eighteenth century, a predominant form of musical writing was the **continuo** (also *basso continuo* or through bass), characterized by the important interplay of melodic and bass lines with inner musical parts serving a chord-filling function. The chief instruments used in realizing the harmony were the harpsichord and organ, and the viola da gamba or cello doubled on the bass line. The standard method of music notation was a form of shorthand with melodic and bass lines filled in and inner parts indicated by numbers representing specific chord structures. All performers were expected to know how to fulfill the composer's intentions, and, particularly, opera singers were expected to embellish the vocal line at appropriate places in an improvisatory manner, somewhat like pop vocalists do today. The peak of Baroque composition was reached with the two masters, J. S. Bach and G. F. Handel.

Caro mio ben, page 173. According to Jon Glenn Paton (*26 Italian Songs and Arias*, Alfred Press, 1991), this favorite Italian song is composed by Tommaso Giordani (1733–1766), rather than Giuseppe Giordani, as incorrectly identified in popular editions derived from the 1890 Parisotti edition. During the 1700s, English enthusiasm for Italian music ran high, especially for operatic works. Giordani, a native of Naples who spent most of his professional career living in London and Dublin, composed this song for Signor Tenducci and a string ensemble to perform on a program presented by the Pantheon and Mr. Abel's Concerts. Our edition, which is a simplified version of standard editions, includes some embellishments intended to enhance the text, as was common performance practice throughout the Baroque Era. However, based on the instructor's and/or performers' preferences, embellishments may be considered optional. The original Italian text communicates a simple expression of heartfelt pain, as experienced by one who is separated from his/her love. The English version remains relatively faithful to the Italian, with some minor exceptions related to the goal of creating a plausible rhyme scheme. "Caro mio ben" should be sung with warm, sincere emotion, all the while striving to maintain sustained legato vocal phrases. (IPA: Fig. C-5, p. 326.)

Cara, cara e dolce, page 176. Sicilian-born Alessandro Scarlatti (1660–1725) received his musical training in Rome. In 1678 he was appointed Maestro di Cappella of San Giacomo degli Incurabili, where he first composed and performed his large-scale oratorio and operatic works. In 1684 at 24 years of age, Scarlatti moved to Naples, where he was appointed Maestro di Cappella at the Naples vice-regal court. For the next two decades, more than half the new operas given at Naples were by Scarlatti, more than 40 works that were performed in prominent theaters. In 1706 he was elected to the Accademia dell' Arcadia, where he most likely met Handel in 1707. Scarlatti's last years were spent in Naples, teaching and composing, primarily cantatas, which ultimately numbered more than 600, most for soprano and continuo. "Cara, cara e dolce"—not to be confused with another Scarlatti aria of similar title ("Cara e dolce")—was first introduced to twentieth century audiences by American conductor/professor John Moriarty in his collection of *Five Scarlatti Arias*, a version that inspired our arrangement. In performing this lovely aria, the primary goal should be to sing with a consistently flowing, legato vocal line and tone throughout, all the while projecting the joy of being free—at last—from a failed love relationship. (IPA: Fig. C-6, p. 327.)

Star vicino (To Be Close), page 236. Formerly attributed to the Italian poet-painter, Salvator Rosa (1615–1673), the authorship of this lovely song is currently in question. The English author-historian Dr. Charles Burney procured some handwritten songs, including some set to Rosa's poems. Assuming Rosa had produced all works, he subsequently included some excerpts from the collection in his book, *A General History of Music*. For the past four decades, research begun by Frank Walker, an English musicologist, has raised serious doubts regarding Rosa's authorship, instead attributing some of the songs to Alessandro Scarlatti, Antonio Cesti, and Giovanni Bononcini. Regardless of the true authorship, the anonymous composer has left a vocal gem for singers to perform. The version included here is patterned after several existing performing editions, utilizing what may be considered interpolated material from measure 20 to the end. The message is the familiar theme of one longing to be with one's beloved, presumably because of a long separation. The first verse is purportedly by Rosa, and Count Pepoli of Bologna may have written the second verse. (IPA: Fig. C-7, p. 327.)

Toglietemi la vita ancor (Oh, Take Away My Breath, My Life), p. 254. Alessandro Scarlatti (1660–1725)

produced numerous operas, including *Pompeo* (1683), from which this aria is extracted. At the time, he was 22 years old and serving as music director to Queen Christina of Sweden, who was in exile from her native Lutheran country because of her conversion to Catholicism. The opera story, which was originally written by Nicolò Minato but revised by an anonymous librettist, is set in Rome during the first century B.C. when the Roman general Pompey has defeated Pontus. Because Pompey has taken the queen of Pontus to Rome as captive, Mitridate, the King of Pontus enters Rome in disguise, searching for his wife. Not finding her, he despairingly states his emotions in this aria, fearing he will never see her again. When performing this aria, the rhythmic pulse must remain vigorous and steady, with slight ritards only at cadences. (IPA: Fig. C-8, p. 328.)

I Attempt from Love's Sickness to Fly, page 193. Considered by most musicologists as England's greatest composer, Purcell (1659–1695) had an uncanny natural gift for writing vocal music. Though some of the texts he set to music are a bit antiquated for modern ears, his songs are considered standards in the modern singer's repertoire. In addition to positions as organist at Westminster Abbey and the Chapel Royal, he had a distinguished career in service to Charles II as principal composer and keeper of the king's instruments.

Written for the masque *Indian Queen* to a text by dramatist John Dryden (1631–1700), this song is sung by Queen Zempoalla. It was later published as a separate song in the collection *Orpheus Brittanicus*. Purcell's baroque affinity for "word painting" is illustrated with the word *fly*, accompanied by a fleeting, florid passage. The word *mien* refers to one's bearing or aspect. The meaning of the song is obvious: One is feverishly coping with lovesickness and would like to break away but can't quite find the courage to act. Performing this song requires a delicate balance between expressive rendering, clear delineation of the musical line, and a minuet-like tempo.

If Music Be the Food of Love, page 202. This is the first of three versions (1692–1695) Purcell set to this text. The text is attributed to H. Heveningham (dates unknown). The song was published in a collection called *Orpheus Britannicus* (London). Only one of two verses is used in this version. As a vocal exercise, this song contains scale work in both descending and ascending patterns at a moderate pace, the only difficulty being a lack of breathing opportunities. To handle this problem, the singer and accompanist must slightly stretch phrases at points where quick breaths are needed. The intoxicated mood is a sensuous and joyous expression of music's ability to create amorous feelings.

Bist du bei mir (If You Are Near), page 170. Although this song is traditionally attributed to Johann

Sebastian Bach (1685–1750), there is some speculation that it is possibly by Gottfried Heinrich Stölzel, one of Bach's contemporaries. To be ascribed authorship of this charming song would be an honor for any composer. J. S. Bach is widely recognized as one of the world's most prominent composers. His professional life was filled with prolific and rich music making as a church organist and composer, and his personal life was filled with producing numerous children. He spent most of his latter career as organist and director of music at Thomaskirche in Leipzig. "Bist du bei mir" is listed as No. 25 in the *Notebook for Anna Magdelena Bach* (BWV 508) as the second of "Drei Arien" (Three Airs). According to most historical accounts, if Bach did write this song for his second wife, Anna Magdelena, it is the only known love song he ever wrote. Because the anonymous text in English translation is a bit obscure— the meaning could refer to both one's beloved as well as God's—this song has been effectively used in funeral services. However, the textual "giveaway" is the familiar use of the German word *du*, which is used only on a personal level of familiarity. A keyboard introduction has been added prior to the entrance of the vocal line. (IPA: Fig. C-9, p. 328.)

Lascia ch'io pianga (Let Me in Weeping) [O Lord, I Pray Thee], page 208. Known internationally as the composer of *Messiah*, next to J. S. Bach Handel (1685–1759) is unquestionably one of the world's most prolific and celebrated composers. Soon after his appointment as Kapellmeister to the Elector of Hannover in 1710, he visited London to produce his opera *Rinaldo* (1711). Having achieved great success in England, he settled there for a lifelong stay, eventually serving his former Hannoverian employer who ascended the English throne as George II. During the remainder of his career, he composed numerous operas for the King's Theater. As opera fell increasingly out of public favor, he turned to producing oratorios, which were essentially operas minus stage trappings. Because Handel displayed a remarkable affinity for vocal composition, he is often referred to as a "singer's composer." According to standard performing practice, singers who have other than the voice types for whom arias were originally written may sing the arias in this anthology. Following are three arias by Handel.

Set to a libretto by Giacomo Rossi, this beautiful aria from *Rinaldo* (act II, scene 4), is sung by Almirena (daughter of Godfrey of Bouillon, leader of the First Crusade), who is in love with Rinaldo (brave knight of the Templars). Under the spell of the sorceress Armida, Almirena sings this song of pathos and longing for freedom. In the style of the period, embellishments have been added to the vocal line, beginning with the B section and continuing throughout the recapitulation of the A section (**da capo**). The singer is free to eliminate these embellishments or otherwise create new ones to enhance textual and vocal expression. An optional religious text is provided for church performance. (IPA: Fig. C-10, p. 328.)

Non lo dirò col labbro (At Evening), page 218. From Handel's opera pastiche *Tolomeo* (1778), with libretto by Nicola Haym (1679–1730), this simple composition bears more resemblance to a song than to an aria. It has become better known to the public as "Silent Worship," a version popularized by the English composer Arthur Somervell (1863–1937). Written in a similar mode of adapting an existing tune to new words— a standard Baroque practice—the English text "At Evening" provides a new tranquil setting extolling the beauty of evening's refreshing rest in preparation for a new day. A literal translation of the original Italian is provided with the IPA transcription. Anyone desiring and willing to create an interesting English text based on the original Italian text is encouraged to give it a try. The idea being expressed is: "I don't dare say what I feel for you, but when I look at you the flames in my eyes reveal my burning passion." (IPA: Fig. C-11, p. 329.)

Oh, Sleep, Why Dost Thou Leave Me? page 199. In the oratorio *Semele* (1744), libretto by W. Congreve, this aria is sung by Semele, a princess of Thebes who longs to be reunited with her beloved. The loss of sleep deprives her of dreams and hopes of being restored to her "wandering love." The statement "O sleep, again deceive me" is a plea that she may at least "dream" of reunification. A religious text ("O Lord, Hear My Prayer") has been added for use in church. Both versions require an ability to sustain a vibrant vocal tone when singing at lower dynamic levels, as with the opening unaccompanied line. To make the long lines a bit easier to sing, some text has been rearranged and repeated (m. 18–19) to lessen the need for having to breathe in the middle of the word "wandering."

The Classical Era

As the tendency for extensive musical elaboration reached its extremes in the mid-eighteenth century, such philosophical ideals as formal elegance, clarity, dignity, order, and correctness of style became moderating influences. Beginning with the famous sons of J. S. Bach, and continuing with composers of the Viennese classic school, such as Franz Josef Haydn, Wolfgang Amadeus Mozart, and Ludwig van Beethoven, the newly emerging piano became the main instrument used for song accompaniment.

Preach Not Me Your Musty Rules, page 221. In the genre of eighteenth-century solo vocal music, Dr. Arne (1710–1778) deserves a place at the front echelon of minor composers. His career consisted of producing several major works for the stage, among them an ambitious opera titled *Artaxerxes*. The composer's music possesses distinct charm and grace, expertly crafted according to the conventional mode of his day, which was predominantly influenced by such dance forms as the minuet and gavotte. Based on John Milton's *Comus* with libretto fashioned by stage director John Dalton, Arne composed his opera *Comus* in 1738. Excerpted from that work, this spirited song is set to a lively dance rhythm and humorous text. The gist of the text is simply "not to worry, follow your heart and senses, be happy and live life to its fullest." A *drone* is a male, non-worker bee; an idler. This song may be sung directly to the audience, even to the point of making eye contact with individuals.

Flocks Are Sporting, page 186. Henry Carey (1689–1743) is recognized for his versatility as an English dramatist, poet, and composer. He began his career as a writer and, in his late 20s, became more interested in composition. His first well-known song, "Sally in Our Alley," written for a staged production, was accomplished with the assistance of a professional composer. Carey's genuine talent for inventing pleasing fresh-sounding melodies resulted in numerous ballad-style songs, a few of which are performed today. "Flocks Are Sporting" is a popular favorite for young sopranos in particular. This version also offers a religious text that may be used for Easter celebrations. The tune could also be adapted to a Christmas carol text (e.g., "Angels Singing") should anyone be interested in inventing an appropriate text. When singing the original Carey text, the mood should be carefree and gay. In contrast, the Easter text needs a more triumphant, celebratory approach, which implies the elimination of all grace notes.

My Lovely Celia, page 214. In contrast to the facile, florid songs of the period, George Monro (1680–1731), a minor English composer, wrote a number of very charming, simple songs that were published in the *Musical Miscellany* (1731). "My Lovely Celia" is imbued with a reserved English sentiment that is also full of warmth and affection. With its short phrases, gracefully moving tempo, and well-contoured melodic line, the song is a fine vocalise for developing legato vocal technique. Though the song is usually performed by young tenors, other voice types may also sing it, including sopranos and mezzo-sopranos. If preferred, the optional words "O, my beloved" may be substituted for "My lovely Celia" at the opening of the song. Sing with a gentle, impassioned ardor throughout, allowing for contrasts in dynamics.

Nel cor più non mi sento (My Heart Has Lost Its Feeling), page 216. In his time, Giovanni Paisiello (1740–1816) was very popular as a comic opera composer. In addition to his *Il Barbieri di Seviglia* (eventually eclipsed by Rossini's opera of the same title), he wrote more than a hundred operas, including *L'Amor contrastato* ("The Hard-Won Love") from which this aria is taken. In the opera, Rachelina, a wealthy mill owner near Naples, sings this aria about the confusion love causes when being pursued by three lovers. At other points in the opera, the melody is also sung by both tenor and baritone suitors, becoming a duet at the end of each solo. This version is a variation of editions currently being used. It is most important to convey a genuine feeling of confused, fluctuating emotions. There's plenty of opportunity to contrast these emotions with subtle facial and body language and to have fun doing it! (IPA: Fig. C-12, p. 329.)

Ridente la calma (May Calm Joy Awaken), page 226. Recent scholarship (Paton 1992) proposed that Wolfgang Amadeus Mozart (1756–1791) composed this version of "Ridente la calma" based on an original composition by his old friend Josef Mysliveček (1737–1781), a successful Czech opera composer. For unknown reasons, around 1773–1775 Mozart undertook a revision of the aria that included a new text, a new second part, and a shortened postlude. The combined result is an exquisite Italianate song of aria-like characteristics. Because the eighteenth-century compositional style presents some minor interpretative problems for novice singers, this edition features some unique "user-friendly" solutions. First, the original $\frac{3}{8}$ time has been converted to $\frac{3}{4}$ time, primarily for easier viewing and studying without impinging on the original artistic intent. Second, all typical embellishments (appoggiaturas, turns, and cadenza) have been written in (indicated with the use of small notes). Third, notes have been added to clarify how certain syllables of the Italian text should be rhythmically voiced using a very fluid connection (see measures 12, 20, 24, 37, 39, 41, et al.). Perform the song with a happy, serene attitude throughout. (IPA: Fig. C-13, p. 329.)

Ich liebe dich (I Love You Dear), page 196. The musical giant Ludwig van Beethoven (1770–1827) is recognized more for his instrumental compositions than for his vocal works. His rebellious, freedom-loving nature caused him to write music that expanded the limits of eighteenth-century classicism, opening the door for the romantic movement of the nineteenth century. As a songwriter of 68 lieder, he was innovative in his use of the piano and helped set the stage for Schubert, Schumann, and those who followed. Often his opera and oratorio writing for the voice is uncomplimentary in its vocal demands, especially in terms of tessitura. However, he wrote many songs capable of being performed well by students, including "Ich liebe dich." Set to a text by Karl Friedrich Herrosee, this gentle, tender song is an expression pledging enduring love through life's ups and downs. In contrast to the typical popular wedding song heard today, this song offers a

The Romantic Era

Social unrest in Europe became increasingly exacerbated during the eighteenth century, reaching a peak with the Napoleonic Wars at the beginning of the nineteenth century. The fall of established monarchies, the advent of the industrial revolution, and the rising prosperity of the common person—juxtaposed with the extreme poverty of others—were some characteristics of an era churning with emotional social issues. In the search for individual freedom of expression, artists in all fields sought to explore and expand the parameters of their art. In music, on one end of the continuum, there was a growth of large-scale musical works, such as massive symphonies and operas. On the other end, there was the growth of intimate musical forms such as the art song, which was primarily intended for friends and colleagues in intimate home performances. The advent of public performances by world-class artists, such as pianist/composer Franz Liszt and singer Jenny Lind, led to the evolution of the soloist moving from the parlor to the stage. The predominant art song during the nineteenth century was the German *lied* (represented herein by three prominent composers: Schubert, Schumann, and Brahms). The French *mélodie* is represented by the two selections "Le Charme," by Chausson, and "Romance," by Debussy.

Vaga luna (Lovely Moon), page 258. Not all the music written in the nineteenth century was innovative in creating a new musical language. For instance, in the first half of the century notable Italian opera composers, such as Gioacchino Rossini (1792–1868), Gaetano Donizetti (1797–1848), and Vincenzo Bellini (1801–1835), were particularly predisposed to advancing the eighteenth-century **bel canto** style. Primarily an opera composer, Bellini wrote arietti, songs similar in style and substance to opera arias, but on a reduced scale. Though he loved poetry, he focused chiefly on the ecstasy of sound created by a curving, flowing melodic line. Composed after 1825, "Vaga luna" is No. 26 in *Aurora d'Italia e di Germania arietta* (Vienna). The version contained here is based on an edition by the famous singer/teacher Pauline Viardot-Garcia in the *'Echoes i'Italie*, Vol. 1 (Paris, 1860s). The text expresses amorous wishes that the all-seeing moon convey one's thoughts of love to the distant beloved. (IPA: Fig. C-15, p. 331.)

An die Musik (To Music), page 165. With more than 600 songs to his credit, Franz Schubert (1797–1828) is justifiably recognized as the most prolific genius of art song composition. His Viennese lifestyle represents the epitome of the nineteenth-century intellectual artist, avidly pursuing his love of music while living in a state of virtual poverty. His greatest contribution to the growth and development of the lied is the integration of text, piano part, and vocal line (melody) into a synthesized whole. Though many of his songs reflect the simple strophic construction of earlier composers, he succeeds in giving the piano accompaniment a major role—other than merely filling out supportive harmonies for the melody. Following are two songs by Schubert.

Schubert's close friend Franz von Schober (1796–1882) wrote the words to this particularly well-known song, which the composer set to music in 1817. Because of the song's great beauty and textual meaning, the National Association of Teachers of Singing traditionally opens every international conference with the entire membership singing it in unison. The poem may be thought of as a hymn of thanksgiving to music, extolling its virtuous influences on human existence. Because performing this song requires solemn dignity and finesse, one should strive to maintain a secure, flowing vocal tone and give careful attention to subtleties in textual meaning. (IPA: Fig. C-16, p. 332.)

Seligkeit (Bliss), page 232. Schubert set "Seligkeit" in 1816 to a poem by Ludwig Heinrich Christoph Hölty (1748–1776), a gifted poet who died prematurely at age 28. Written simply in strophic form, the light-hearted melodies of the vocal part and the piano accompaniment pass back and forth in a joyful interplay. Although numerous singers have performed this simple lied, perhaps the most memorable renditions, both live concerts and recordings, can be attributed to the great German soprano Elizabeth Schumann. Although this upbeat song needs to be performed straightforwardly, subtle variations of each verse are needed to create dramatic contrast and interest. The piano introduction/interlude provides an opportunity to create and maintain dramatic interest when you are not singing, so resist any tendency to merely "bide time." (IPA: Fig. C-17, p. 333.)

Du bist wie eine Blume (You Are So Like a Flower), page 184. Though not quite as prolific as Schubert, Robert Schumann (1810–1856) is often cited as the most representative romantic composer of lieder. As a writer he was widely known for co-founding the *Neue Zeitschrift für Musik*, a journal devoted to promoting the cause of new music. Many of Schumann's songs were inspired by his love for Clara Wieck, daughter of his piano teacher Herr Wieck, who initially vehemently opposed their relationship. This poem by the highly respected Heinrich Heine (1797–1856) is one of his most frequently set poems. Because of its compact construction with interweaving of piano and voice (plus text), this little gem is one of Schumann's most frequently performed works. The performing attitude should be one of absolute devotion and adoration of one's beloved, while giving attention to maintaining a legato style throughout. (IPA: Fig. C-18, p. 333.)

Le Charme (The Charm), page 212. Though Ernest Chausson (1855–1899) is not ranked among the major composers, his contributions to the French mélodie repertoire are highly respected among art song enthusiasts. In his influential administrative position as secretary of the Société de Nationale de Musique he did much to further the cause of French music. Most of his later songs are somewhat musically and interpretatively difficult, but "Le Charme" (1879), a song from the composer's early period that is set to a poem from *Chanson des heures* by Armand Silvestre, gives the singer an opportunity to sample the composer's highly individual use of harmonies and rhythms in a moderately easy format. This song must be sung smoothly and with suppleness according to clear indications of dynamics and tempo in the score. The basic story is recalling the first encounter with one's sweetheart, when it was "instant love." (IPA: Fig. C-19, p. 334.)

Romance (Romance), page 230. The compositional style of Claude Debussy (1862–1918) is closely associated with *impressionism*, an artistic movement prevalent in France circa 1890–1910 that favored softly focused, somewhat "blurred" images in describing a scene or expressing emotions. In addition to visual art influences, French poets helped shape his musical characteristics, notably the mysticism and sensuality of symbolist poet Paul Verlaine. "Romance" (1891), composed to a poem by minor French poet Paul Bourget, is representative of Debussy's early style of impressionistic writing. The song is characterized by graceful declamatory musical phrasing that contours the textual rhythms, and the harmonic treatment enhances the overall impressionistic mood of the text. The sensitive nature of the song calls for a supple vocal line, with a slight rubato throughout and variable dynamics according to the specific markings in the score. (IPA: Fig. C-20, p. 334.)

The Modern Era

At the turn of the twentieth century, advancing technologies affected every aspect of human existence, including music. Between the two world wars, the radical concepts of atonality and irregular meter were incorporated into musical composition, effectively creating a large chasm in the music world between conservative and radical forces. Though radical experimentation abated during the 1940s and 1950s, the increasing impact of electronic technologies on composers and audiences caused experimentation to accelerate in the 1960s. The two prominent trends of art song in the twentieth century are derived from the traditional branches of neoclassicism and neoromanticism. Because most singers and audiences are generally conservative in musical preferences, most frequently performed songs exhibit appealing melodic, textual, rhythmic, and harmonic components. In particular, the contemporary British and American songs in this anthology share these fundamental characteristics, as well as others, including Italian composers such as Puccini.

E l'uccellino, page 188. Giacomo Puccini (1858–1924) was essentially an opera composer whose art song output was limited in scope. However, he did create a few art songs comparable in quality to those of such renowned late nineteenth-century composers as Robert Schumann ("Du bist wie eine Blume," p. 184) and Claude Debussy ("Romance," p. 230). "E l'uccellino" fares very well in comparison to notable lullabies, such as the famous "Wiegenlied" by Johannes Brahms. According to Puccini scholar, Michael Kaye, this tender folk-like lullaby was composed for the infant son of a close family friend ("al bambino Memmo Lippi"), and advertised in the *Gazetta Musicale di Milano* (February 8, 1900) as a song for mezzo-soprano or baritone. Because the vocal range and performance characteristics are easily manageable, any voice type should be able to perform this charming song effectively. Performers should approach the song gently and gracefully, but not too quietly. Throughout the song, the singer needs to sustain an energized vocal tone, while maintaining a visual focus on a sleeping infant. (IPA: Fig. C-21, p. 335.)

The Side Show, page 247. Undeniably one of America's most individualistic and inventive composers, Charles Ives (1874–1954) experimented with unorthodox harmonies and sonorities long before it was fashionable. Primarily self-taught, he supported his music "habit" as an insurance executive. He was finally given prominent recognition when awarded the Pulitzer Prize for his *Third Symphony*. With the exception of several very traditional, singable songs, many of his approximately 100 songs are musically difficult to master. "The Side Show," text and music by Ives, is a very short song about a song: "Is That Mr. Riley, Who Keeps [manages] the Hotel." The fluctuating $\frac{3}{4}$ and $\frac{2}{4}$ meter depicts the irregularity in the turning of the merry-go-round as an old horse pulls it, producing a sound that resembles a Russian dance tune. It should be sung matter-of-factly and straight-facedly, using the optional high notes if preferred.

The Call, page 238. The foremost British composer of the first half of the twentieth century, Ralph Vaughan Williams (1872–1958) is recognized for his extensive use of British folk-song melodic and rhythmic patterns. As this setting of a poem by clergyman poet George Herbert (1593–1633) aptly illustrates, he set the English language to music in an impeccable manner. "The Call," from *Five Mystical Songs*, was originally conceived for baritone and piano, but may be used by any voice type capable of singing it in the key presented. *Way,*

Truth, and *Life; Light, Feast,* and *Strength;* and *Joy, Love,* and *Heart* are all symbolic references to the deity (Christ or God) as one fervently prays for divine guidance. As you sing the song, be aware of the fluctuating meters and sustain a very legato tone.

Dream Valley, page 180. Roger Quilter (1877–1953), known for his refined, conservative compositional style, is one of the most beloved British art song composers. Several of his 112 well-crafted songs are considered standard repertoire for singers, from avocational to professional levels. Many were written for his favorite singer, Gervase Elwes, who also premiered them. As one of Quilter's more popular compositions, "Dream Valley" represents his characteristic writing style, which is exemplified by flowing melodic lines set to texts of high quality and rich harmonic colorations in the piano accompaniment. Quilter's exquisite setting of William Blake's melancholy poem creates an appropriate dreamlike atmosphere, achieved by his simple harmonic treatment, relaxed tempi, and gently flowing melodies. The second stanza, which begins at measure 13, is a freely improvised treatment of the first stanza. One possible interpretation of the poem may be that daydreams are the result of conscious fantasies, whereas night dreams are influenced more by subconscious fears and urges. Although low dynamic levels and a peaceful mood are suggested, the singer should maintain an energized, vibrant tone throughout.

Weep You No More, Sad Fountains, page 261. This tender Quilter song is No. 1 of *Seven Elizabethan Lyrics,* Opus 12 (1908), set to an anonymous text taken from John Dowland's *Third Book of Ayres.* The song is intended as a lover's profound expression, and attention is focused on one's beloved who is sleeping. The word *fountains* refers to the eyes of the beloved. In a soothing, comforting manner, the singer should convey a tranquil mood for restful sleep and restoration.

A Memory, page 168. Rudolph Ganz (1877–1972) was a well-known Swiss American pianist, conductor, composer, and pedagogue. He spent his musical career as a concert pianist, conductor of the St. Louis Symphony Orchestra, teacher/administrator of Chicago Musical College (later Roosevelt University), and composer. His adeptness at song composition was undoubtedly inspired and nourished by his sequential marriages to two singers. Because information concerning Minnie K. Breid is limited, it is assumed she was a minor poet. "A Memory" (1919) uses through-composed form with simple harmonic techniques. Originally written in the key of G Major, the Song Anthology presents the song in F Major. The mood of the song is wistful, a longing for someone whose presence is intensely experienced, but only in the keen imagination of memory.

The Pasture, page 244. The American pianist and composer Charles Naginski (1909–1940) attended the Julliard School to study and teach composition. Because of his untimely death from drowning at age 31, his compositional output is limited to a few symphonic works, two string quartets, and several songs. "The Pasture" (1940) was written for Paula Frisch, a well-known Danish American soprano who championed modern international song literature. Much of the success of the song is due to the charming poem by Robert Frost (1874–1963), one of America's most gifted poets. Frost's poetic language is based on a combination of humor and seriousness that was common to the folk of rural New England, where he lived for most of his adult life. The musical material is straightforward in its support of the cheerful nature of the text. The playful piano accompaniment moves along in a skipping mood, pausing only when reference is made to "fetch the little calf." Cleaning the pasture spring to keep it clear of debris is a regular farm chore to guarantee clean drinking water. The person singing can be portrayed as either a young person speaking to a friend or sibling or as a young parent speaking to a child.

The Daisies, page 240. One of America's most outstanding composers, Samuel Barber (1910–1981) has bequeathed a treasured body of song repertoire representative of the very best in art song composition. He was the recipient of numerous honors and awards, including the prestigious Pulitzer Prize. Set to the poem "The Daisies," by the Irish author James Stephens (1882–1950), this brief, exquisite song is folk-like in its simplicity. The text is self-explanatory; the only performance suggestions are for the singer to keep it moving along lightly and gracefully with no noticeable awkward meter changes. For female singers, it should be perfectly acceptable to substitute *he* for *she* in measure 21.

Heavenly Grass, page 190. Paul Bowles (b. 1910) is known as a folk music specialist and writer of incidental stage music. His other career is that of novelist, and his most successful publication is *The Sheltering Sky* (1949). "Heavenly Grass" is from *Blue Mountains Ballads,* a collection of folk-style songs set to texts by Tennessee Williams (1911–1983). The meaning of the poem is somewhat obscure and free to interpretation. A rather obvious interpretation can be based on the religious belief that we come from God (heaven), live on earth, and long to eventually return home to God. In other words, we are all angels who spend some time on earth as a way of experiencing the human condition. One can almost imagine the ethereal world of clouds and light in the placid opening section, the almost abrupt, dramatic change (m. 14) when coming down to earth, and the longing "itch" to return "home" in the last seven measures.

It's All I Bring Today, page 206. Ernst Bacon (1898–1990) enjoyed a long and versatile professional career in his native United States—as concert pianist, conductor, administrator, artist/teacher, writer, and composer. After completing his musical studies at the

University of Chicago and Northwestern University, he served as assistant conductor of the Rochester Opera and taught piano at Eastman. Later on he served as dean and professor of piano at the University of South Carolina–Spartanburg, followed by a directorship at Syracuse School of Music. His deep interest in song composition was strongly influenced by American writers, notably nineteenth-century poets Walt Whitman and Emily Dickinson, the latter whose eloquent poem inspired this lovely song. Written in a traditional neo-romantic style, Bacon sets Dickinson's poem simply and sensitively. Presented from either a male or female perspective, the poem seems to express sincere love and devotion—a total surrender to one's beloved in a pastoral setting on a peaceful, pleasant day. This delicate song should be performed as smoothly and tenderly as possible, with special attention given to the high opening pitches (measures 1 and 15) at the beginning of the descending phrases. Initiate both high notes gracefully, avoiding strong, loud accents.

This Little Rose, page 248. Songwriter, conductor, and pianist William Roy (1928–2003) was a native of Detroit, Michigan. As a child he received a stage education at the Hollywood Professional School and became a child actor in movies. Later Roy studied music with several reputable instructors and developed into an accomplished pianist, eventually serving as an accompanist to cabaret star Julie Wilson, and later as writer, arranger, and conductor for the nightclub act of Bernadette Peters in Las Vegas. Roy produced several memorable Julius Monk nightclub revues, in addition to several musicals that played outside of New York. "This Little Rose" was written for his Broadway musical *Maggie*, about which little information is available. The music publisher, G. Schirmer, included this song in an early American art song anthology, and it has been widely performed over the years, primarily by voice students but also by some professional singers. Its simple melody and flowing harmonic treatment well suit the brief, descriptive poem by Emily Dickinson (1830–1886), one of America's most illustrious and prodigious poets, with an impressive output of 800 poems. This song requires a sensitive legato treatment, with sufficient give-and-take in tempo, according to score markings. The fermata over the last beat in m.37 on the word "easy" is an editorial optional. The meaning can be taken literally, or metaphorically, in that all human life is ephemeral, and like the rose, is destined to fade and die.

INFORMATION ABOUT THE MUSICAL THEATER SONGS

The popularity of American and British musical theater has become a love affair with the general public in these two countries and has gradually spread all over the world, especially throughout continental Europe. In many of the provincial German opera houses it has become standard practice to include at least one musical in the performing repertoire of the annual 10–month season. In the United States, many regional companies regularly produce *musicals*, though sometimes only in the summer. In addition to professional activity, numerous performances are produced under the auspices of educational institutions and community groups. In almost every community (or at least within a reasonable commuting distance) the average American has an opportunity to attend a musical show, at least occasionally.

Current musical comedy is directly descended from the burlesque, extravaganza, and comic opera prominent in London during the 1890s. These works were characterized by having a loose plot that combined comic and romantic interests and a musical score of catchy songs, ensembles, and dances. In general, both **operetta** and musical comedy are still characterized as lighthearted musical theater pieces based on entertaining stories, appealingly accessible music, and spoken dialogue. A prime example of an early operetta song is "Tipsy Song."

Tipsy Song, page 292. Jacques Offenbach (1819–1880), a French composer of German heritage, is celebrated as one of the most outstanding late-nineteenth century composers of popular music, especially operetta. Among his numerous stage works is *La Périchole* (1868), set to a libretto by the renowned Ludovic Halévy (1834–1908). Set in eighteenth-century Peru, the story is centered around Périchole and Piquillo, street singers/lovers struggling to earn a living in Lima, which is ruled by the eccentric viceroy, Don Andres de Ribera. Much smitten by Périchole, the roving viceroy takes advantage of her destitute condition by offering her a position in the palace as a lady-in-waiting to his nonexistent wife. However, since only married women are allowed to live in the palace, the viceroy arranges a "marriage of convenience" between Périchole and the wretched Piquillo. Following the official wedding, the married couple (unrecognized by one another) enjoy an unaccustomed feast of much food and drink. Both become inebriated, prompting Périchole to sing about her tipsy condition in this simple aria. (*Note:* This selection is provided in the anthology because it offers singers an opportunity to "loosen up" and "let go" of performing inhibitions; it is not an endorsement of drunkenness, nor is it intended to make fun of those who have a drinking problem.) The appropriate attitude for this aria is one of being pleasantly *tipsy*, or slightly off-balance, not falling-down drunk. (IPA: Fig. C-22, p. 336.)

During the 1920s and 1930s, a plethora of shows by such composers as George Gershwin, Jerome Kern, and Vincent Youmans solidified the pattern of success for the musical plays that were extremely popular on and off Broadway. From the 1940s through the 1960s, the "golden age" of musical theater, there was an enormous output of first-class shows by such acclaimed composer/lyricist teams as Richard Rodgers and Oscar Hammerstein II, and Frederick Lowe and Alan Jay Lerner. In more recent times such popular composers as Andrew Lloyd Webber and Stephen Sondheim have produced some outstanding musicals.

The reason for emphasizing shows produced during the 1940s through the 1960s in this anthology is based on the respectable level of vocal, musical, and artistic qualities inherent in these works. Although these musicals provide some opportunities for character voices, a majority of the songs require a moderately high degree of vocal skills. The songs in this anthology are selected for their educational potential in the development of vocal, musical, and dramatic skills. According to standard performing practice, any voice type may perform these songs, regardless of the original role designation in the musicals. The only criterion should be whether the song is suitable for an individual singer's composite capabilities.

'S Wonderful, page 284. Born of Russian Jewish immigrant parents, George Gershwin (1898–1937) and his brother Ira Gershwin (1896–1983) collaborated on the production of several musicals, including *Of Thee I Sing*, for which they received the Pulitzer Prize, and *Funny Face*, for which this clever song was written. Fred and Adele Astaire portrayed the roles of the lovers, Peter Thurston and Frankie, respectively. The lyrics play upon typical American speech colloquialisms, such as slurring and contracting words. For example, the very proper "It is wonderful" can be partially shortened to "It's wonderful" and finally can be fully abbreviated to "'S wonderful." The song is intended to be sung in a carefree, playful manner, and may be performed either as a solo or with a "he" and a "she" singing to one another as indicated in the score. For persons who have difficulty with subtleties in American English, certain words may present some interpretative difficulties, such as *fash* meaning "fashion"; *pash* meaning "passion"; *emosh* meaning "emotion"; and *devosh* meaning "devotion." *Four leaf clover time* means "good luck time." Enjoy!

Oh, What a Beautiful Mornin', page 275. Composer Rodgers (1902–1979) and lyricist Hammerstein (1895–1960) were the most prolific and successful musical comedy duo team during the 1940s and 1950s. From a total of nine musicals, five are still considered monuments of the American musical theater, including *Oklahoma, Carousel, South Pacific, The King and I*, and *The Sound of Music*. The musical *Oklahoma* (1943), the first collaborative effort of Rodgers and Hammerstein, was highly successful, with the rural setting and the down-home story striking a familiar chord in the hearts of Americans. The song is sung at the beginning of the

show by the young man, Curly, as he arrives to court Laurey at her farm home. He's a positive, outgoing type and is happy over his prospects of seeing her again. As is the case with most musical show songs, there's nothing wrong with a Laurey singing the song either. This song is a delight for anyone to sing and is a great way to start a new day.

Almost Like Being in Love, page 264. Frederick Loewe (1904–1988) was an accomplished piano virtuoso from Berlin who became an aficionado of American music when he began playing in nightclubs in New York City as a young man. When he teamed up with Alan Jay Lerner (1918–1986), a talented scriptwriter with a wealthy background (Lerner Shops), the alliance produced several hit musicals, including *Brigadoon* in 1947. The success of this endearingly sentimental show was a combination of the enchanting story and the fetching music. Tommy, on a hunting trip from New York City to Scotland, sings "Almost Like Being In Love" after meeting the village lass Fiona for the first time. The song became an instant hit and secured the reputations of Loewe and Lerner. The song should be sung with exuberance and ecstasy, as though falling in love for the first time.

Time After Time, page 281. Composer Jule Styne (1905–1994), who grew up in the slums of London as a piano prodigy, was forced to relinquish his concert pianist ambitions due to an accident with a drill press. Shifting his interests to burlesque and popular music, he moved to the United States where he managed his own band in south Chicago, then worked in New York as a vocal coach, and eventually ended up in Hollywood composing music for B movies. His collaboration with prominent songwriter-musician Sammy Cahn (1913–1993) was the result of Cahn's close association with Frank Sinatra, the male lead in the 1947 movie musical, *It Happened in Brooklyn*. In the movie plot, Danny Miller (Frank Sinatra) has spent four years in the army, all the while thinking nostalgically about his native Brooklyn. Though at first disappointed upon his return after the war, Danny soon finds an apartment with his friend, Nick, and lands a singing job in a music store. Soon he meets Leo, a talented pianist and his teacher Anne (Kathryn Grayson), whose aspires to be an opera singer. When Jamie, an English composer friend, arrives for a visit, Danny introduces him to Brooklyn and helps him compose modern swing music. The four friends collaborate in helping Leo win the Brooklyn music scholarship. Danny sings this tender love song to his sweetheart, Anne. The song requires an easygoing, flowing vocal line and an unaffected, yet expressive textual delivery.

On a Clear Day, page 272. In the musical *On a Clear Day You Can See Forever*, lyricist Alan Jay Lerner joined up with composer Burton Lane (1912–1997) to produce a story set in New York City. The song is sung by Daisy Gambel, a highly susceptible and somewhat "kooky" young woman who claims she is also Melinda, an eighteenth-century wench. An affair gradually develops with her psychiatrist/hypnotist Dr. Mark Bruckner, who falls in love with her. In performing the song, imagine a clear day in the city, when the smog has dissipated, viewing the blue skies and smelling the fresh air. Then, too, there's a parallel meaning relating to how your mental and emotional life affects the way things appear and ultimately influence you. When completely lucid and happy, you can see forever. This is a very happy song, full of encouragement and hope.

Put On a Happy Face, page 278. Charles Strouse (b. 1928), classically trained composer and jazz pianist, teamed up with Lee Adams (b. 1924) to produce *Bye Bye Birdie* (1961), a musical based loosely on the emerging popularity of rock-and-roller Elvis Presley. Another successful collaboration was "Those Were the Days," the theme song for *All in the Family*, one of the best-known sitcoms in television history. In the musical, Albert Peters is the enthusiastic agent ("music business bum") of Conrad Birdie, rock star. He sings this "toe-tapping" song early in the show to reinforce his confidence that his promotional schemes will ultimately bear fruit. The only suggestion is to sing it straight with solid vocal technique, avoiding any temptation to create a "character voice."

Till There Was You, page 288. Serving the dual capacities of lyricist and composer, Meredith Willson (1902–1984) established his musical reputation with the big hit *The Music Man* (1957), a traditional musical evoking the life of a small American town at the turn of the century. The story presents Harold Hill, an evangelistic music salesman who arrives in town to hawk musical instruments and ends up falling in love with the prudish and lovely Marian (the librarian). They each sing this charming old-fashioned love song at different times in the show as an expression of their true feelings about one another. Strive for simplicity and sincerity when singing this song, and maintain a flowing musical line, avoiding any tendency toward "crooning." Because the one verse may be repeated, it will need a slightly different treatment to make it interesting. It would also work to have a "he" and "she" sing the song, each taking a turn, beginning with the woman. At the pickup to measure 33 and lasting to the end, the two singers might harmonize a closing duet, effectively dramatizing the romantic angle.

Try to Remember, page 294. Composer Harvey Schmidt (b. 1929), and lyricist Tom Jones (b. 1928), met while attending the University of Texas. Their first collaboration was a college show entitled *Hipsy-Boo*, and

their first professional venture was a one-act version of *Fantasticks* for Bernard College's summer theater program. In 1960 a two-act version debuted off-Broadway, eventually gaining sufficient positive acclaim to be awarded the Vernon Rice prize for outstanding off-Broadway production. "Try to Remember," the opening song sung by the narrator, El Gallo, became a hit tune. Sung from the perspective of a mature person (one over 30), the song asks you to try to remember how it felt to be young and in love for the first time. The bittersweet, nostalgic mood should remind you of a sweetly remembered past, of times gone by but fondly remembered. The challenge with singing the same music three times is to make each verse slightly different to suit the subtle changes of the text.

Why Should I Wake Up?, page 298. The musical *Cabaret*, with music by John Kander (b. 1927) and text by Fred Ebb (1933–2004), made its Broadway debut in 1966, with an extended run of 1,165 performances. Kander, a native of Missouri, received his musical training at Oberlin College and Columbia University, and began his professional career as an accompanist in New York. He gradually developed a strong reputation as a composer of songs and musicals. His professional partnership with lyricist Ebb resulted in two movies and 16 musicals, with *Cabaret* recognized as their most famous collaboration. In the show's plot, Clifford Bradshaw, a one-book U.S. traveler living temporarily in tumultuous pre-WWII Berlin, sings this song upon awakening and realizing that Sally Bowles, a beautiful young English woman who has been fired from her singing job at the Kit Kat Klub, is sharing his apartment and bed. At a later point in the story, he has a strong desire to leave Berlin and return to America, taking the pregnant Sally with him. At the song's beginning the mood is dreamy—an enchanting, unreal experience shared with one's newfound love. The vocal line and text should be sung very smoothly, with a sense of gentle stretching and yawning. When approaching the end of the first full section (mm.29–35), the phrases broaden a bit, as though mustering energy to get out of bed. But then there's a return to the beginning musical/textual mood, and the impulse slows again. At m.51 the change of key is a slight wake-up signal, with the emotional level picking up and changing to being more awake, yet reluctant to let go of the dreamy effect.

Any Dream Will Do, page 268. Sir Andrew Lloyd Webber (b. 1948) has been called by some the "Sir Arthur Sullivan of the Rock Age," a testament to his popularity as a composer of popular music with a classical twist. His many notable stage works are revered worldwide—for example, the highly celebrated musical, *The Phantom of the Opera*. Webber received his musical training at the Royal College of Music, where he studied piano, violin, and french horn. In collaboration with

Tim Rice, a law student and lyricist, the duo created their first musical, *Joseph and the Amazing Technicolor Dreamcoat*, a liberal adaptation that combined Biblical scripture with country music and French chanson. Written in 1968 for a student performance at a London school, *Joseph* soon was moved to the West End Theater, where it had a successful professional run, including a record album and national television in 1972. Joseph, the protagonist, sings "Any Dream Will Do" at the conclusion of the show, when reunited with his brothers. From the Bible we learn that Joseph, the highly favored eleventh son of Jacob and Rachel, is given a many-colored coat. Joseph's envious brothers sell him into Egyptian slavery, reporting to their parents that he has been murdered. As an interpreter of dreams, Joseph rises from slavery to serve wisely and successfully as the Pharaoh's prime minister. When his brothers are sent to Egypt to buy corn, Joseph recognizes them, conceals his identity, and sends them back with money hidden in their bags. When they next return, he reveals himself to them, treats them kindly, and offers them a home in Egypt. The text of the song speaks of Joseph's dreams, with references to his mournful parents, prized coat, descent into slavery, and desire to experience his original dreams.

Appendix C

FOREIGN LANGUAGE SONG TEXTS: IPA AND LITERAL TRANSLATIONS

There is perhaps no more controversial subject in voice study than that of correct diction. Although experts generally agree on most fundamental vowel and consonant sounds, some particular phonemes are open to question. Such factors as a singer's vocal technique, regional speech differences within a single country, a composer's unique textual setting, and contradictory authoritative information (language dictionaries) must be considered when approaching matters of diction. In general, classical stage diction is the standard used in presenting IPA singing texts. For example, because of the peculiar characteristics of the Swabian folk dialect, Brahms's arrangement of the German folk song "Da unten im Tale" presents peculiar phoneticization problems (see Web site).

All foreign-language song texts included in this anthology are presented in this appendix in a simplified IPA format. In preparation for using these transcriptions, each area of concern (regarding use of IPA symbols) will be briefly discussed.

Syllabic Duration

Because most syllabic durations are determined by the manner in which the composer sets the text to music, only problematic vowel durations are indicated in this book. The [ː] symbol, indicating a prolonged vowel sound, is used only in those cases where the longer sounding vowels need emphasizing, as when two or more vowels are voiced to a word set to one note. Two examples are the Italian word *mio* ("my"), which is presented as [miːɔ], and the German word *rein* ("pure"), which is presented as [rɑːɪn]. This procedure helps singers avoid the common tendency of prematurely voicing second vowels in diphthongs.

Syllabic Accents

Accents of important syllables are commonly indicated by underlinings in IPA transcriptions. However, because composers normally determine syllabic accent by rhythmic and musical means, such symbols or markings are not used.

Glottal Onsets

The glottal onset symbol [/] for words beginning with a vowel is not used. In practically all circumstances, gentle glottal onsets are typically used in articulating German words beginning with vowels that occur within a sentence, as well as for certain English words that need emphasis and clarity. However, except in very rare instances of dramatic expression, glottal onsets are not used in Italian, Spanish, and French.

Elisions

Slur markings indicating word connections are used occasionally. In such cases, elisions are indicated with the slur symbol [‿]as with the two connected Italian words *è un* ("is a") which are indicated as [ɛ‿un]. Another example of using a slur indication for connecting two words is [ply zœ̃] for *plus un*.

Exploded and Imploded Consonants

Singers must give attention to such consonants as [k], [p], and [t] which are "exploded" (more air released) in English and German but imploded (minimal air release) in Italian, Spanish, and French.

Special IPA/Diction Matters

In most foreign languages, the tongue-flipped [ɾ] is used in lieu of the general American "r." Though it is not used in the IPA transcriptions below, the rolled or trilled [r̄] occurs occasionally in foreign texts to indicate more vigorous speech delivery; for example, "crudely cieli" in "Toglietemi la vita ancor." Usually, "r's" are rolled at the beginning and ending of words, or in the middle of words when occurring before a consonant; for example, "to*r*mento" in "Nel cor più non mi sento."

The Spanish songs "Niño precioso" and "Con qué la lavaré" present some special challenges with the pronunciation of e's and o's, which are generally more closed than Italian, but not as closed as German, for example. Also, "v" is pronounced more like [β], which is less precise than the American "v." The same holds true for "d's," which are pronounced somewhat similarly to the voiceless phoneme [ð]. Essentially, "v's" and "d's" will sound more authentic if they are softened. Please note that the more sophisticated Castillian pronuciation is used for certain consonants in the Spanish folksong, "Con qué la lavaré," whereas a Central/South American Spanish pronunciation is used in the Nicaraguan folksong,"Niño precioso."

All song texts are assigned figure numbers according to the order of occurrence in the informational notes.

Explanation of International Phonetic Transcriptions

The IPA transcriptions consist of three separate lines for each line of verse, as follows:

kɑrɔ miːɔ bɛn	the IPA symbols/phonemes
Caro mio ben	the original text, in this case Italian
Dear, my beloved	the word-by-word translation

In addition, there is a singing version (My dearest love), which is located in the musical score.

SONG TEXT: IPA TRANSCRIPTIONS AND TRANSLATIONS

Figure C-1 Shalom, Chaverim! [ʃalɔm xavɛrim]

ʃalɔm	xavɛrim	ʃalɔm	lə	xit	raot	ʃalɔm
Shalom,	**chavarim,**	**shalom.**	**Le**	**hit**	**raot,**	**shalom.**
Farewell,	*friends,*	*farewell.*	*Until we meet again,*			*farewell.*

Figure C-2 Vive L'Amour [vivə la muɾ]

vivə	la	muɾ	vivə	la	kɔ̃paɲi
Vive	**l' amour,**		**vive**	**la**	**compagnie!**
Long live [the] love, long live [the] fellowship!					

Figure C-3 Con qué la lavaré (koŋ ke la laβare]

koŋ	ke	la	laβare	la	teθ	ðe	la	mi	kara
Con	**qué**	**la**	**lavaré**	**la**	**tez**	**de**	**la**	**mi**	**cara,**
With	*what*	*it*	*will wash*	*the*	*skin*	*of*	*-the*	*my*	*face,*

koŋ	ke	la laβare	koŋ	ke	la laβare
Con	**qué**	**la lavaré,**	**con**	**qué**	**la lavaré,**
With	*what*	*it will wash,*	*with*	*what*	*it will wash*

ke	βiβo	mal	penaða
que	**vivo**	**mal**	**penada.**
That	*I live*	*badly*	*punished.*

laβanse	las	kasaðas	kon	aɣa	ðe	limones
Lávanse	**las**	**casadas**	**con**	**agua**	**de**	**limones;**
Wash	*the*	*matrons*	*with*	*water*	*of*	*lemons;*
(The married women wash themselves with lemon water.)						

laβome	jo	kwitaða	kon	penas	i	ðolores
lávome	**yo,**	**cuitada,**	**con**	**penas**	**y**	**dolores.**
I wash	*myself,*	*I sorrowful*	*with*	*pain*	*and*	*sufferings.*

Figure C-4 **Niño precioso** (niɲo presjoso)

niɲo	presjoso	mas	kel	armiɲo
Niño	**precioso,**	**mas**	**que el**	**armiño,**
Baby boy	*precious,*	*more*	*than*	*ermine,*

risw</br>eɲo	niɲo	djoz	del	amor
Risueño	**niño,**	**Dios**	**del**	**amor.**
Smiling	*baby boy,*	*God*	*of*	*love.*

dwerme	traŋkilo	dwerme‿entretanto	
Duerme	**tranquilo,**	**Duerme**	**entretanto**
Sleep	*peacefully,*	*sleep*	*meanwhile*

eleβa	uŋ	kanto	mi‿	umilde	βos
Eleva	**un**	**canto,**	**mi**	**humilde**	**voz.**
Lifts	*a*	*song,*	*my*	*humble*	*voice.*

dwerme	tʃikitito	ke	oi	ɑse	friːɔ
Duerme,	**chiquitito,**	**que**	**hoy**	**hace**	**frio.**
Sleep,	*little one,*	*that*	*today*	*is*	*cold.*

dwerme	tʃikitito	jo	βelɑre
Duerme,	**chiquitito,**	**jo**	**velaré.**
Sleep,	*little one,*	*I*	*will watch.*

Figure C-5 **Caro mio ben** (kaɾo miːo bɛn)

kaɾo	miːo	bɛn	il	tuo	fɛdel
Caro	**mio**	**ben**	**Il**	**tuo**	**fedel**
Dear,	*my*	*beloved*	*[The]*	*your*	*faithful one*

krɛdimi‿	almen	sospiɾa‿	oɲor
Credimi	**almen**	**Sospira**	**ognor.**
Believe me at least,		*Sighs*	*always.*

sɛntsa	di	te	tʃɛsːa	krudɛl
Senza	**di**	**te**	**Cessa,**	**crudel,**
Without [of] you			*Cease, cruel-one,*	

laŋgwiʃɛ‿	il	kɔr	tanto	rigor
Languisce	**il**	**cor.**	**Tanto**	**rigor!**
Languishes the heart.			*So much severity.*	

Figure C-6 Cara, cara e dolce [kɑɾa, kɑɾa e doltʃɛ]

kɑɾa,	kɑɾa ‿ e	doltʃɛ	libɛɾta
Cara,	**cara e**	**dolce**	**libertà,**
Dear,	*dear and*	*sweet*	*liberty,*

lɑlma	miːa	kɔnsɔli	tu
L'alma	**mia**	**consoli**	**tu;**
[the]	*my*	*console*	*[you];*
(console my spirit)			

pju	nɔn	vivɛ ‿ in	sɛrvitu
Più	**non**	**vive in**	**servitù**
more	*not*	*it-lives in*	*servitude*
(it no longer lives in servitude)			

sil	mːio	kɔɾ	ʃɔlto	sɛn	vɑ
S'il	**mio**	**cor**	**sciolto**	**s'en**	**va.**
if-[the]	*my*	*heart*	*free itself*	*there*	*goes.*

vola	fudːdʒi	puɾɛ	vola	fudːdʒi	puɾ	dɑ	mɛ
Vola,	**fuggi**	**pure,**	**vola**	**fuggi**	**pur'**	**da**	**me,**
Fly,	*flee then*	*alone,*	*flee*	*then*	*from*	*me,*	

fɑ	rɛtɾato	diːɔ	dɑmor
Fa	**retrato**	**Dio**	**d'amor.**
Make	*retreat*	*(the) God*	*of love.*

e	dʒa	libɛɾo ‿ il	mːio	kɔɾ
E	**già**	**libero il**	**mio**	**cor**
Is	*already*	*free*	*(the)*	*my* *heart*

se	pju	lɑtːtʃi ‿ il	pjɛ	nɔn ‿ ɑ
Se	**più**	**lacci il**	**pié**	**non ha.**
if	*more*	*snares the*	*foot*	*not has.*
(if the foot has no more snares.)				

Figure C-7 Star vicino (stɑɾ vitʃinɔ)

stɑɾ	vitʃino ‿ al	bɛl	idɔl	kɛ	sama	e ‿ il	pju	vagɔ	dilɛtːtɔ	dɑmor
Star	**vicino al**	**bel**	**idol**	**che**	**s'ama,**	**È il**	**piu**	**vago**	**diletto**	**d'amor!**
To be	*near the*	*beautiful*	*idol*	*one*	*loves,*	*Is the*	*most*	*charming*	*delight*	*of love!*

stɑɾ	lɔntano	kɔlɛːi	kɛ	si	brama	ɛ	dɑmoɾɛ ‿ il	pju	mɛstɔ	dɔlor
Star	**lontano**	**colei**	**che**	**si**	**brama,**	**È**	**d'amore il**	**più**	**mesto**	**dolor!**
To	*be far*	*from her*	*that*	*one*	*desires,*	*Is*	*of love the*	*most*	*sad*	*affliction!*

Figure C-8 Toglietemi la vita ancor (tɔʎɛtɛmi la vita‿aŋkɔr)

tɔʎɛtɛmi	la	vita‿aŋkɔr	krudeli	tʃɛli
Toglietemi	**la**	**vita ancor,**	**crudeli**	**cieli**
Take away	*the*	*life from me,*	*cruel*	*heavens*

sɛ	mi	vɔlɛtɛ	rapi	rɛːil	kɔr
se	**mi**	**volete**	**rapire**	**il**	**cor.**
If	*from me*	*you wish*	*to steal*	*the*	*heart.*

nɛgatɛmi	i	raːi	dɛl	di	sɛvɛrɛ	sfɛrɛ
Negatemi	**i**	**rai**	**del**	**di,**	**severe**	**sfere,**
Deny to me	*the*	*light*	*of*	*day,*	*severe*	*stars,*

sɛ	vagɛ	sjɛtɛ	dɛl	miːɔ	dɔlɔr
se	**vaghe**	**siete**	**del**	**mio**	**dolor.**
If	*glad*	*you are*	*of*	*my*	*sorrow.*

Figure C-9 Bist du bei mir (bɪst du baːɪ mir)

bɪst	du	baːɪ	mir	ge	ɪç	mit	frɔːydən
Bist	**du**	**bei**	**mir,**	**geh**	**ich**	**mit**	**Freuden**
Are	*you*	*with*	*me,*	*go*	*I*	*with*	*joy*

tsʊm	ʃtɛrbən	ʊnt	tsu	maːɪnər	ru
zum	**Sterben**	**und**	**zu**	**meiner**	**Ruh!**
to	*dying*	*and*	*to*	*my*	*rest!*

ɑx	vi	fɛrgnykt	ver	zo	maːɪn	ɛndə
Ach,	**wie**	**vergnügt**	**wär**	**so**	**mein**	**Ende,**
Ah,	*how*	*pleasant*	*would be*	*thus*	*my*	*end,*

ɛs	drʏktən	daːɪnə	ʃønən	hɛndə	mir	di	gɛtrɔːyən	aːʊgən	tsu
es	**drückten**	**deine**	**schönen**	**Hände**	**mir**	**die**	**getreuen**	**Augen**	**zu!**
it	*closed*	*your*	*beloved*	*hands*	*me*	*the*	*faithful*	*eyes*	*to (shut)!*

Figure C-10 Lascia ch'io pianga (laʃa kiːɔ pjaŋga)

laʃa	kiːɔ	pjaŋga	la	dura	sɔrtɛ	e	kɛ	sɔspiri	la	libɛrta
Lascia	**ch'io**	**pianga**	**la**	**dura**	**sorte**	**e**	**che**	**sospiri**	**la**	**libertà;**
Allow	*that I*	*weep*	*the*	*harsh*	*fate*	*and*	*that*	*I sigh (for)*	*the*	*liberty;*

il	dwɔlɔ‿infraŋga	kwɛstɛ	ritɔrtɛ	de	mjɛːi	martiri	sol	pɛr	pjɛta	si
Il	**doulo infranga**	**queste**	**ritorte,**	**de**	**miei**	**martiri**	**sol**	**per**	**pietà,**	**si, (etc.)**
The	*grief shatter*	*these*	*chains,*	*of*	*my*	*torments*	*if only*	*for*	*pity,*	*yes, (etc.)*

Figure C-11 **Non lo dirò col labbro** (nɔn lɔ dirɔ kɔl labːbrɔ)

nɔn	lɔ	dirɔ	kɔl	labːbrɔ	ke	tantɔ	ardir	nɔn‿a
Non	**lo**	**dirò**	**col**	**labbro**	**che**	**tanto**	**ardir**	**non ha.**
Not	*will*	*I say*	*with*	*(the) lips*	*which*	*so much*	*risk*	*not have.*

fɔrse	kɔn	le	favilːle	dɛl‿	avide	pupilːle
Forse	**con**	**le**	**faville**	**dell**	**avide**	**pupille,**
Perhaps	*with*	*the*	*sparks*	*of*	*avid*	*pupils,*

per	dir	kome	tutːtɔ	ardɔ	lɔ	zgwardɔ	parlɛra
per	**dir**	**come**	**tutto**	**ardo**	**lo**	**sguardo**	**parlerà:**
to	*speak*	*how*	*everything*	*flames*	*the*	*look*	*will tell:*

Figure C-12 **Nel cor piu non mi sento** (nɛl kɔr pju nɔn mi sɛntɔ)

nɛl	kɔr	pju	nɔn	mi	sɛntɔ	brilːlar	la	dʒɔventu
Nel	**cor**	**più**	**non**	**mi**	**sento**	**brillar**	**la**	**gioventù;**
In the	*heart*	*more*	*not*	*myself*	*feel*	*sparkle*	*the*	*youth;*

kadʒon	dɛl	miːɔ	tormentɔ	amor	sɛːi	kɔlpa	tu
Cagion	**del**	**mio**	**tormento,**	**amor**	**sei**	**colpa**	**tu.**
Cause	*of*	*my*	*torment,*	*Love,*	*are*	*guilty*	*you.*

mi	pitːtsiki	mi	stutːtsiki	mi	pundʒiki	mi	mastiki
Mi	**pizzichi,**	**mi**	**stuzzichi,**	**mi**	**pungichi,**	**mi**	**mastichi;**
Me	*you pinch,*	*me*	*you tease,*	*me*	*you prick,*	*me*	*you bite;*

ke	kɔza‿ɛ	kwesta‿ɔːimɛ	pjɛta
Che	**cosa è**	**questa, ohimè?**	**Pietà!**
What	*thing is*	*this, alas?*	*Pity!*

amo	rɛ‿un	tʃertɔ	ke	ke	disperar	mi	fa
Amor	**è un**	**certo**	**che,**	**che**	**disperar**	**mi**	**fa!**
Love	*is a*	*certain*	*something,*	*which*	*despair*	*me*	*makes!*

Figure C-13 **Ridente la calma** (ridɛntɛ la kalma)

ridɛntɛ	la	kalma	nɛl‿	lalma	si	dɛsti,
Ridente	**la**	**calma**	**nell'**	**alma**	**si**	**desti,**
Smiling	*the*	*calm*	*in the*	*soul*	*itself*	*awaken,*

ne	resti	un	seɲɔ	di	zdeɲɔ‿e	timor.
ne	**resti**	**un**	**segno**	**di**	**sdegno e**	**timor.**
nor	*let remain*	*a*	*trace*	*of*	*anger and*	*fear.*

tu	vjɛni	fratːtantɔ	a	strindʒer	miːɔ	bɛnɛ
tu	**vieni**	**frattanto**	**a**	**stringer,**	**mio**	**bene,**
You	*come*	*meanwhile*	*to*	*tighten,*	*my*	*beloved,*

lɛ	doltʃe	katɛnɛ	si	grate‿al	miːɔ	kɔr
le	**dolce**	**catene**	**si**	**grate al**	**mio**	**cor.**
the	*sweet*	*chains*	*so*	*welcome to*	*my*	*heart.*

Figure C-14 **Ich liebe dich** (ɪç libə dɪç)

ɪç	libə	dɪç	zo	vi	du	mɪç	am	abənt	ʊnd	am	mɔrgən
Ich	**liebe**	**dich,**	**so**	**wie**	**du**	**mich,**	**am**	**Abend**	**und**	**am**	**Morgen,**
I	*love*	*you,*	*so*	*as*	*you*	*me,*	*in*	*evening*	*and*	*in*	*morning,*

nɔx	var	kaɪn	tak	vo	du	ʊnt	ɪç	nɪçt	taːɪltən	ʊnzrə	ʒɔrgən
noch	**'war**	**kein**	**Tag,**	**wo**	**du**	**und**	**ich**	**nicht**	**theilten**	**uns're**	**Sorgen.**
there	*was*	*no*	*day,*	*where*	*you*	*and*	*I*	*not*	*shared*	*our*	*sorrows.*

aːʊx	varən	zi	fyr	dɪç	ʊnt	mɪç	getaːɪlt	laːɪçt	zu	ɛrtraɡən
Auch	**waren**	**sie**	**für**	**dich**	**und**	**mich**	**getheilt**	**leicht**	**zu**	**ertragen;**
Also	*were*	*they*	*for*	*you*	*and*	*me*	*shared*	*easy*	*to*	*endure;*

du	trøstətəst	im	kʊmmər	mɪç	ɪç	vaːɪnt	ɪn	daːɪnə	klagən
du	**tröstetest**	**im**	**Kummer**	**mich,**	**ich**	**weint'**	**in**	**deine**	**Klagen,**
you	*comforted*	*in*	*sorrow*	*me,*	*I*	*cried*	*in*	*your*	*laments,*

drʊm	gɔttəs	zegən	ybər	dir	du	maːɪnəs	lebəns	frɔːydə
D'rum	**Gottes**	**Segen**	**über**	**dir,**	**du**	**meines**	**Lebens**	**Freude,**
Therefore	*God's*	*blessings*	*upon*	*you,*	*you,*	*my*	*life's*	*joy.*

gɔt	ʃʏtsə	dɪç	ɛrhalt	dɪç	mir	ʃʏts	ʊnt	ɛrhalt	ʊns	baːɪdə
Gott	**schütze**	**dich,**	**erhalt'**	**dich**	**mir,**	**schütz'**	**und**	**erhalt'**	**uns**	**beide!**
God	*protect*	*you,*	*keep*	*you*	*me,*	*protect*	*and*	*keep*	*us*	*both!*

Figure C-15   **Vaga luna** (vɑgɑ lunɑ)

vaga luna ke inardʒɛnti kwɛstɛ ɾivɛ e kwɛsti fjɔɾi
Vaga luna che inargenti queste rive e questi fiori
Lovely moon, that silvers these bands and these flowers

ed inspiɾi‿ ed‿ inspiɾi‿ aʎi‿ ɛlɛmenti il liŋgwadːʒɔ dɛlːamor
Ed inspiri, ed inspiri agli elementi, il linguaggio dell'amor,
And breathes, and breathes into the elements, the language of the love,

tɛstimɔnjo‿ or sɛːi tu sola del miːɔ fɛrvidɔ dɛziɾ
Testimonio or sei tu sola del mio fervido desir,
Witness now are you alone of-the my fervid desire,

ed‿a lɛi kɛ minːamoɾa kɔntɑ‿i palpiti‿e‿ i sɔspir
Ed a lei che m'innamora conta i palpiti e i sospir.
And to her who me-makes-fall-in-love tell the tremblings and the sighs.

dilːlɛ puɾ kɛ lɔntanantsa il miːɔ dwɔl non pwɔ lɛniɾ
Dille pur che lontananza il mio duol, non può lenir,
Tell her only, that distance, the my grief, not-I can to-her assuage,

kɛ sɛ nutɾɔ‿ una spɛɾantsa ɛlːɑ‿ɛ sol si nɛlːavːveniɾ
Che se nutro una speranza, ella è sol, si, nell'avvenir.
That if I nourish one hope, she is only, yes, in-the-future.

dilːlɛ puɾ kɛ dʒɔɾnɔ‿e seɾa kɔntɔ lorɛ del dɔlor
Dille pur che giorno e sera conto l'ore del dolor;
Tell-her just that day and evening I-count the-hours of-the sadness;

kɛ‿ una spɛmɛ luziŋgjɛɾa mi kɔnfɔɾta nɛlːamor
Che una speme lusinghiera mi conforta nell'amor.
That a hope enticing me comforts in-the love.

Figure C-16   **An die Musik** (ɑn di muzik)

du	hɔldə	kʊnst	ɪn	vifil	grɑːʊən	ʃtʊndən
Du	**holde**	**Kunst,**	**in**	**wieviel**	**grauen**	**Stunden,**
You	*lovely*	*art,*	*in*	*how many*	*gray*	*hours,*

vo	mɪç	dɛs	lebəns	vɪldər	krɑːɪs	ʊmʃtrɪkt
Wo	**mich**	**des**	**Lebens**	**wilder**	**Kreis**	**umstrickt,**
Where	*me*	*the*	*life's*	*wild*	*ring*	*around-binds,*

hast	du	mɑːɪn	hɛrts	tsu	vɑrmər	lip	ɛntsʊndən
Hast	**du**	**mein**	**Herz**	**zu**	**warmer**	**Lieb'**	**entzunden,**
Have	*you*	*my*	*heart*	*to*	*warm*	*love*	*kindled,*

hast	mɪç	ɪn	ɑːɪnə	bɛsrə	vɛlt	ɛntrʏkt
Hast	**mich**	**in**	**eine**	**bessre**	**Welt**	**entrückt!**
Have	*me*	*into*	*a*	*better*	*world*	*wafted away!*

ɔft	hat	ɑːɪn	zɔːyftsər	dɑːɪnər	harf	ɛntflɔssən
Oft	**hat**	**ein**	**Seufzer,**	**deiner**	**Harf**	**entflossen,**
Often	*has*	*a*	*sigh,*	*your*	*harp*	*flowed away,*

ɑːɪn	zysər	haːɪligər	akkɔrt	fɔn	dir
Ein	**süsser,**	**heiliger**	**Akkord**	**von**	**dir,**
A	*sweet,*	*holy*	*chord*	*from*	*you,*

den	hɪmməl	bɛssrər	tsɑːɪtən	mir	ɛrʃlɔssən
Den	**himmel**	**bessrer**	**Zeiten**	**mir**	**erschlossen,**
The	*heavens*	*a better*	*time*	*to-me*	*show (open up),*

du	hɔldə	kʊnst	ɪç	daŋkə	dir	dɑfyr
Du	**holde**	**Kunst,**	**ich**	**danke**	**dir**	**dafür!**
You	*lovely*	*art,*	*I*	*thank*	*you*	*for that!*

Figure C-17   Seligkeit (zelıçkaːıt)

frɔːydən	zɔndər	tsal	blyn	ım	hımməlsal
Freuden	**sonder**	**Zahl**	**blühn**	**im**	**Himmelssahl!**
Joys	*without*	*number*	*bloom*	*in*	*Heaven's hall!*

eŋəln	ʊnt	fɛrklɛrtən	wi	di	fɛtər	lertən
Engeln	**und**	**Verklärten,**	**wie**	**die**	**Väter**	**lehrten,**
Angels	*and*	*(the) transfigured,*	*as*	*the*	*fathers*	*taught.*

o	da	møçt	ıç	zaːın	ʊnt	mıç	eviç	frɔːyn
O,	**da**	**möcht**	**ich**	**sein,**	**und**	**mich**	**ewig**	**freun!**
O	*there*	*would*	*I*	*be,*	*and*	*to me*	*eternally*	*joyful!*

jedəm	lɛçhɛlt	traːʊt	aːınə	hımɛlsbraːʊt
Jedem	**lächelt**	**traut**	**eine**	**Himmelsbraut;**
Upon	*all smiles*	*trustingly*	*a*	*heavenly bride.*

harf	ʊnt	psaltər	klıŋət	ʊnt	man	tantzt	ʊnt	zıŋət
Harf	**und**	**Psalter**	**klinget,**	**und**	**man**	**tanzt**	**und**	**singet.**
Harp	*and*	*psalter*	*sound,*	*and*	*people*	*dance*	*and*	*sing.*

o	da	møçt	ıç	zaːın	ʊnt	mıç	eviç	frɔːyn
O,	**da**	**möcht**	**ich**	**sein,**	**und**	**mich**	**ewig**	**freun!**
O	*there*	*would*	*I*	*be,*	*and*	*to me*	*eternally*	*joyful!*

libər	blaːıp	ıç	hir	lɛçɛlt	laːʊra	mir
Lieber	**bleib**	**ich**	**hier,**	**lächelt**	**Laura**	**mir,**
Rather	*remain*	*I*	*here,*	*smiles*	*Laura*	*to me,*

aːınən	blık	der	zagət	das	ıç	aːʊsgɛklagət
Einen	**Blick,**	**der**	**saget,**	**dass**	**ich**	**ausgeklaget.**
A	*look*	*which*	*says*	*that*	*I*	*need not worry.*

zelıç	dan	mıt	ir	blaːıp	ıç	eviç	hir
Selig	**dann**	**mit**	**ihr,**	**bleib**	**ich**	**ewig**	**hier!**
Blissful	*then*	*with*	*her,*	*remain*	*I*	*eternally*	*here!*

Figure C-18   Du bist wie eine Blume (du bıst vi aːınə blumə)

du	bıst	vi	aːınə	blumə	zo	hɔlt	ʊnt	ʃøn	ʊnt	raːın
Du	**bist**	**wie**	**eine**	**Blume,**	**so**	**hold**	**und**	**schön**	**und**	**rein;**
You	*are*	*as*	*a*	*flower;*	*so*	*tender;*	*so*	*lovely*	*and*	*pure.*

ıç	ʃaːʊ	dıç	an	ʊnt	vemut	ʃlaːıçt	mir	ıns	hɛrts	hınaːın
Ich	**schau'**	**dich**	**an,**	**und**	**Wehmuth**	**schleicht**	**mir**	**in's**	**Herz**	**hinein.**
I	*gaze*	*at*	*you,*	*and*	*sadness*	*fills*	*me*	*in the*	*heart*	*herein.*

mir	ıst	als	ɔp	ıç	di	hɛndə	aːʊfs	haːʊpt	dir	legən	zɔlt
Mir	**ist,**	**als**	**ob**	**ich**	**die**	**Hände**	**auf's**	**Haupt**	**dir**	**legen**	**sollt',**
To me	*is*	*as*	*though*	*I*	*the*	*hands*	*on the*	*head*	*of yours*	*lay*	*should,*

betənt	das	gɔt	dıç	ɛrhaltə	zo	raːın	ʊnt	ʃøn	ʊnt	hɔlt
betend,	**dass**	**Gott**	**dich**	**erhalte**	**so**	**rein,**	**und**	**schön**	**und**	**hold.**
praying	*that*	*God*	*you*	*will keep*	*so*	*pure,*	*and*	*lovely*	*and*	*tender.*

Figure C-19 Le Charme (lə ʃɑrm)

kɑ̃	tɔ̃	suriʀə	mə	syʀpri	ʒə	sɑ̃ti	fʀɛmir	tu	mɔ̃‿nɛtʀə
Quand	**ton**	**sourire**	**me**	**surprit,**	**Je**	**sentis**	**fremir**	**tout**	**mon être,**
When	*you*	*smile*	*me*	*surprised,*	*I*	*felt*	*to-quiver*	*all*	*my being,*

mɛ	sə	ki	dɔ̃tɛ	mɔ̃‿	nɛspri	ʒə	nə	py	dabɔr	lə	kɔnɛtʀə
Mais	**ce**	**qui**	**domptait**	**mon**	**esprit,**	**Je**	**ne**	**pus**	**d'abord**	**le**	**connaître.**
But	*that*	*which*	*tamed*	*my*	*spirit,*	*I*	*not*	*could*	*at first*	*it*	*to-know.*

kɑ	tɔ̃	ʀəgar	tɔ̃ba	syr	mwa	ʒə	sɑ̃tis	mɔ̃‿	namə	sə	fɔ̃dʀə
Quand	**ton**	**regard**	**tomba**	**sur**	**moi,**	**Je**	**sentis**	**mon**	**âme**	**se**	**fondre,**
When	*your*	*glance*	*fell*	*upon*	*me,*	*I*	*felt*	*my*	*soul*	*itself*	*to-melt,*

mɛ	sə	kə	səʀɛ	sɛ‿	temwa	ʒə	nə	py	dabɔ‿	rɑ̃	repɔ̃dʀə
Mais	**ce**	**que**	**serait**	**cet**	**émoi**	**Je**	**ne**	**pus**	**d'abord**	**en**	**répondre.**
But	*this*	*what*	*would be*	*this*	*emotion*	*I*	*not*	*could*	*at once*	*to it*	*respond.*

sə	ki	mə	vɛ̃ki‿	ta	ʒamɛ	sə	fy‿	tœ̃	ply	duluʀø	ʃarmə
Ce	**qui**	**me**	**vainquit**	**à**	**jamais,**	**Ce**	**fut**	**un**	**plus**	**douloureux**	**charme;**
That	*which*	*me*	*conquered*	*for*	*ever,*	*That*	*was*	*a*	*more*	*painful*	*charm;*

e	ʒə	ne	sy	kə	ʒə‿tɛmɛ	kɑ̃	vwajɑ̃	ta	pʀəmjɛʀə	larmə
Et	**je**	**n'ai**	**su**	**que**	**je t'aimais,**	**qu'en**	**voyant**	**ta**	**première**	**larme.**
And	*I*	*only*	*knew*	*that*	*I you loved,*	*when*	*seeing*	*your*	*first*	*tear.*

Figure C-20 Romance (ʀɔmɑ̃s)

lala	mevapɔre	e	sufʀɑ̃tə	lamə	dusə	la‿	mɔdɔrɑ̃tə
l'âme	**évaporée**	**et**	**souffrante,**	**l'âme**	**douce,**	**l'âme**	**odorante,**
The soul	*fleeting*	*and*	*suffering,*	*the soul*	*gentle,*	*the soul*	*fragrant,*

de	li	sdivɛ̃	kə	je	kœji	dɑ̃	lə	jardɛ̃	də	ta	pɑ̃se
Des	**lis**	**divins**	**que**	**j'ai**	**cueillis**	**dans**	**le**	**jardin**	**de**	**ta**	**pensée,**
Of (the)	*lilies*	*divine*	*that*	*I have*	*gathered*	*in*	*the*	*graden*	*of*	*your*	*thought,*

u	dɔ̃	le	vɑ̃	lɔ̃	til	ʃase	sɛ‿	tɑ‿	madɔrablə	de	lis
Où	**donc**	**les**	**vents**	**l'ont-ils**		**chassée,**	**cette**	**âme**	**adorable**	**des**	**lis?**
Where	*then*	*the*	*winds*	*it have they*		*chased,*	*this*	*soul*	*adorable*	*of the*	*lilies?*

nɛ‿til	ply‿	zœ̃	parfœ̃	ki	rɛstə	də	la	syavite	selɛstə
N'est-il	**plus**	**un**	**parfum**	**qui**	**reste**	**de**	**la**	**suavité**	**céleste,**
Is there no	*longer*	*a*	*perfume*	*that*	*remains*	*of*	*the*	*sweetness*	*celestial,*

de	jur‿	zu	ty	mɑ̃vəlɔpe	dynə	vapœr	syʀnatyʀɛlə
Des	**jours**	**où**	**tu**	**m'enveloppais**	**d'une**	**vapeur**	**surnaturelle,**
O the	*days*	*when*	*you*	*me enveloped*	*in a*	*vapor*	*supernatural,*

fɛtə	dɛspwar	damur	fidɛlə	də	beatityd	e	də	pɛ
Faite	**d'espoir,**	**d'amour**	**fidèle,**	**de**	**béatitude**	**et**	**de**	**paix?**
Made	*of hope,*	*of love*	*faithful,*	*of*	*beatitude*	*and*	*of*	*peace?*

Figure C-21   E l'uccellino [e lutːtʃelːlinɔ]

e   lutːtʃelːlinɔ   kanta   sulːla   frɔnda
E   l'uccellino   canta   sulla   fronda;
And   the little bird   sings on the leafy   branch;

dɔrmi   trankwilːlɔ   bokːkutːtʃa   damɔrɛ
Dormi   tranquillo,   boccuccia   d'amore;
Sleep   peacefully,   little (mouth of) love;

pjɛgala   dʒu   kwelːla   tɛstina   bjonda
Piegala   giù   quella   testina   bionda,
Put   down   your   head   fair

delːla   tuːa   mamːma   pozala   sul   kwɔrɛ
Della   tua   mamma   posala   sul   cuore.
Of   your   mama,   put it on   the   heart.
(Rest your head on your mamma's heart).

e   lutːtʃelːlinɔ   kanta   su   kwɛl   ramɔ
E   l'uccelino   canta   su   quell   ramo,
And   the little bird   sings   on   that   branch:

tantɛ   kozinɛ   bɛlːlɛ‿imparɛrai
Tante   cosine   belle   imparerai,
So many   dear things beautiful you will learn,

ma   sɛ   vɔrːr̃ai   konoʃɛr   kwantiːɔ   tamɔ
Ma   se   vorrai   conoscer   quant'io   t'amo,
But   if you want   to know   how much   I love you,

ɲesːsunɔ‿al   mondɔ   potra   dirlɔ   mai
Nessuno   al   mondo   potrà   dirlo   mai!
No one   in the world   could   tell you   ever!!

e   lutːtʃelːlinɔ   kantal   tʃɛl   serenɔ
E   l'uccellino   canta al   ciel   sereno:
The   little bird   sings in the   sky   clear:

dɔrmi   tɛzɔrɔ   miːɔ   kwi   sul   miːɔ   senɔ
Dormi   tesoro   mio   qui   sul   mio   seno.
Sleep,   treasure   mine,   here   upon   my   breast.

ɑ	kɛl	dine	ʒə	vjɛ̃	də	fɛrə	e	kɛl	vɛ̃‿nɛkstrɑɔrdinɛrə
Ah!	**quel**	**dîner**	**je**	**viens**	**de**	**faire,**	**Et**	**quel**	**vin extraordinaire,**
Ah!	*What*	*dining,*	*I*	*come*	*to*	*make,*	*And*	*what*	*wine extraordinary,*

ʒɑ‿	ne	tɑ	by	mɛ	tɑ̃	tɑ̃	tɑ̃	kə	ʒə	krwa	bjɛ̃	kə	mɛ̃tənɑ̃
J'en	**ai**	**tant**	**bu,**	**mais**	**tant,**	**tant,**	**tant,**	**Que**	**je**	**crois**	**bien**	**que**	**maintenant.**
That	*so*	*much*	*drink,*	*but*	*so much,*	*much,*	*much,*	*as*	*I*	*believe*	*well*	*that*	*at present.*

ʒə	sɥi‿zɶ̃	pø	gri‿zɶ̃	pø	grizə	mɛ	ʃyt
Je	**suis un**	**peu**	**grise**	**un**	**peu**	**grise,**	**Mais**	**chut!**
I	*am a*	*little*	*tipsy,*	*a*	*little*	*tipsy,*	*but*	*hush!*

fo	pɑ	kɔ̃	lə	dizə	ʃyt	fo	pa	fo	pa	ʃyt
faut	**pas**	**qu'on**	**le**	**dise,**	**chut!**	**faut**	**pas,**	**faut**	**pas.**	**Chut!**
Want	*walk*	*which*	*the*	*-say,*	*hush*	*want*	*walk,*	*want*	*walk.*	*Hush!*

si	ma	parɔlə	ɛ‿tɶ̃	pø	vagə	si	tu‿	tɑ̃	marʃɑ̃	ʒə	zigzagə
Si	**ma**	**parole**	**est**	**un**	**peu**	**vague,**	**Si**	**tout**	**en**	**marchant**	**je**	**zigzague,**
If	*my*	*speech*	*is*	*a*	*little*	*vague,*	*If*	*all*	*like*	*tradesman*	*I*	*zig zag.*

e	si	mɔ̃	nɶ‿	jɛ	tegrijar	il	nə	fo	sɑ̃‿	netɔne	kar
Et	**si**	**mon**	**oeil**	**est**	**égrillard,**	**Il**	**ne**	**faut**	**s'en**	**étonner**	**car.**
And	*if*	*my*	*look*	*is*	*lewd,*	*It*	*not*	*you*	*astonish*	*because.*	

ʒə	sɥi‿zɶ̃	pø	gri‿zɶ̃	pø	grizə	mɛ	ʃyt
Je	**suis un**	**peu**	**grise**	**un**	**peu**	**grise,**	**Mais**	**chut!**
I	*am a*	*little*	*tipsy,*	*a*	*little*	*tipsy,*	*but*	*hush!*

fo	pɑ	kɔ̃	lə	dizə	ʃyt	fo	pɑ	fo	pɑ	ʃyt
faut	**pas**	**qu'on**	**le**	**dise,**	**chut!**	**faut**	**pas,**	**faut**	**pas.**	**Chut!**
Want	*walk*	*which*	*the*	*say,*	*hush*	*want*	*walk,*	*want*	*walk.*	*Hush!*

Glossary

Some terms in this glossary are referenced in the text;
others are mentioned on the sheet music in the Song Anthology.

A

a cappella: Singing without instrumental accompaniment; originated with choral church music performed in sixteenth-century Europe.

a tempo: Indicates return to normal tempo after an interruption or temporary change of tempo.

abdomen (abdominal area): Portion of the body lying between the pelvis and the thorax (chest cavity), with the exception of the back.

abduction: Drawing apart of the vocal folds from the midline position or opening of the glottis, as occurs with breathing.

accelerando: Becoming faster.

accent: Emphasis on one note or chord.

accompaniment: Separate part or parts that accompany a solo or ensemble, such as a keyboard (piano) instrument.

acoustics: Science of audible sound, including its production, transmission, and effects.

ad libitum, ad lib.: At liberty, freely, and usually slowly.

adagio: A tempo slower than andante.

Adam's apple: Common term for the visible protrusion of the larynx (thyroid cartilage) in the neck, mostly observable in males.

adduction: Drawing together of the vocal folds or closing of the glottis in the act of phonation.

agility: In singing, the ability to perform fast-moving scales and arpeggios with ease and clarity.

agonist: Anatomically, a prime mover muscle that is opposed in action by another muscle called the antagonist.

al fine: To the end, that is, repeat until reaching the word *fine*.

alla breve: Performed with one beat per half note, usually two beats to a measure.

allargando: Becoming broader and slower.

allegretto: In a somewhat lively tempo, but less quick than allegro.

allegro: In a lively tempo.

alto: Low female voice, usually used in choral music.

alveolar ridge: Upper dental ridge where speech sounds occur when the apex of the tongue touches it, for example "d," "l," and "t."

amplitude: Magnitude or range of movement of a vibrating object.

anatomy: Scientific study of the structure of the human body.

andante: In a slow tempo, similar to a moderate walking pace.

andantino: In a moderately slow tempo but usually faster than andante.

animando: Becoming faster (animated).

antagonist: Anatomically, a muscle or muscle group that opposes the primary countermovement of the agonist muscle or muscle group.

appoggiatura: In modern practice, a rhythmically strong dissonant note that resolves to a consonant note, usually to emphasize dramatic intent of the text.

appoggio: Development of a coordinated, dynamic balance among the processes of respiration, phonation, and resonation in singing.

aria (air): Refers primarily to Italian vocal composition; a solo composition for voice in an opera, oratorio, or cantata.

arpeggio (arpeggios): Notes of a chord played or sung in succession in ascending or descending order.

art song: Vocal composition that combines voice, text, and instrumental accompaniment in an artistic manner and style.

articulation: Physiological process of producing consonants in speech and singing.

articulators: Speech organs—jaw, tongue, lips, teeth, soft palate, and hard palate—that work to modify the acoustic properties of the vocal tract.

arytenoid cartilages: Derived from the Greek word *ladle*, the two matching pyramidal-shaped cartilages connecting the larynx and the arytenoid muscle and acting as primary activators in phonation.

aspirate: Articulation of a speech sound with audible friction, for example, the use of the consonant "h" to induce airflow.

aspirato: Singing style based on using "h's" to articulate fast moving notes.

assai: Very much.

B

baritone: Male voice of medium range and vocal color, between bass and tenor.

baroque: Musical style that existed from approximately 1600–1750, represented by such composers as Monteverdi, Purcell, Scarlatti, Bach, and Handel.

bass: Lowest male voice type; also used to describe both the lowest note in a chord and the low-pitched string instrument by that name.

bel canto: Literally translated as "beautiful singing" in reference to a vocal style that emphasizes purity of tone and flexibility; originated in seventeenth-century Italy and remained strong through the first part of the nineteenth century with such composers as Bellini, Rossini, and Donizetti.

belting: Style of pop singing where the chest voice is pushed upward beyond its natural limits without gradual blending with the head voice.

bleat: Fast, tremulous tone (nine or more pulses per second) resembling the sound of a goat and possibly caused by pharyngeal constrictor tensions.

breath management: Efficient handling of the breath cycle in producing vocal tone.

bronchi: Bifurcation of the trachea into two branches leading to the lungs.

bronchiole: Smallest division of the bronchial tree within the lungs, branching off from the bronchi.

C

cadenza: Elaborate ornamental musical passage exhibiting the skills of a solo performer; usually appears at the end of an aria.

cantabile: In a lyric, legato style.

cantata: Literally meaning "sung"; a chamber-sized secular or sacred vocal composition for solo instrument with other musical forces, for example, chorus and/or instrumentalists.

cartilage: Nonvascular body tissue more flexible than bone.

catch breath: Quick, partial intake of air, usually in fast tempo music.

chest register (chest voice): Heavy voice mechanism (register) existing primarily in the low vocal range and marked by sensations of vibrations in the chest.

chiaroscuro: "Bright-dark" tonal characteristics of a dynamically coordinated and balanced voice.

chord: Two or more pitches sounded simultaneously.

chorus (choir): Composed of many singers, usually balanced between sopranos, altos, tenors, and basses.

classical (classicism): Musical style of clarity, dignity, and balanced form that existed from approximately 1750–1825, represented by such composers as Haydn, Mozart, and Beethoven; also refers to music of high artistic intent and permanence.

coda: Literally meaning "tail"; concluding section of a composition.

cognates: Consonants produced with the same place and manner of articulation, differing only by unvoiced or voiced characteristics, e.g., [p] or [b].

coloratura: Elaborate ornamentation or embellishment, including fast passages and trills, both written and improvised.

coloratura soprano: The highest-pitched voice type, of lyrical tone quality, and capable of performing fast-moving scales and arpeggios, primarily associated with operatic and oratorio repertoire containing coloratura passages.

compression (phase): In acoustics, the portion of a sound wave in which the air particles set in motion by a vibrator are dense because they are moving close together, in contrast to the less dense rarefaction wave that follows.

con anima: With soul and spirit.

con espressione: With expression.

con moto: With movement.

consonant: Speech sound created when articulating organs obstruct breath flow.

continuant: Speech sound sustained with a single breath, for example "m," "n," "ng," "z," and "s."

continuo (basso continuo): In baroque music, a bass part written in shorthand notation for an accompaniment to be filled in with chords; usually played by a keyboard instrument (organ or harpsichord) and a bass instrument (cello).

contralto: Lowest and rarest female voice used in solo singing.

costal: Pertaining to rib or costa.

crescendo (cresc.): Becoming louder.

cricoid cartilage: Lower circular cartilage of the larynx located at the top of the trachea.

cricothyroid muscles (cricothyroids): Muscles that attach to the front of the cricoid cartilage and serve to lower the thyroid cartilage in assisting the adjustment of the vocal-folds for higher pitches (head voice registration).

D

da capo (D.C.): Literally meaning "from the head" or "beginning"; return to the beginning and then continue to *fine* (end).

da capo aria (form): Three sections consisting of two contrasting sections (A and B) and a repetition of the first (A), usually with embellishments of the melodic line.

dal segno (D.S.): Return to the D.S. sign 𝄋 and continue to the end.

decibel: Acoustical unit for measuring the relative loudness of sound; the 1 unit is the smallest degree of intensity perceived by the human ear and 130 marks the threshold of pain toleration.

declamatory: An impassioned dramatic style of rhetorical speech and singing.

decrescendo (decresc.): Gradually getting softer.

diaphragm: Large dome-shaped partition comprising muscle tendon and sinews; facilitates breathing and separates the abdomen (stomach) from the thorax (chest).

diaphragmatic-costal breathing: Combined involvement of the abdominal muscles, diaphragm, and intercostal (rib) muscles in breathing.

diction: Comprehensive manner and style in which language is rendered according to established standards of word usage and pronunciation.

diminuendo: Becoming softer.

diphthong: Combination of two vowel sounds on one syllable, for example "sigh," "night," and "say."

dolce: Sweetly.

dramatic voice: Heavy in quality and large in size.

duet: Musical composition for two performers.

dynamics: Degrees of loudness and softness.

E

energy: The biological force or power that expands one's physical and mental capacity for living.

ensemble: Group of performing musicians.

enunciation: Act of pronouncing syllables, words, or sentences in an articulate manner; also associated with definite statements, declarations, or proclamations.

epigastrium: Triangular portion of the high abdominal area at the base of the sternum and directly below the ribs.

epiglottis: Leaf-shaped cartilage located between the root of the tongue and the entrance to the larynx; responsible for protecting the larynx from foreign matter (food) that could otherwise get into the lungs.

exhalation (expiration): That part of the breath cycle when air is expelled.

expression: Act of communicating thoughts and feelings to others.

extrinsic: Meaning "external" or "on the outside"; for example, neck muscles that support and influence laryngeal action.

F

falsetto: Associated primarily with the high register and light quality of the male voice; produced by using only the medial compression of the vocal folds.

faucial pillars (fauces): Two folds on either side of the pharynx, between which lie the tonsils; the narrow passage from mouth to pharynx that is situated between the velum and tongue base; the space encapsulated by the soft palate, the palatine arches, and the tongue base (see Fig. 8-2).

fermata: Pause, hold, or wait on a note, chord, or rest sustaining the duration longer than normal for dramatic effect; sometimes called a "bird's eye" (⌢).

fine (Italian): End, close.

flute/whistle register: Highest vocal range in the female voice, sometimes referred to as "squeak" or coloratura register.

focus: Term borrowed from optics, referring to the concentration and clarity of tone.

folk song: Familiar song of simple musical and textual content, created and modified through person-to-person transmission without being written down.

form: (See song form)

formants: Regions of prominent energy distributions (overtones) in a vocalized tone that determine the characteristic qualities of vowels, as well as individual vocal quality.

forte (f): Loudly.

forte-piano (fp): Playing or singing loudly, immediately followed by a softer dynamic.

fortissimo (ff): Very loud.

frequency: Number of vibrations or cycles per second that determine pitch; the faster the vibrations per second, the higher the pitch.

fundamental: Lowest frequency of a complex sound wave, the frequency of which usually determines what is perceived by the listener as pitch.

G

glide: Vocal sounds caused by the movement or "gliding" of either the tongue or the lips or both, for example, "w," "r," and "l."

glottals: Vowels voiced with a sharp onset (attack) by building up breath pressure and releasing it abruptly in either a gentle or harsh manner.

glottis: Space between the vocal folds.

H

hard palate: Anterior bony portion of the roof of the mouth.

harmony: Chordal, or vertical, structure of a musical composition.

head register (voice): Adjustment of the laryngeal mechanism that produces a lighter tonal quality, with sensations experienced in the head; suitable for soft singing and for the upper part of the voice range.

hertz (Hz): Unit of measurement of cycles per second, for example, 440 Hz (A4); named for the physicist Gustav Hertz.

hymn: Simple religious song of praise, thanks, or plea.

hyoid bone: U-shaped bone located at the base of the tongue and at the top of the larynx.

hyperfunction: Use of any body mechanism with excessive tension, as can occur in any part of the vocal mechanism.

hypofunction: Insufficient activity in any body mechanism, as can occur in any part of the vocal mechanism.

I

inhalation (inspiration): That part of the breath cycle when air is taken into the lungs.

intensity: Amplitude of pressure variations resulting from vibratory impulses passing through an elastic medium such as air or water; magnitude of loudness or volume; depth of emotional expression.

intercostal: The short external and internal muscles between the ribs.

intercostal muscles (external and internal): Three sets of muscles between the ribs that control their raising and lowering.

interpretation: Performer's personal artistic re-creation and realization of a composer's musical and dramatic intentions.

interval: Distance in pitch between two tones.

intonation: Degree of accuracy in producing pitches.

intrinsic: Meaning "internal" or "on the inside"; for example, intrinsic muscles of the larynx.

K

key: Main ("key") note or tonal center of a composition to which all its notes are related and on which the work normally ends.

L

largo: Broadly.

laryngeal collar: The epilaryngeal vestibule or muscular ring located at the top of the larynx composed of the aryepiglottic folds, the epiglottis, and the arytenoid cartilages.

larynx: An organ of the respiratory tract situated in the throat and neck above the trachea (windpipe); composed of cartilage and muscles and containing a pair of vocal folds that vibrate to produce voice.

legato: Smoothly and connected, without a discernible break in sound.

leggiero: Lightly.

lied: German word for "song," used in reference to art songs by such German composers as Schubert, Schumann, Brahms, and Wolf.

lieder (plural for lied): German art songs.

ligament: Strong band of tissue connecting the articular extremities of bone.

lip-buzz: A vocal tone produced when air is blown through the lips, causing them to vibrate, as when voicing "B-b-b-b-b buh, it's cold."

lyric voice: Light in quality and moderate in size.

M

ma non troppo: Meaning "but not too much."

major scale: Musical scale with a major-third interval between the first and third notes.

marcato: Stressed, accented.

melody: Succession of tones perceived as a musical line.

messa di voce: To crescendo (increase) and decrescendo (diminish) a sustained pitch (tone) from soft-to-loud-to-soft dynamic levels.

meter: Division of music into measures or bars, each with a specific number of beats or pulses, for example, $\frac{2}{2}$, $\frac{2}{4}$, $\frac{4}{4}$, $\frac{3}{4}$, $\frac{6}{8}$.

metronome: Mechanical device that maintains a steady beat at any tempo, slow to fast.

mezzo forte (mf):   Moderately loud; less loud than *forte*.

mezzo piano (mp):   Moderately soft; less soft than *piano*.

mezzo-soprano: Female voice of medium range and somewhat darker tone color, usually found in the performance of opera and oratorio.

minor scale: Musical scale with a minor-third interval between the first and third notes.

mixed (middle) register: Blending and dynamic balancing of chest and head register mechanisms in the middle range of the voice.

moderato: Medium tempo.

molto: Very much.

morendo: Dying away.

muscular antagonism: Anatomically, a balanced tension created when a muscle or muscle group opposes the primary countermovement of the agonist muscle or muscle group.

musicology: Professional study of all aspects of music history, literature, theory, and philosophy.

N

nasal cavity: The area of the vocal tract known as the *nasopharynx*, located above the velum and extending to the nostrils.

nasal cavity port: Passage from the pharynx into the nasal cavity at the point where the velum (soft palate) is capable of touching the back wall of the nasopharynx.

notation: System of symbols used for writing music.

O

octave: Eight-note interval between a note and the nearest note above or below of the same name.

onset: Initiation of vocal-fold vibration in response to airflow.

opera: Theatrical work using scenery, props, costumes, lighting, dance, text, and vocal and instrumental music with staged dramatization; usually sung throughout.

opera buffa: Comic opera.

operetta: Theatrical work similar to an opera (see above), but shorter and lighter in subject matter and musical substance; uses spoken dialogue.

opus (Op.):   Used to indicate the chronological position of a composition within a composer's entire output, for example, Op. 1, no. 4.

oratorio: Large composition based on a religious text for soloists, chorus, and instrumentalists and usually concertized rather than staged.

ornament: Extra notes serving to decorate or embellish a melody.

ossify: To become bone; for example, when cartilage turns into bone.

overtones: Upper harmonics that, in conjunction with the fundamental, make up a complex musical tone.

P

palate: Roof of the mouth, divided into hard (front) and soft (back).

passage zone (zona di passaggio):   Series of pitches in the middle voice wherein several tones can be sung by varying register principles.

pharynx (throat):   That portion of the vocal tract and alimentary canal situated immediately behind the mouth and esophagus, comprising three connecting chambers: (1) the laryngopharynx, which is the space immediately above the vocal folds, (2) the oropharynx, which extends from the hyoid bone to the terminal point of the soft palate, and (3) the nasopharynx, which lies directly behind the nose and above the soft palate.

phonation: Vibration of the vocal folds to produce sound.

phonemes: Small unit of speech sounds (vowels or consonants) that collectively compose a linguistic or phonetic system.

phrase: Series of notes sung or played as a single musical and expressive unit, analogous to a clause or sentence in verbal language.

phrasing: Art of shaping a musical phrase expressively, including places for breathing.

physiology: Scientific study of the functioning of the parts of the human body.

piano (p):   Softly; also used as a name for the pianoforte keyboard instrument.

pitch: Property of tone resulting from frequency of vibrations; for example, 440 vibrations per second will produce the pitch A4.

più: More.

pivotal zone (zona di passaggio):   Approximate point or pitches of register transition.

placement: Subjective term used to describe vibratory sensations experienced during singing, usually in the facial mask.

plosive: Speech sound caused by a complete stop, closure, and release of air by either the glottis or the organs of articulation, for example, some forms of "b," "p," "t," "d," "k," and "g."

poco a poco: Little by little.

poco meno mosso: A little less motion, slower.

portamento: Connection between two pitches produced by maintaining the vowel performed on the first pitch while slurring, usually at the last moment, to the second pitch.

presto: Very fast; faster than *allegro*.

pulse (beat):   Regular beat that is the foundation of a steady tempo.

R

rallentando (rall.):   Becoming gradually slower.

range: Distance between the lowest and highest notes of a song or a person's voice.

rarefaction phase: In acoustics, the portion of a sound wave in which the air particles set in motion by a vibrator are less dense because they are moving farther apart, in contrast to the preceding dense compression phase.

recitative: Sung music that closely follows the inflections, tempi, and phrasings of speech and is used to convey dramatic action prior to an aria or a composition for vocal ensemble.

register: Series of consecutive, homogeneous tone qualities, the origin of which can be traced to a special kind of biochemical (muscular) action.

Renaissance: The period following the Middle Ages, approximately 1425–1600, when art, literature, and science were revived, humanism spread, and classical values restored.

repertoire: List of pieces that a musician or group of musicians have learned and are ready to perform.

resonance: Spontaneous reinforcement and amplification of tonal vibrations (energy) occurring whenever a cavity is tuned to the natural fundamental frequency (pitch).

resonator: Sympathetically vibrating surface or cavity that amplifies and dampens overtones.

respiration: Exchange of internal and external gases during the complete breath cycle.

rhythm: Whole feeling of movement in music in time, with patterns of organization according to duration, regularity, and variation of notes above the underlying meter.

ritardando (rit.): Becoming gradually slower.

ritenuto (rit.): Held back.

romantic (romanticism): Musical style during the nineteenth century based on strong subjective emotions and represented by such composers as Schumann, Verdi, and Wagner.

round: Musical piece formed by three to four voice parts repeating the same melody three to four times, entering at regular intervals, and blending into a harmonious unit.

S

scale: Series of rising pitches arranged in order of frequency of vibrations, most commonly with seven tones per octave.

sempre: Always.

singer's formant: The desirable tonal "ring" produced by a singer whose formants form a peak in the spectral envelope at around 2500–3200 Hz.

sinus cavities: Generally, a recess or depression; for example, the sinus of Morgani or in this case the paranasal sinuses in the region of the forehead.

soft palate: Muscular membrane (velum) in the roof of the mouth behind the hard palate.

song cycle: Group of songs with a similar subject or style, planned to be performed as a unit.

song form: Structure and organization of all elements involved in a musical composition: strophic (stanzas); two-part (AB); three-part (ABA); and through-composed (all new material) are the major song forms.

soprano: Highest female voice and highest part of a choir.

sostenuto: In a sustained, connected manner.

sound: Movement of air particles set in motion by a vibrator, transported to an ear, and perceived as tone or noise.

sound wave: Movement of air particles in concentric spheres (compression and rarefaction waves) within an elastic medium; consists of four basic elements—frequency, amplitude, duration, and form.

Sprechstimme (also **Sprechgesang**): A type of exaggerated vocalization, halfway between song and speech.

staccato: Detached.

sternum: Breast bone in the center of the chest to which the ribs attach.

straight tone: Static, vibratoless tone which is caused by manipulative control of the larynx.

strap muscles: Muscles connecting the hyoid bone (above these muscles) to the sternum below, and connecting to the pharyngeal musculature behind; they function to stabilize the larynx.

strophic: Songs constructed in stanzas, each sung to the same melody, as in hymns.

subglottic: Below the glottis.

subito: Suddenly.

T

technic (technique): Procedures and methods used in acquiring skills and executing tasks; involves using exercises designed to help the necessary muscular coordination, strength, and skill for proper performance.

tempo: Rate of speed in music.

tenor: Highest male voice.

tenuto (ten.): Held, slightly lengthened.

tessitura: Particular range of a composition (song or aria) that is most consistently used, as opposed to the total range or compass of a composition; also refers to the comfortable singing range of the voice.

thorax (chest cavity): That portion of the torso situated between the neck and the abdomen which houses the breathing organs within the framework of the ribs, costal cartilages, and the sternum.

through-composed: Song form constructed of new material throughout with no repetitive material.

thyroarytenoid muscles (thyroids): The paired muscles that form the main body of the vocal folds, originating below the thyroidal notch and inserting into each arytenoid cartilage; associated primarily with chest voice registration.

thyroid cartilage (Adam's apple): Largest, single cartilage of the larynx; contains the vocal folds.

timbre: Distinctive quality and character of a tone, resulting from the combined effect of the fundamental and its overtones.

tone: Musical sound of a definite pitch and quality.

trachea: Commonly referred to as the windpipe; a cartilaginous tube through which air passes to and from the lungs.

tranquillo: Peacefully.

tremolo: Vibrato with rate of speed faster and more narrow than the six to seven oscillations per second of efficiently produced tone.

trill: Intended oscillation of pitch; oscillation of a semitone or more that is produced by movement of the larynx.

triphthong: Combination of three vowel sounds on one syllable, for example, "air," "ear," and "our."

U

Umlaut: A German word that refers to mixed vowels, single phonemes comprising two vowels sounded as one, and typically found in German, French, and Scandinavian languages.

unison: Two or more performers sounding the same pitch.

unvoiced: Consonants produced without vocal-fold vibration; for example, "h," "f," "p," "s," "t," and "k."

V

velum: Membranous partition and muscular portion of the soft palate.

ventricle: Small cavity or pouch; for example, the laryngeal sinuses known as the ventricle of Morgani, situated between the true and false folds.

verse: Portion of a song where the music remains the same while the words change with each repetition.

vibrato: Natural pitch variant of six to seven neurological, physically produced pulses per second that occur when the voice is well-coordinated and balanced.

viscera (abdominal cavity): Soft internal organs of the body, notably those of the trunk; for example, the intestines.

vocal folds: Lower part of the thyroarytenoid muscles, or true folds (cords, bands, or lips).

vocal fry: Sometimes referred to as "the scrape of the glottis" because of the frying quality produced on the lowest vocal pitches when lacking sufficient airflow.

vocal range: The compass of pitches (low to high) capable of being performed by a particular voice type.

vocal tract (two interpretations): The entire respiratory system that constitutes the vocal process, from the lower abdominal muscle to the palatal muscles; the combined vocal resonators, extending from the vocal-folds in the larynx to the lips, and encompassing the oropharynx (mouth and throat cavities), plus occasional access to the nasopharynx (nasal cavity).

vocalise: Vocal exercise designed to accomplish specific vocal and musical tasks.

voiced: Vocal-fold sounds set in motion by airflow; also refers to consonants produced by vocal-fold vibration.

volume: "Loudness of sound," best measured in terms of acoustic energy or intensity.

vowel: Speech sound produced when breath is not stopped (see consonants); for example "ee," "ay," "ah," "oh," and "oo."

vowel modification: Vowel adjustments made according to pitch levels throughout a singer's full vocal range; allows for tone equalization.

W

wobble: Undesirable, slower-than-normal vibrato pattern, or oscillation of pitch.

Y

yodeling: Style of singing a melody with frequent leaps and glides mixed with normal singing, usually improvised by the performer and commonly heard in Austrian, Bavarian, Swiss, and country-western music.

Z

zart: Tender, gentle.

Index